FUNNY STUFF

Why was the piano player arrested?
Because he got into treble.

A note left for a pianist by his wife:
"Gone Chopin, have Liszt, Bach in a minuet."

Do you think, Professor, that my wife should take up the piano as a career?
No, I think she should put down the lid as a favor.

Why was the piano invented?
So the musician would have a place to put his beer.

What did the piano player say to the tightrope walker?
You better C sharp or you'll B flat!

Why are a pianist's fingers like lightning?
They rarely strike the same place twice.

Piano Tuner: I'm here to tune the piano.
Music Teacher: But we didn't send for you.
Piano Tuner: No, the people who live across the street did.

What happens when a pianist plays the blues backwards?
His wife comes back to him, his dog returns to life, and he gets out of prison.

At a posh wedding reception in Beverly Hills the pianist fell into the swimming pool and yelled: "Help me! I can't swim!" One of the other guests said: "So what? I can't play the piano, and you don't hear me complaining."

"Haven't I seen your face before?" a judge demanded, looking down at the defendant.
"You have, Your Honor," the man answered hopefully. "I gave your son piano lessons last year."
"Ah yes," recalled the judge. "Twenty years!"

Did you hear about the stupid pianist who kept banging his head against the keys?
He was playing by ear.

What do you get when you drop a piano down a mine shaft?
A flat minor.

The audience at a piano recital was appalled when a telephone rang just off stage. Without missing a note, the soloist glanced towards the wings and called: "If that's my agent, tell him I'm working!"

CONTENTS

INTRODUCTION

ABOUT THIS BOOK

Welcome to *All About Piano*. This book is designed to help you play the piano or electric keyboard, and have fun doing it! Maybe you've already fooled around with the piano, and you're excited by the sounds, and want to learn more. Or maybe you've always wanted to learn, but you're intimidated because you think it's too difficult. Or maybe you were turned off the piano during the lessons you had when you were younger, but now you're ready to start up again. Well, whatever your situation, this book will help get you playing the piano in no time!

It's important to mix "organized learning" with some good old "goofing off": playing what your ears and fingers feel like doing. That's one way we always stay in touch with the "fun" element of playing piano. And remember, above all, this is supposed to be fun! However, organized learning helps develop your skills, so you'll ultimately be able to play more tunes and styles, and have even more fun (and maybe even get paid occasionally!).

The following are some different ways you can use this book:

- as a method or teaching/learning aid if you are a beginner
- as a reference and a source of new ideas if you are already a more experienced player
- as a way to learn more about the piano, some famous pianists, and music in general.

Maybe you already have a piano or keyboard instrument, but if you need some help buying one, we'll cover the various types of keyboards available, to help you decide which is right for you. The techniques in this book apply to electronic keyboard instruments, as well as the good old-fashioned acoustic piano (sometimes referred to as a "steam piano" in musician circles!).

This book is divided into different sections or parts. You can work through the book from beginning to end, or jump into any section you wish. You can easily review material from an earlier section, as needed.

Section 1: **Preparing** gets you acquainted with the "nuts and bolts" of how acoustic and electric pianos work. We'll see how the black and white keys are laid out, and how to use the pedals. We'll also cover how to sit at the piano, as well as how to develop good practice habits (so that we can learn to play all the fun stuff in this book more quickly!).

Section 2: **Playing, Part 1** gets you started on your journey at the piano. We'll unlock the mysteries of music notation, so you'll know how to relate the notes on the paper to the keys on the keyboard. We'll learn how piano music is organized into a "Grand Staff," and is divided into bars or measures. Then we'll start to play some well-known songs, first with each hand separately, then combining both hands. Along the way, we'll learn about scales and key signatures, and how to add left-hand chords to a melody played in the right hand. Using these techniques, you'll be playing professional arrangements of famous songs sooner than you think!

Section 3: **Playing, Part 2** develops more advanced piano techniques in a step-by-step method. We'll learn about "seventh" chords, and how to re-arrange chords into "inversions." We'll also learn how to move the hands to new positions on the keyboard as needed, while playing well-known classical and pop tunes. Then we'll learn how to create on-the-spot arrangements of songs from "fake books," both for accompanying a vocalist or another instrumentalist, and for playing the melody of the song (which will hopefully then be recognized by our adoring public!).

We'll also work more with scales and fingerings, in preparation for playing improvised solos over chord changes.

Section 4: **Styles** introduces the techniques you'll need to play in various musical styles: boogie-woogie, rock 'n' roll, blues, jazz, pop/rock, country, and classical. When creating your own arrangements, you need to use the techniques and tricks appropriate for each style. To put it another way, if you think you're playing rock 'n' roll, but your audience thinks you're playing a country ballad, you may have a problem! So using famous pieces and some original tunes, we'll look at all of these styles and see what makes each of them "tick."

Section 5: **Songs** contains five full piano parts for famous songs in different styles (which are all included on the CD). There is a wealth of information here, as you can compare the note-for-note transcriptions with the recorded versions to get the "inside scoop" on how the professionals create those special sounds on the piano.

Section 6: **The Gig** gives you a lot of real-world information to help take your performance to the next level, whether it's a cool jazz gig, a high-energy rock 'n' roll set, or a classical recital. Here we cover the preparation for the performance, sound check, etiquette, interaction with other musicians, even how to "fake it" and use showmanship when necessary! We'll also delve into the playing opportunities available for piano players, including solo performance, joining or forming a band, and the different types of gigs that are out there for you to pursue. "Playing out" can be a uniquely rewarding experience, making all those hours of practice worthwhile! Finally, we'll explore recording techniques for the piano, both acoustic and electronic.

Section 7: **Instruments and Care** introduces the different types and brands of pianos, both acoustic and electronic. Buying a piano or keyboard instrument is an important decision. If you buy an acoustic, should you go for a grand or an upright? If you prefer electronic, should you go for a digital piano, a "workstation"-type synthesizer, a controller-and-module setup, or a computer-based software piano? We'll help you navigate through all the jargon, and put you "in control" of the purchase process so that you end up with the equipment that is right for you and your situation. This section also discusses how to treat your instrument once you've got it home. You'll need to consider issues such as sunlight, temperature, humidity, ventilation, and so forth. We'll also get into piano cleaning, tuning, and repairs, as well as moving your acoustic piano from one location to another (always hire a qualified professional for this job!).

Section 8: **Who's Who** gives you information on eight great piano players, spanning the eras from classical through to jazz, and on to pop and rock. Recommended listening examples are also included for each artist. Hopefully, you'll find these profiles interesting and inspiring, and that they will motivate you to check out some of their compositions and recorded works.

ABOUT THE CD

On the accompanying CD, you'll find demonstrations of most of the exercises and songs in this book (including all of the full-song arrangements in Section 5). Many of the solo piano examples feature the left-hand piano part on the left channel, and the right-hand piano part on the right channel, for easy "hands separate" practice (just turn down the left or right channel).

There are also a number of tracks with a full band accompaniment as well as the piano. For these tracks, the rhythm section is on the left channel, and the piano is on the right channel, so that you can easily play along with the band by turning down the right channel. Please refer to the CD track listing at the end of the book for further information. It is recommended that you "try out" all songs and examples first, before you listen to the CD. Also, playing along with the band is a great way to impress all your friends!

Section 5 songs and classical pieces were recorded by Hal Leonard musicians. All other tracks were recorded by Mark Harrison.

ICON LEGEND

Included in every *All About* book are several icons to help you on your way. Keep an eye out for these.

AUDIO
This icon signals you to a track on the accompanying CD.

TRY THIS
Included with this icon are various bits of helpful advice about piano playing.

EXTRAS
This includes additional information on various topics that may be interesting and useful, but not necessarily essential.

DON'T FORGET
There's a lot of information in this book that may be difficult to remember. This refresher will help you stay the course.

DANGER!
Here, you'll learn how to avoid injury and keep your equipment from going on the fritz.

ORIGINS
Interesting little historical blurbs are included for fun and background information.

NUTS & BOLTS
Included with this last icon are tidbits on the fundamentals or building blocks of music.

SECTION 1

Preparing

CHAPTER 1
GETTING TO KNOW THE PIANO

What's Ahead:

- The difference between acoustic and electronic pianos
- Finding your way around on the keyboard
- How to use the pedals

ACOUSTIC AND ELECTRONIC PIANOS

First of all, what do we mean by an *acoustic* or *electronic* piano? Well, an acoustic piano doesn't need to be plugged in anywhere. When you strike a key, a felt-covered "hammer" strikes the strings to produce the sound that we hear. In other words, this is purely a physical, acoustic process. By contrast, when you strike a key on an electronic keyboard, the sound is generated electronically (or "digitally"). As opposed to the sound occurring naturally in the room (as with the acoustic piano), the electronic piano's signal needs to be fed to a speaker system in order to be heard. The speakers might be located on the electric piano itself (as with many "home keyboards") or they may be part of a separate amplification system (more common in professional setups).

A lot of people use the term *keyboard* to refer to an electronic instrument (as opposed to acoustic). This can be confusing, as the arrangement of black and white keys on both acoustic and electronic instruments is also known as the keyboard. Later in Section 7, we'll go into much more detail about all the different types of acoustic and electric instruments available. For now, here is a quick summary of the pros and cons of acoustic vs. electronic instruments:

Acoustic *Pros:* Distinctive and unique sound… the "real thing."
Physical responsiveness and sensitivity not easy to duplicate with electronic instruments.

Cons: Higher cost, higher maintenance, take up more space, harder to move, harder to record.

Electric *Pros:* Lower cost, lower maintenance, smaller footprint, better portability, easier to record, continually better approximations of the "real thing" (duplicating the sound of the piano).

Cons: Keyboards often lack the weight, responsiveness, and sensitivity of the real piano, and need electricity and a speaker system!

origins

The term *piano* is actually an abbreviation for *pianoforte*, which in Italian means "soft-loud." This instrument was invented in the early 18th century by Bartolomeo Cristofori, and for the first time enabled notes to be played with great dynamic range (softly or loudly). The predecessor of the piano was the harpsichord, which had a consistent volume level and a more primitive, "plucked" metallic sound.

In the paragraph comparing acoustic to electric instruments, reference was made to the "physical responsiveness" of the acoustic piano. Because of the weight of the keys and the physical process by which the sound is created on the piano, the keys feel heavy to push down, especially when compared to some electronic pianos and keyboards. Some modern (electronic) keyboards feature a "weighted action" which purports to duplicate the feel of the real acoustic piano keyboard. However, there is much variation between makes and models, and what will be right for one player will feel totally "wrong" to another.

If you primarily play or practice on electronic keyboards, DO NOT expect to be able to make an immediate transition to the heavier "weight" of the acoustic piano, particularly for extended periods of playing time.

Acoustic pianos almost always have 88 keys, equivalent to 7-octaves and a bit... (More about octaves shortly.) The largest electronic keyboards may have 88 keys, but keyboards with either 61 or 76 keys are also common.

See Chapter 25 for more about various types of pianos.

BENCHES AND CHAIRS

When you're learning, it's generally accepted that you should be seated while playing, as this helps you learn the correct position for your hands and arms (more about positions and posture in the next chapter). So whether you're playing an acoustic or electric instrument, you'll want to get hold of a good bench or chair.

In some rock or fusion music situations, a standing keyboard player can contribute to the energy and visual appeal of the live performance. I performed with a hard rock band in various venues along Hollywood's Sunset Strip in the early '90s, and I always stood up. However, on almost all other occasions (particularly the jazz and fusion gigs I have done in recent years), I have been seated when performing.

A piano bench is normally three feet wide, with a flat surface, either wooden or padded (the latter is definitely more comfortable for those long practice sessions!). Also, the better benches have an adjustable height feature, which can be very helpful for your position and posture.

The main differences between the piano chair and the bench, is that the chair has a back, and is not as wide. The better chairs have padding, and some also allow you to adjust the height. Having the back, though, can be something of a double-edged sword, as it may be tempting to slump against it, rather than developing a "straight-spine" position (more on this later). Most piano benches are also a bit taller than your average dinner-table chair, and height is very important as we will see in the next chapter.

FINDING THE WHITE AND BLACK KEYS

If you go to your instrument and look down at the keys, you'll notice that some are white and some are black, and that they are arranged in a pattern like this:

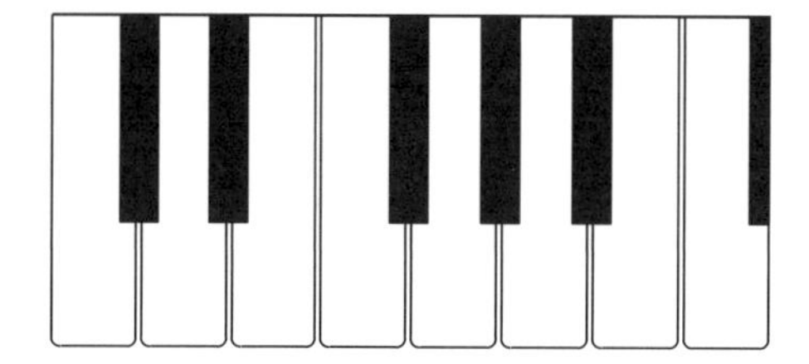

You'll also notice that the black keys are grouped together, in sets of "two" and "three," repeatedly up and down the keyboard. This is very handy (not to say essential!) as it enables us to identify the notes, and where we are on the keyboard. Or, to put it another way: if the keys just alternated "white-black-white-black" all the way up and down the keyboard, we'd be hopelessly lost (and I would probably be in another line of work… !).

Next, we're going to be introduced to the *music alphabet*. This refers to the letters A, B, C, D, E, F, and G that we use to label the white keys. You'll never need to go beyond the letter G, as we "wrap around" again to use the letter A. So, if someone asks you to find an H on the piano keyboard, you can safely assume that he or she is kidding around (or that they're in desperate need of this book!). Now we'll look at the previous diagram again, this time with the letters of the music alphabet added:

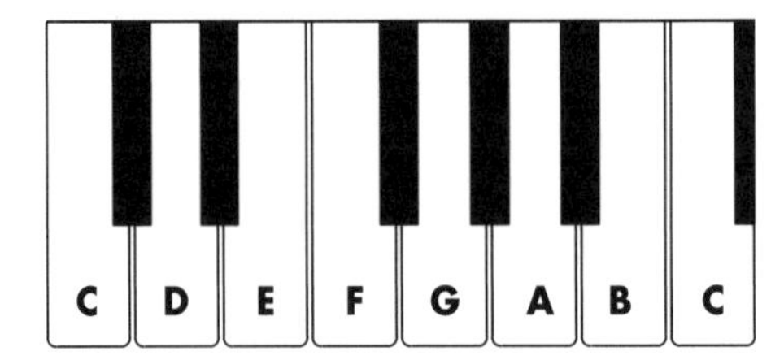

You'll notice that this diagram starts and ends on the note C. It just so happens that the white keys on the keyboard collectively make up a *C major scale* (much more about this later on!). As we said before, notice that after we use the letter name G, we start at the beginning of the music alphabet again to use the letter name A. This set of seven letter names repeats all the way up (to the right, or forwards in the alphabet) and down (to the left, or backwards in the alphabet) the keyboard.

Now we are going use the position of each white key relative to the black keys (i.e., to the sets of "two" or "three" black keys) to identify each white key:

The note **C** is always to the left of the group of 2 black keys.
The note **D** is always in the middle of the group of 2 black keys.
The note **E** is always to the right of the group of 2 black keys.
The note **F** is always to the left of the group of 3 black keys.
The note **G** is always between the 1st and 2nd key within the group of 3 black keys.
The note **A** is always between the 2nd and 3rd key within the group of 3 black keys.
The note **B** is always to the right of the group of 3 black keys.

Now we'll play a fun exercise to help you locate where these white keys are on the keyboard. Start with any letter of the music alphabet, let's say D. Then find and play the lowest (leftmost) D on your keyboard. Once you've done that, play each D successively moving up the keyboard, ending with the highest D. Next, repeat this exercise with all letter names (jump around the alphabet too!) until you've covered all the notes!

Next, we'll look at the note names for the black keys on the keyboard. These will use the same letter names (A up to G), but with either a "sharp" or "flat" sign added:

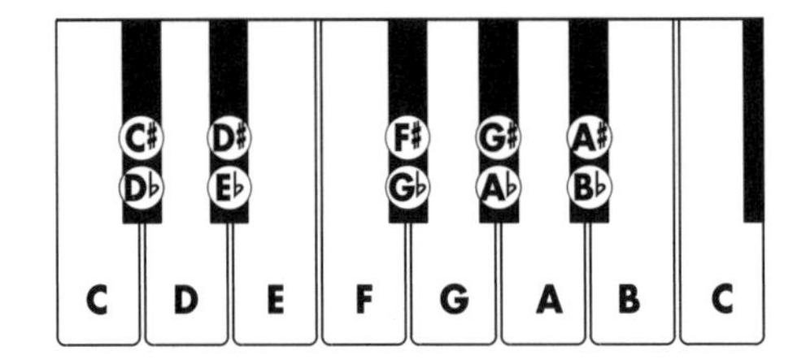

The term *sharp* (♯) means to raise the pitch of the note, and the term *flat* (♭) means to lower the pitch. When we move to the right on the keyboard, the notes become progressively higher in pitch. When we move to the left on the keyboard, the notes become progressively lower.

Note that each black key has been given two names, for example, the black key in between C and D can be called either C♯ (C sharp) or D♭ (D flat). In other words, we can sharp (or raise) the pitch C to get to C♯, or we can flat (or lower) the pitch D to get to D♭.

The term *enharmonic* is used to describe the same pitch having more than one name. For example, the note names C♯ and D♭ are *enharmonic equivalents*. (You can impress your friends at parties by talking about enharmonics!)

You might be thinking, *why would we need to have more than one name for the same note? Wouldn't one name be enough?* Well, believe it or not, depending on which *key* or *scale* we are using (much more about keys and scales later on!), we may prefer to use one name or the other—stay tuned!

Now we'll introduce our first music interval term, the *half step*. If we move from any key on the keyboard to the nearest note (black or white) on the right or left, this distance is referred to as a half step interval. For example, if we start on the note C, the next highest note (i.e., nearest note to the right) is the black key between C and D. This black key, known as C♯ or D♭, is therefore a half step higher than the note C.

When we *sharp* a note (by adding the "♯" suffix to the note name), we are raising the pitch by a half step, and when we *flat* a note (by adding the "♭" suffix to the note name) we are lowering the pitch by a half step.

Another interval term we'll learn about is the *octave*. This is the distance between any note and the next-occurring note of the same name, either to the right (higher) or to the left (lower). For example, in the keyboard diagram, the interval between the C on the left and the C on the right is an octave. Go ahead and count the number of octaves on your instrument. On an acoustic piano and most digital pianos, you'll have a little over seven octaves to play with.

You may also notice that certain pairs of white keys on the keyboard don't have a black key in between them (a consequence of the black keys being grouped into sets of "two" and "three" as we have seen). E–F and B–C, the two pairs of white keys, are a half step apart.

If you count, starting from the C on the left of the diagram to the C on the right, you'll find that there are *twelve half steps in one octave*. This is a fundamental relationship upon which Western music is generally based!

HOW TO USE THE PEDALS

Finally, we'll explore the pedals available on your instrument. Acoustic pianos generally have three pedals, whereas, digital pianos will have either one, two, or three, depending upon the make and model you are using.

The most important pedal on all types is the *sustain pedal* (also known as the *damper* pedal). This is the pedal farthest to the right on pianos that have more than one pedal. On an acoustic piano, when you depress and then release a key, the sound stops because the dampers mute the strings to stop the vibrations. However, when the sustain pedal is depressed, the dampers are "disabled" so that the sound continues after you release the key on the keyboard, at least until the sound fades away naturally. This creates a full and resonant sound, as more notes can then be heard simultaneously.

On electronic keyboards, the musical effect of the sustain pedal is the same, but as these instruments do not have internal moving parts such as dampers, this effect is re-created electronically. On some keyboards, the sustain pedal is a separate piece of equipment that is plugged into a jack socket on the back of the instrument.

The sustain pedal is used in all styles of popular music (especially ballads and new age music) and is also needed for classical music, especially that from the Romantic era onwards (i.e., Chopin and Liszt). When using the sustain pedal, it's important to depress and release it at the right times, otherwise the results will be muddy or indistinct, with too many notes "running into" one another—more about this later.

When people talk about "the pedal," they are referring to the sustain (or damper) pedal. Also, when using the pedal, try to keep your heel on the floor rather than lifting your whole foot.

On to the other pedals (if you have them!): The left-most pedal on acoustic pianos (and on electronic keyboards with more than one pedal) is known as the "soft" pedal (*una corda*) because (surprise, surprise) it makes the piano sound softer. On an acoustic piano, this is actually achieved by moving all of the keys and hammers a little bit to the right, resulting in a softer sound as the strings are struck in a different place. Again, on an electronic keyboard, this effect is re-created electronically.

Acoustic pianos (and some of the fancier digital pianos) also have a middle pedal. This can have one of two functions:

- It can function as a *sostenuto* (which can be thought of as a "selective sustain") pedal. Depressing this pedal will sustain any notes currently held down on the keyboard, but any other notes played afterwards will not be sustained. This pedal is seldom used in pop styles, but comes in handy for certain classical pieces. Many upright pianos may instead have a variation on the sostenuto in the form of a "partial" or "bass sustain" pedal. This pedal acts just like the damper, but only on the lower half (or so) of the keyboard.
- On some upright pianos, the middle pedal functions as a "practice" pedal, inserting a layer of felt between the hammers and strings, creating a very quiet (and rather muffled) sound. This can be helpful if you don't want to disturb your neighbors while practicing. You can think of this as the "pre-digital age" version of the headphone output!

CHAPTER 2
GOOD POSTURE AND PRACTICE HABITS

What's Ahead:

- The correct posture for your back, arms, and hands
- "Warming up" before performing
- Getting the most out of your practice time

BEST POSITIONS FOR YOUR BACK, ARMS, AND HANDS

The key to having good posture is to be comfortable, but not to be hunched over or slumped in front of the keyboard. Your back should be fairly straight, and your hands, arms, wrists, and shoulder and back muscles should all be relaxed. You should resist any tendency to lean too far forward, and your feet should be resting on the floor. To check that you are sitting at the correct height, your hands and forearms should be parallel to the floor, with the fingers touching the keys, as shown.

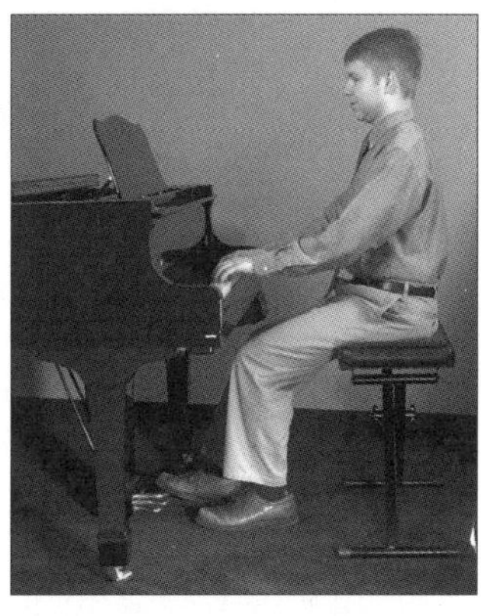

The height of your bench or chair is also important. As shown in the photo, the bench should be high enough so that your forearms are approximately level, with a slight slant downward, toward the keys. A shorter chair would cause the forearms to slant up, producing the need for the wrists to bend down in order to play—bad for the wrists. So, if you do not have a bench that is tall enough, use a phonebook to sit on.

You might be thinking, "Gee, all that posture stuff sounds boring. I just want to play!" Well, guess what? You'll be able to play much better, and, therefore, play more fun and interesting pieces, if you have good posture!

If you have bad posture (slumped or slouched back, forearms not parallel to floor, too much tension in wrists and/or fingers, etc.), then a number of bad things can happen: backache, cramped hands, even carpal tunnel syndrome. So, good posture is essential (and will enable you to enjoy playing a whole lot more!).

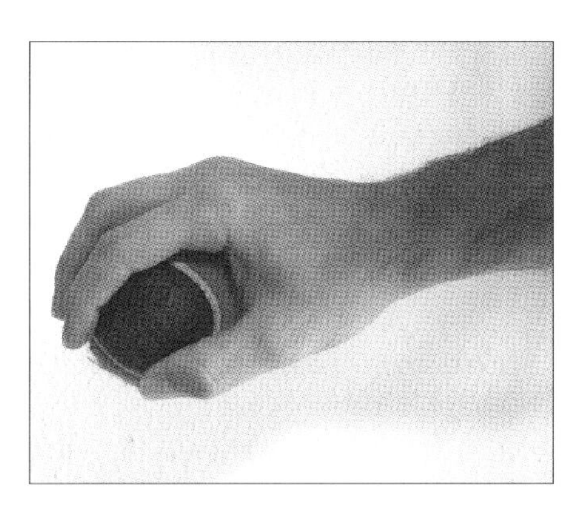

The position of the hands and fingers while playing deserves a special mention here. You should try to keep your fingers curved and your wrists straight, in line with your hands (not a bent wrist). You'll build better stamina and technique this way, as well as have better access to all the keys on the keyboard.

One way to learn this position is to hold a tennis ball in each hand. This way you will naturally curve the fingers, as shown here:

Again, do not tense up when learning this position. Keep the wrist, hand, and fingers as relaxed as possible.

WARMING UP BEFORE PLAYING

It's hard to overestimate the importance of warming up before a performance, whether you're playing for some friends at a party, or playing at Madison Square Garden! When I play gigs with my jazz-fusion group (Mark Harrison Quintet) here in Los Angeles, I always fit in between 1–2 hours of warm-ups before I head out to the gig. Apart from anything else, I'm lucky enough to have some top pros in my band, and so I need to be at the "top of my game" to keep up with my guys!

Here are some ideas for what to play during warm-ups:

- **Scale exercises** – For example, play some major scales ascending and descending, for at least two octaves (more about major scales and fingerings in Chapter 7).
- **Arpeggio exercises** – An arpeggio is the notes of a chord, played one-at-a-time, or "broken chord" style (much more about chords and arpeggios later on).
- **Hanon exercises** – These are excellent exercises for technique in general, and very good for warm-ups. Most music stores sell these (the full title is *Hanon–The Virtuoso Pianist In 60 Exercises*). These exercises very ingeniously build up finger independence, and strengthen the so-called "weak fingers" (the ring and pinkie fingers in each hand).
- **Pieces to perform** – You can run over sections or excerpts of pieces that you are going to perform, for some extra reassurance… but this is NOT the time to obsess over or magnify small details of what you are about to play—the time for learning or practicing the tunes has passed—you need to "go with what you have," and focus on the performance!

GETTING THE MOST OUT OF YOUR PRACTICE

Here's a topic you may find even less thrilling than posture: practicing! (I can hear the groans from here). Well, I'm afraid that whether you play rock, jazz, or classical, you're going to need practice in order to get anywhere worthwhile. The trick is *how* to get the best value out of your precious practice time, especially these days, when time is so hard to find. I am going to suggest some practice habits which will help make your practice time productive, and even fun (who knew?).

One question I am asked a lot by piano students is, "how much practice do I need?" It's hard to give a general answer to that question, as circumstances and goals will obviously vary between different players. That said, if you are a beginning to intermediate player working through this book, then I think you should aim for no less than three hours of practice time per week. Ideally, this should be divided up evenly, i.e., around half an hour per day, although it's not a problem if some sessions are longer than others. However, missing three days in a row of practice, and then trying to make it up with a two-hour cram session is not the best way to go (and not the healthiest). You'll learn best if you keep it up each day, even if some days are only ten minutes or so.

Here are some ways to get the most out of practicing:

- **Have (or set) goals and priorities for your practice session.** For example, in a half-hour session, you might work for five or more minutes on technique (say some scales and/or Hanon exercises), five or more minutes on sight-reading (playing some music "at sight" without having seen it before—start with very simple examples first!), and then the remaining time on the piece or pieces you are currently learning, whether you're working step-by-step through this book, or working with a teacher.
- **Aim to play the pieces you're working on, as smoothly and clearly as possible.** Isolate any "rough spots" and work on these until you can play them without pausing. This will often require finding the correct hand position and fingering needed, as we will see in various examples in this book.

- **Play at an even tempo and slow the piece down as needed.** I sometimes hear students rush through pieces too fast, then stumble over some notes, then resume playing (too fast again), and so on. This is exactly the WRONG way to go about it! You should find a comfortable tempo (without any stumbles), even if the tempo is really slow. This will help you play more evenly, as well as help to get the piece into your "muscle memory" so that your hands will begin to learn it. Then you can gradually increase the tempo as your facility improves, without pauses or mistakes.
- **Practice pieces with hands separately as needed.** Separating the two hands allows you to focus on one hand at a time. Then, when you re-combine the hands, you'll have a "head start," as you'll be familiar with the individual parts. Actually, in popular styles such as blues and rock, the left-hand part is often rather repetitive, so practicing this part separately can help get the left hand on "auto-pilot."
- **Practice with a metronome as needed.** A metronome is a machine which emits a steady "ticking" sound at whatever tempo (speed) you set it. Listen hard when playing along to make sure that you are not slowing down or speeding up. For beginning players, you should be using a metronome for at least 50% of your practice time on each session. Metronome practice will also go a long way in helping you play tunes in a continuous fashion, without pausing or stumbling (again, keep it slow at first).
- **Always try to "look ahead" in the music.** You should become familiar enough with the piece so that you are able to look ahead in the music. That way you'll more easily be able to anticipate interval skips, hand position changes, and so on, and will, therefore, be less prone to stumbling as you play through the piece.
- **Always try to keep going when practicing a performance.** When you see a tune for the first time, it's normal to be a little uncertain and make mistakes as you practice it. But, once you have learned the piece (using the various techniques we've talked about), the next stage is to "practice the performance." Do your best to convey the emotion and expressiveness of the music, and above all keep going even if you make a mistake. If there is still some work to do on certain sections of the piece, isolate and work on them afterwards.
- **Make sure you are relaxed while practicing.** Don't forget all that posture stuff we talked about earlier in this chapter! Don't tense up: make sure your arms, wrists, and fingers are all relaxed. Take a pause or short break every so often to relax before starting up again.
- **Find the right practice environment.** You should practice in a quiet place, free from interruptions, phones ringing, etc. If your piano or keyboard is in a room where you can close the door (if there are other people in the house), close it! Try not to think about all the other things you've had to deal with that day, and instead take a moment to calm down and focus on the task at hand! Also try to find a time of day when you have some energy and are not too tired. I have some students who practice first thing in the morning before they go off to work. For them this works better than trying to find time at the end of the day, when they are more tired and would be less productive. So, figure out a schedule that works for you, and do your best to stick with it!
- **Don't get discouraged.** If the piece you're working on has a part that you don't seem to be making any headway on, leave it and come back to it later. Sometimes we can run into the law of "diminishing returns" in our practice, i.e., we get burned out on a particular section that doesn't seem to be improving. Often when we come back to it, a fresh start can yield some progress.

Good luck with your practicing!

SECTION 2

Playing, Part 1

CHAPTER 3
NOTATION AND RHYTHMS

What's Ahead:

- Introducing treble and bass clefs, and the "Grand Staff"
- Separating music into bars
- Rhythmic values and counting

Now we'll begin to unlock the mysteries of music notation. The good news is that this is actually easier than you think. Once you learn and understand the rules, it all starts to make sense. Music notation will tell you which notes to play, how long the notes are played, and when to play them (among other things). If you know all this stuff already, skip on to Chapter 4 where you can start playing some tunes! But for those of you who are new to the material, or just need a refresher… here we go!

THE MUSICAL STAFF

We'll start out with the *musical staff*, which is a collection of five parallel lines, like this:

When notes are written on the staff, they can be written on the lines (the "line notes") or on the spaces between the lines ("space notes"). You remember back in Chapter 1, we defined the music alphabet (using the letters A–G) to label the notes on the keyboard. So now we need some way to relate these letter names to the lines and spaces on the music staff, so that we know which note corresponds to each line or space. This is achieved by using a *clef*, which is a symbol placed at the beginning of the music staff to let us know how the letters in the music alphabet are allocated to the staff lines and spaces. Pretty cool huh!

THE TREBLE CLEF

The first clef we'll be looking at is the *treble clef*. This is used to represent the upper portion of the keyboard—notes normally played with the right hand:

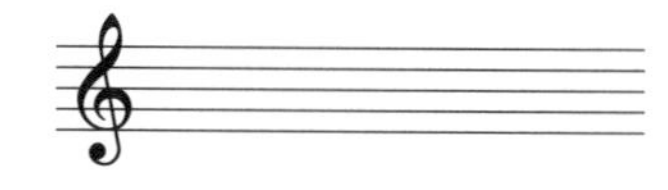

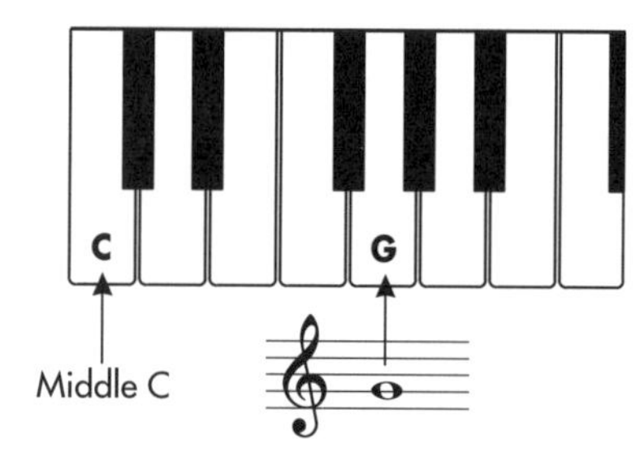

This clef is a *G clef*. If you take a close look at the clef symbol, you'll notice the lower part of the symbol circles around the second line from the bottom of the staff. This clef is telling you that the second staff line from the bottom represents the note G. Once we know that, we can easily work out which letter names are allocated to the remaining line and space notes on the staff. Let's now relate the clef to the notes on the keyboard, as follows:

You remember from Chapter 1 that the note G was found between the first 2 black keys in the set of three black keys together. It turns out that the G on the second staff line (from the bottom) of the treble clef, is not just "any old G"—it is specifically the G above *middle C*. This all-important reference note we call *middle C* is the C which is found in the middle of the piano keyboard. Go ahead and find it on your instrument!

We said earlier that "line" and "space" notes can be written on the musical staff. Let's now take a look at the line and space notes used in the treble clef:

We've already shown that the second "line note" in the left-hand diagram is G. The other letter names are allocated to the remaining lines and spaces on the staff, according to the musical alphabet. For example, the next note above G on the keyboard is A (as we "wrap around" to the start of the alphabet), and if you look in the right-hand diagram, the note A is the second note shown (a "space note"), which is the next note moving up the staff from G.

Some people like to use mnemonic sayings to learn or remember the line and space notes on the staff. For example, the line notes in the treble clef **E–G–B–D–F** could correspond to the phrase "**E**very **G**ood **B**oy **D**oes **F**ine." Also, the space notes **F–A–C–E** spell the word "face," of course. Now, as this is a book primarily for beginners, it would be easy for me to recommend that you use these mnemonics (and indeed, other beginner books do exactly that). But the truth is, while they may be fun and handy at the very initial stages of learning, they are not suitable as a long-term way to learn and memorize your notes. Sorry... ! It's actually better to develop a more relative or "positional" technique to learn the note names, particularly when we develop the "Grand Staff," combining both hands (more about this shortly).

So far we've only been dealing with the white-key names and their location on the treble clef staff (or "treble staff"). Next, we'll see how to notate the black keys. Back in Chapter 1 we named the black keys with either a sharp (♯) or a flat (♭). Now we'll see how these notes are notated on the staff, as follows:

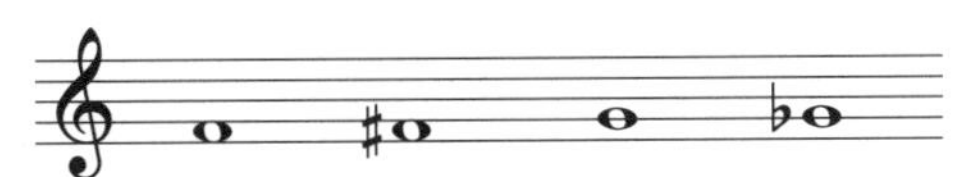

The first note shown above is F, and then the next note is F♯. Notice that this is still in the "F space," but now with a sharp sign (♯) to its left. Similarly, following the G, we have a G♭, which is still on the "G line," but now with a flat sign (♭) to its left.

Notice how both the sharp and flat signs are exactly on the same line or space as the note they are affecting. When you're writing your own music, remember not to write them too high or too low, relative to the note! I'll sometimes even see this mistake being made by experienced musicians... just a small point, but something to be aware of.

THE BASS CLEF

On to our next clef, the *bass clef*. This is used to represent the lower portion of the keyboard—notes normally played with the left hand:

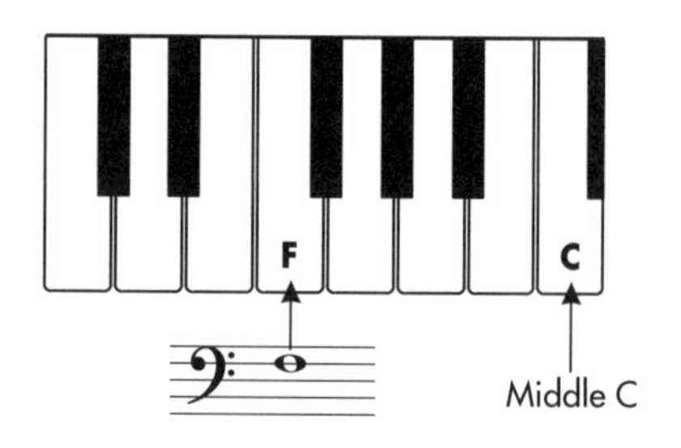

This clef is an *F clef*. If you take a close look at the clef symbol, you'll notice that the clef seems to be attached to the second line from the top of the staff, with two dots on either side. This tells you that the second staff line from the top represents the note F. Once we know that, we can easily work out which letter names are allocated to the remaining line and space notes on the staff. So let's now relate this clef to the notes on the keyboard, as follows:

We saw in Chapter 1 that the note F was found to the left of the set of three black keys. The F on the second staff line from the top of the bass clef is actually the F below middle C on the keyboard.

Now we'll take a look at the line and space notes used in the bass clef:

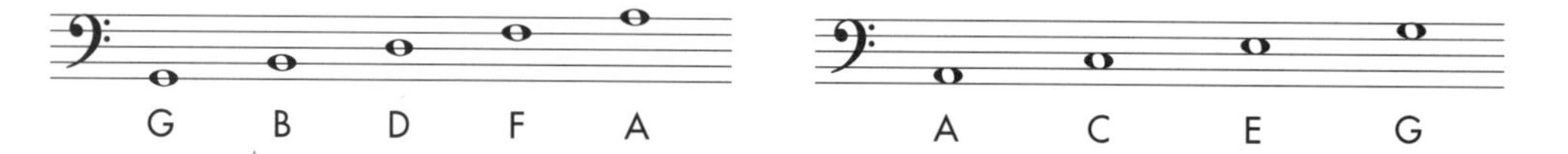

Note that the fourth "line note" in the left-hand diagram is an F, as this is on the second line from the top of the staff (between the two dots in the clef symbol). The other letter names are allocated to the remaining lines and spaces on the staff, according to the musical alphabet.

Again, it's possible to use mnemonics to get acquainted with the notes in the bass clef. For example, the line notes in the bass clef **G–B–D–F–A** could correspond to the phrase "**G**ood **B**oys **D**o **F**ine **A**lways," and the space notes in the bass clef **A–C–E–G** could correspond to the phrase "**A**ll **C**ows **E**at **G**rass."

THE GRAND STAFF

Fasten your seat belts... now it's time to join the treble and bass clefs together to create what is known as the *grand staff*. This is normally how piano music is written, with the right hand playing the treble clef part, and the left hand playing the bass clef part. Notice there is now a line connecting the two staffs (or *staves*) together, and also a bracket is added, signifying that they are "grouped" together.

MIDDLE C AND LEDGER LINES

Now we come back to the note *middle C*, which I mentioned earlier. It turns out that this note is just a little below the treble clef, and just a little above the bass clef. So we need to extend the clefs by adding another small staff line (known as a *ledger* line) to accommodate this note:

It's important to understand that *both* of the notes shown above are actually middle C. We know that the bottom line note in the treble clef is E. Well, if we go down one letter name to D, this note would sit right below the bottom staff line, and then one further note down to C would need an extra staff line below, which is exactly what the ledger line is. Similarly, we know that the top line note in the bass clef is A. Then if we go up one letter name to B, this note would sit right above the top staff line, and then one further note up to C would again need the extra staff line or ledger line.

Middle C is both the first ledger line below the treble clef, *and* the first ledger line above the bass clef. This important relationship will help you get oriented to the grand staff.

LEARNING THE NOTE NAMES IN TREBLE AND BASS CLEFS

Now we'll develop some techniques to begin learning the note names across the range of the treble and bass clefs (or "grand staff"). In my classes and books, I often talk about developing "guideposts" to help you recognize the notes. Our first set of guideposts consists of all the C notes (… not $100 bills!) within a four-octave range, centered around middle C, as follows:

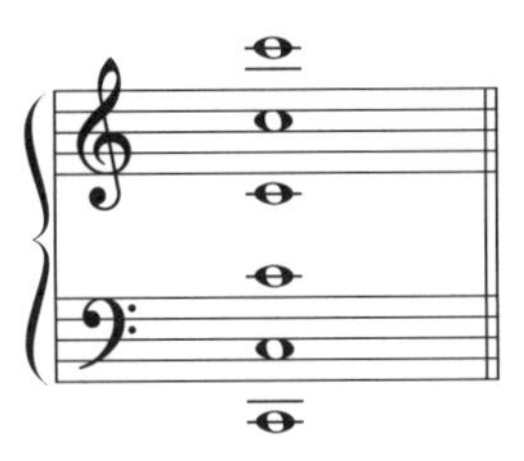

Comparing this to the previous diagram, notice that the middle C's are still there, but now we have some extra notes. We remember that the third space of the treble clef is also C (this is an octave above middle C), and that the second space of the bass clef is again C (this is an octave below middle C). The notes at the very top and bottom are also C's, and require two ledger lines each, as they are above and below the staffs, respectively.

Find and play all of these C's on your piano. (Don't forget that the note C is to the left of the set of two black keys). Play middle C with your right hand (it doesn't matter with which finger, for now!), then play the C an octave above that, then the C an octave above again. Next, play middle C with your left hand, then play the C an octave below that, then the C an octave below again. Congratulations! You just played all the notes in the above example.

Now, learning and memorizing where these C's are on the grand staff is fairly easy. Notice that there is a "mirror-image" or symmetrical relationship on either side (above and below) of middle C. These "guideposts" are handy when figuring out other notes on the grand staff—at least you could count up or down within the music alphabet, from the nearest C. The next stage is to add and memorize some more guideposts. How about adding all of the G's within this four-octave range? Let's try it:

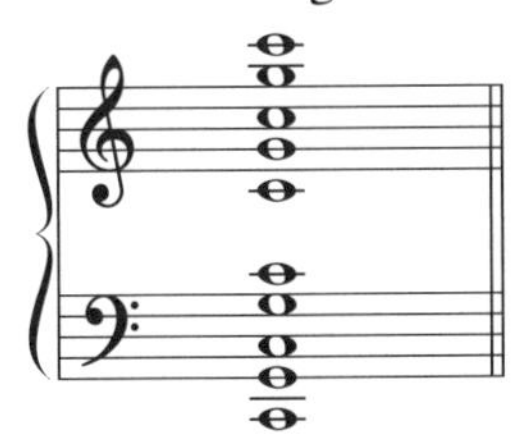

Now this stack of notes looks a bit more intense, but all we've done is add two G's in the treble clef (on the second line, and right above the top line) and two G's in the bass clef (in the top space, and on the bottom line). Although these are not exactly symmetrical on either side of middle C—well, they're pretty darn close—I think they're fairly easy to memorize visually.

Now go ahead and play all of these C's and G's on your piano. You guessed it, start with middle C in the right hand, then the G above that, then the C above that, and so on. Then play middle C with your left hand, then the G below that, then the C below that, and so on. As you're finding these notes on the keyboard, make sure you also read and relate to the written notation example.

Once you've memorized these notes, and you're trying to figure out other notes on either the treble or bass staves, remember that you'll never be more than two notes away from a C or a G, and you can work up or down the music alphabet as needed. This is, of course, only a temporary method (i.e., until you gradually learn all of the notes individually), however, it's still *way* better than fooling around with mnemonics for note names… at least in my humble opinion!

Let's now "fill in all the blanks" and take a look at look at all of the notes between the lowest and highest Cs shown in the previous examples:

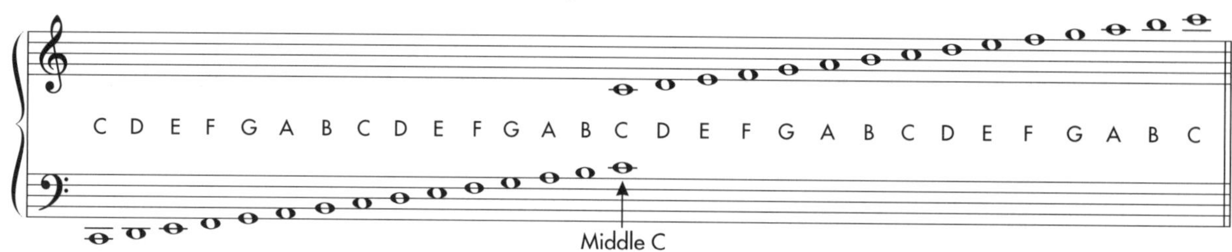

You should make it a goal to learn all of these notes individually. On the road toward this goal, learning the "guideposts" in the previous examples will definitely help you. Ninety percent (or more) of the music that you read and play will be within this 4-octave range. (However, you should still dust those keys at the top and bottom of your piano!)

SEPARATING MUSIC INTO MEASURES

So far we've just been concerned with the pitches of the notes (i.e., how high or low they are) and where they are positioned on the staff. Now we'll learn about the vital part that rhythm plays in music, and in how we notate the music. Most styles of music have a rhythmic *beat* or *pulse* to them. When you tap your feet along with a piece of music, most likely you are tapping along with the beat. These beats are then grouped into *measures* (or *bars*) when the music is notated. Here is an example of a treble staff with bar lines separating the measures:

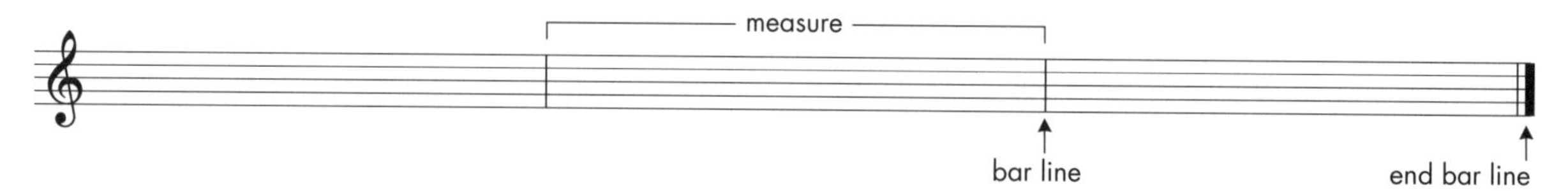

Notice at the end that we have two bar lines, one thin and one thick. This "double bar line" is known as the final bar line or final double bar, and is used to show the end of the song. In future musical examples, you may see two thin bar lines at the end. This is used to show the end of a section of music, but not the "end end."

4/4 TIME SIGNATURE

Much of the music that you will play will have *four beats in each measure*. This means that, when we count the beats, after we get to 4 we will go back to 1: "1, 2, 3, 4, 1, 2, 3, 4," etc. By now you're probably thinking that we need a way to let whoever's reading the music know how many beats there are in each measure. Well, you'd be right. This is called a *time signature* and is placed right after the clef sign, as follows:

The *top* number of the time signature (4 in this case) indicates *how many beats* there are in each measure. These beats are where you would normally tap your foot! The *bottom* number of the time signature (again 4 in this case) indicates what *rhythmic value* is assigned to the beat.

We're about to be introduced to different rhythmic values (i.e., note lengths) such as quarter notes, half notes, and whole notes. The 4 at the bottom of the time signature means that each beat in the measure will be a quarter note. The 4/4 time signature, therefore means that there are four quarter-note beats per measure. More about quarter notes in a minute…

The 4/4 time signature is also referred to as "common time," probably because it is overwhelmingly the most common time signature in music. "Common time" also has its own symbol:

So any time you see this "C" symbol used as a time signature, that's equivalent to 4/4 time. You may see either one—they both mean the same thing.

INTRODUCING NOTE LENGTHS

Now we need to get into *note lengths*—how many beats each note lasts. Let's first have a look at the *quarter note*, which lasts for one beat, and is written with a black (or "filled in") notehead, and a long stem attached:

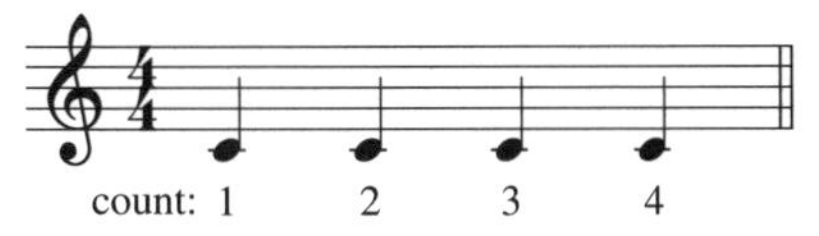

Play these quarter notes on your piano, using the thumb of the right hand. Count out loud "1, 2, 3, 4" as you play (holding each note for one beat).

So why is this called a quarter note (I hear you ask)? Well, we already said that music most often uses the 4/4 time signature (i.e., has four beats per measure). So, in this case, the note lasting for one beat is also a quarter of the measure. Next, we'll look at the *half note*, which lasts for two beats (or half of the 4/4 measure), and is written with a white (or "empty") notehead, and a long stem attached:

Play these half notes on your piano, using the thumb of the right hand. Count out loud "1, 2, 3, 4" as you play (and play the notes on "1" and "3," holding each note for two beats).

You've probably noticed that both the quarter notes and half notes have stems, in this case to the right of each note, and going upwards. However, once the notehead gets to the middle line of the staff or above, the stem is then on the left of the note and goes downwards.

Next, we have the whole note which lasts for four beats and is written with a white (or "empty") notehead, and no stem:

Play this whole note on your piano, using the thumb of the right hand. Count out loud "1, 2, 3, 4" as you play. Start playing right on count "1," and hold it for four beats.

Similar logic is again behind the naming of the whole note: it lasts for four beats, and is also the whole of a 4/4 measure.

Back in Jolly Olde England (where I'm originally from, before I moved to California in the 1980s), they have these rather odd names for different note durations. Instead of quarter note they say "crotchet;" instead of half note they say "minim;" and...wait for it... instead of whole note they say (... drum roll...) "semibreve." Gotta love those Brits... anyway, be thankful that you're using the good ol' American system. It's way more logical and easy to use!

COUNTING RHYTHMS WITH QUARTER, HALF, AND WHOLE NOTES

Next, we have an example written in 4/4 time (combining different rhythmic values), and we'll see how to "count our way" through it.

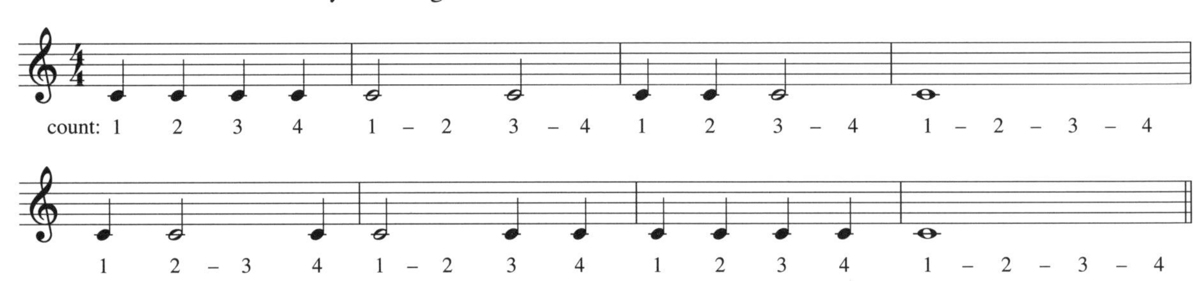

Notice the counting under the staff. We have one number (equal to one beat) under each quarter note, two numbers (equal to two beats) under each half note, and four numbers (equal to four beats) under each whole note.

Listen to **track 1** on the CD, and try to play these rhythms while counting along. Notice that there is one count-off measure on the CD before the music starts—four clicks to let you know the tempo, and where to come in.

The sum of all the rhythmic values in each measure has to add up to the time signature (in this case four beats). For example, in the third measure above, we have two quarter notes (1 beat each), and one half note (2 beats): 1 + 1 + 2 = 4 beats total, so we're OK.

INTRODUCING RESTS

Sometimes one hand or the other will take a break, rather than keep playing continuously. This is shown in the music with rests, which let you know how many beats of silence should be "played" (or not played). Here are some examples:

These rests last for one, two, and four beats, respectively. Finally, in this chapter, we'll combine some notes and rests together, again just playing middle C with the right thumb for now:

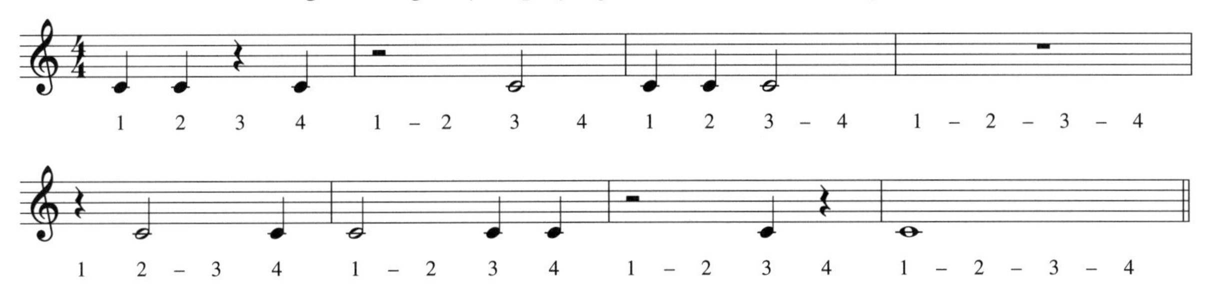

Listen to **track 2** on the CD and try to play the example while counting along. Make sure you *play* the notes, but *don't play* during the rests. Again, there is one "count-off measure" on the CD before the music starts. Also notice how the tempo remains the same, even on the rests. (Rests are just as important as notes, so don't rush them, and, especially, don't ignore them!)

The sum of all the rhythmic values (now including notes and rests) in each measure has to add up to the time signature. For example, in the seventh measure above, we have one half rest (2 beats), one quarter note (1 beat) and one quarter rest (1 beat): 2 + 1 + 1 = 4 beats total, so again, we're OK.

CHAPTER 4

RIGHT-HAND SONGS IN C POSITION

What's Ahead:

- Fingers and finger numbers
- The right-hand C Position
- Pickup measures

FINGERS AND FINGER NUMBERS

In this chapter, we finally get to play some songs! So far we've found out how to read and recognize note names and lengths when reading music. But, I hear you ask, "How do I know which fingers to use on the notes?" Good question! After all, we have five fingers in each hand (unless you're the piano player in the movie *Gattaca*!), and beginning-level players often need some guidance as to which fingers to use.

The songs in the next few chapters all have the fingerings marked next to the notes. These fingerings consist of the numbers: 1, 2, 3, 4, and 5, corresponding to the fingers (on either hand) as follows:

1 Thumb
2 Index finger
3 Middle finger
4 "Ring" finger
5 Pinkie, or little finger

Here is a visual reference of these finger numbers, for the right hand:

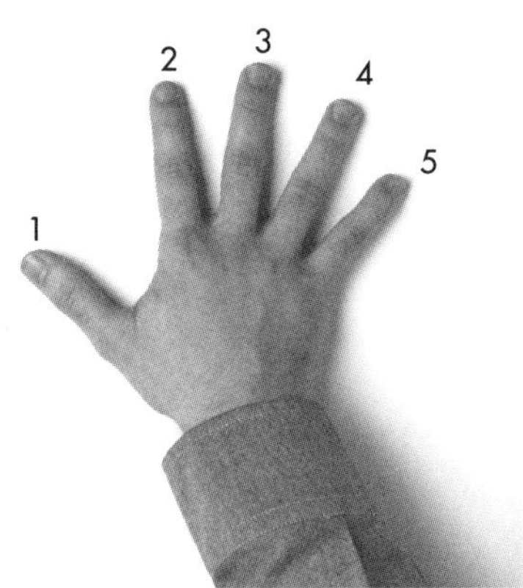

THE RIGHT-HAND C POSITION

Hand positions are very important when playing the piano. A hand position allows the pianist to access a particular group of notes (for example, C-D-E-F-G) on the keyboard. Within that group, different fingerings (using finger numbers 1 through 5) will be used. If the piece of music needs notes that are not accessible within the current hand position, then the hand will be moved to a new position, and so on.

For the next couple of chapters, we're going to stick with songs that are all contained within one hand position, as an easy way to get started. Then later, we'll move on to songs that need hand position changes.

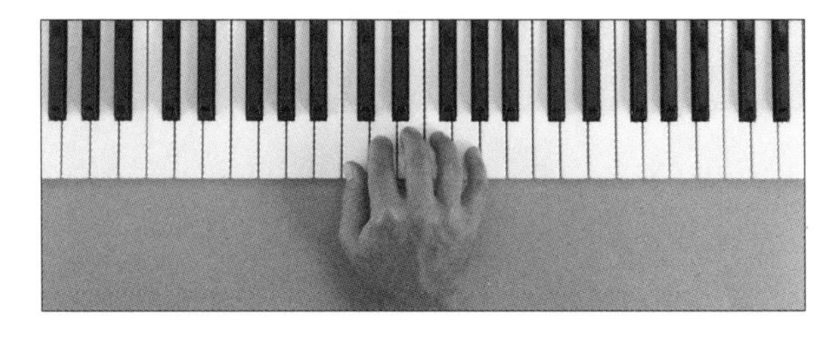

The first hand position we're going to use is the right-hand *C Position.* For this you'll rest the thumb of the right hand on middle C, and the pinkie on the G above middle C, with the other fingers evenly spread out on the white keys in between.

Now we're going to play our first song in right-hand *C Position*, "Go Tell Aunt Rhody." Try playing the song on your own first, without listening to the CD, using the fingering numbers above each note (as opposed to below, where our "counting" numbers would go). Practice it a few times to get the feel of it.

audio tracks 3

Go Tell Aunt Rhody

Traditional

fingers: 3 3 2 1 2 4 3 2 1

counts: 1 – 2 3 4

Go tell Aunt Rho - dy, go tell Aunt Rho - dy,

5 4 3 1 2 4 3 2 1

go tell Aunt Rho - dy the old grey goose is dead.

How'd it go? Now that you've played it a couple of times, have a listen to **track 3**. How close were you to the recording? Try playing along with the CD track now.

Count the rhythms as you play through this song with **track 3**. Again, you'll hear the four "clicks" before the song starts, and you can count "1, 2, 3, 4" during this count-off measure. The first measure of counting is written in for you, and you may pencil in the rest. If you get stuck, turn back to Chapter 3 to remind yourself how we did this.

Pretty strange lyrics in this song, huh?! (none of this "I love you" stuff...) When you're comfortable playing through the piece without counting, try singing the lyrics while you play. Don't worry if you don't have the greatest singing voice, you're just having fun (and besides, singing along while you are playing is a really good "ear training" exercise).

PICKUP MEASURES

Notice that in the last song, the very first melody note began on beat 1 of the first measure. "So what?" I hear you say, "Why wouldn't it?" Well, believe it or not, there are a lot of songs that start part-way into the first measure (in other words, on either beat 2, 3, or 4). We could write one or more rests at the beginning of the first measure to indicate this, but in practice, composers normally use a "pickup measure" instead, which omits the rests at the beginning (you're already silent before you start playing, right?). So, in the first measure of the next example, instead of the four beats we would expect in 4/4 time, notice there are only three beats. This is the pickup measure you've heard so much about, with the first melody note (C) falling on beat 2 of the measure.

...On to our next song in *C Position*, "When the Saints Go Marching In." Practice the tune on your own first, and remember to follow the finger numbers. After you've played it a bit, have a listen to **track 4** on the CD, and play along.

When the Saints Go Marching In

Words by Katherine E. Purvis
Music by James M. Black

Oh when the saints go march - ing in,
oh when the saints go march - ing in,
oh Lord I want to be in that num - ber
when the saints go march - ing in.

Watch out for the pickup measure as you listen to this song on the CD. You will actually hear five metronome clicks before the first melody note. The first four clicks are beats 1, 2, 3, and 4 of the count-off measure, and then the next click is beat 1 of the pickup measure (the “missing” beat) before the melody actually starts, on beat 2. Cool huh!

This is also our first song containing a mixture of notes and rests. Make sure you observe (i.e., don’t play during) the rests, and count your way through each measure as needed. You may write in the counts below the notes as you did before if it helps. Have fun!

CHAPTER 5
LEFT-HAND SONGS IN C POSITION

What's Ahead:
- Fingers and finger numbers
- The left-hand C Position

FINGERS AND FINGER NUMBERS

Now we'll start to play some songs using the left hand. Again, we'll be using the finger numbers 1, 2, 3, 4, and 5 to refer to the fingers (thumb through pinkie). Here's a visual reference of these numbers, for the left hand:

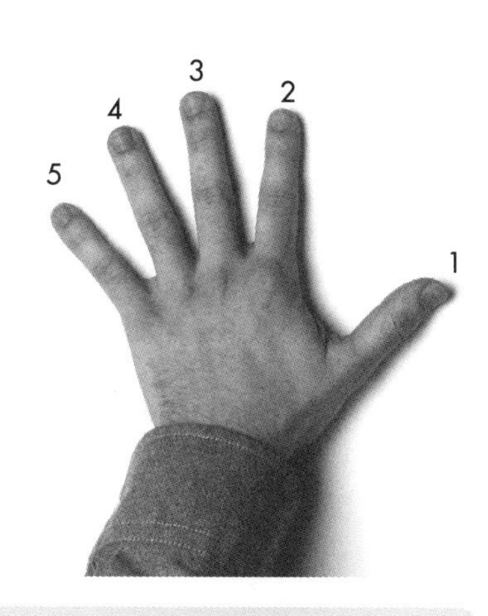

Quite a lot of beginners and self-taught players have a much weaker left hand than right hand, in terms of technique and dexterity (not to mention note recognition in bass clef!). So it's good that we start working on your left hand right away, in order for you to stay on track and develop both hands at the same pace.

Like most right-handed people, I would normally use my right hand for the mouse or trackball when working on the computer. Anyway, several years ago I noticed that the combination of my piano playing with all the work I was doing on the computer, was making my right hand and wrist very fatigued and sore. So I made a conscious decision to switch all my mouse and trackball operations to my left hand. This felt very weird at first, but it soon became natural, and now it feels odd doing these things with my right hand! Anyway, this helped to "even out the load" between my hands, and was a major benefit. You may wish to consider switching tasks to your left hand, to build up independence and strength in your left hand, and also to lighten the load for the right hand, if needed!

THE LEFT-HAND C POSITION

Next, we'll put the left hand in *C Position*. For this, you'll rest the pinkie of the left hand on the C below middle C, and the thumb on the G below middle C, with the other fingers evenly spread out on the white keys in between:

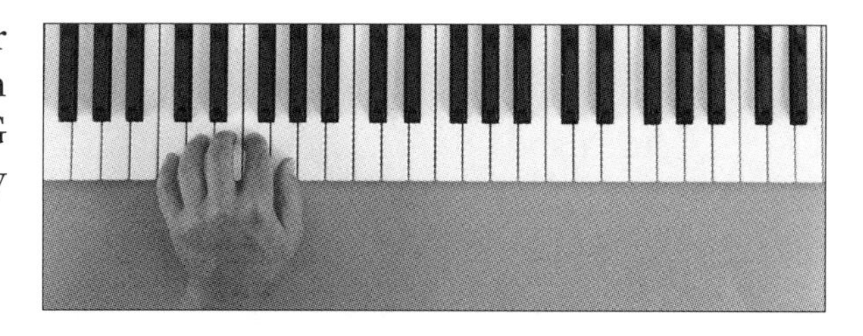

Now we're going to play our first song in left-hand *C Position*, "Dry Bones." Look it over, then get your hand into place and give it a go, remembering all the same things we concentrated on with the right-hand songs: fingering, counting, even tempo, singing along, etc. After that, have a listen to **track 5** on the CD, and then play along.

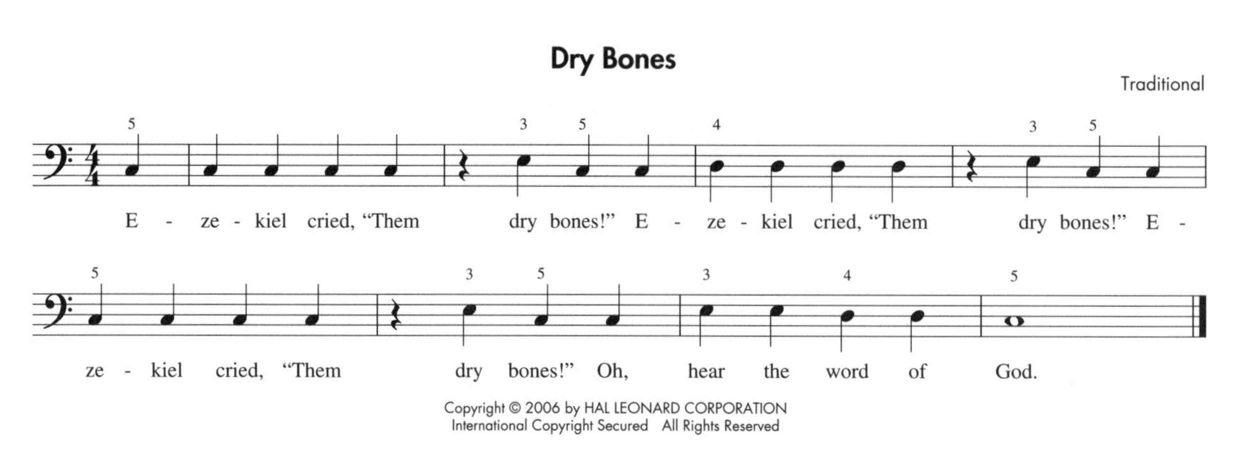

Notice we again have a "pickup measure" at the beginning of this song. Even though the normal 4/4 time signature is shown at the beginning of the first line, there is only one beat in the first measure. This first note is, therefore, beat 4 of the measure, so we're actually resting for the first three beats.

Now on to our next song using the left-hand *C Position*, "Home Sweet Home." Give it a whirl, and then listen to **track 6** on the CD:

Yup, you guessed it—there's another pickup measure at the start of this song, this time we have C and D being played on beats 3 and 4.

All of these songs have fingerings added, so make sure that you use them, and stay within the hand position shown. Have fun!

CHAPTER 6

MORE NOTATION AND RHYTHMS

What's Ahead:

- Introducing eighth notes and rests
- Counting rhythms with eighth notes
- Dotted notes, ties, and triplets
- "Straight" and "swing" feels
- Introducing sixteenth notes and rests
- Counting rhythms with sixteenth notes

INTRODUCING EIGHTH NOTES

Continuing our work from Chapter 3, where we started to look at different note lengths (quarter notes, half notes, etc.), we're next going to look at the *eighth note*, which lasts for half a beat. The eighth note is written with a black (or "filled in") notehead, a long stem attached, and either a "flag" if the note is by itself, or a "beam" if the note is joined to other notes. Sometimes the beam may join two eighth notes together within one beat, or the beam may join four eighth notes within two successive beats.

The next example shows the various ways eighth notes could be notated (flags and beams) as a demonstration, but normally, the entire example would be notated as in the second measure. Later on, we will learn the reasons for using flags and different beam groups. For now, let's play some eighth notes!

Notice the rhythmic counting underneath the staff, which now uses an "&" between each of the beat numbers.

"And" (&) is what we count for notes that fall halfway between the beat.

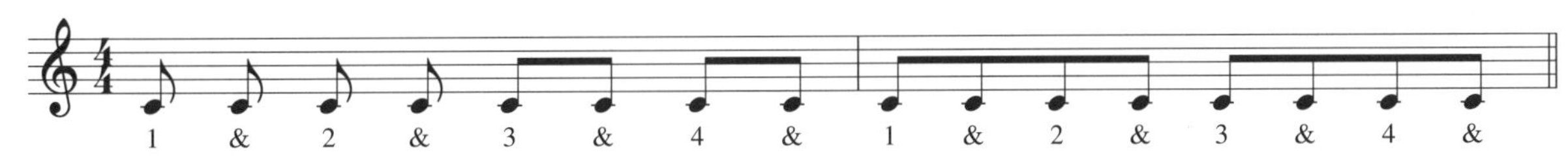

Listen to **track 7** on the CD, and then play this eighth-note pattern while counting along. As usual, you have one "count-off measure" on the CD before the music starts, and the click is on every quarter-note beat. This means that you will be playing in between the clicks when playing on the "&'s," as shown above.

In situations where eighth notes are used, the notes falling on the beats (i.e., on 1, 2, 3, or 4) are referred to as *downbeats*, and the notes falling on the "&'s," in between, are referred to as *upbeats*. Also, the eighth note following beat 1 is referred to as the "'and' of 1." The eighth note following beat 2 is referred to as the "'and' of 2," and so on. So now you know…

So why are these guys called "eighth notes?" Well, we saw in Chapter 3 that note lengths were named according to what fraction they used of a 4/4 measure (for example, a quarter note takes up a quarter of a 4/4 measure). So an eighth note (lasting half of one beat) takes up one-eighth of a 4/4 measure. Eighth notes may also be beamed (or joined) to other smaller note values, such as sixteenth notes (more about sixteenths soon).

INTRODUCING DOTTED NOTES

Now we will go boldly into the realm of dotted notes! Whenever a dot is placed after a note, it adds half as much again to the rhythmic value or length (or if you're a math whiz, it multiplies the existing length by 1.5). Let's check out the following example:

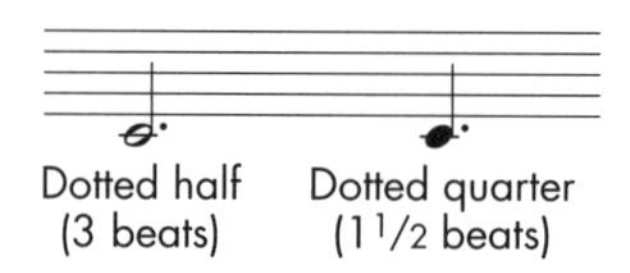

Without the dot, the first note above would just be a half note (lasting for 2 beats). But with addition of the dot, we add half as much again to the original length, so the note now lasts for 3 beats. Similarly, without the dot, the second note would just be a quarter note (lasting for 1 beat). But with the dot, we add half as much again to the original length, so the note now lasts for 1 1/2 beats.

Next, we will see some typical ways in which these dotted notes can be used in a melody. If we use a dotted half note (3 beats) together with a quarter note (1 beat), the resulting total of four beats will fill a 4/4 measure. If we use a dotted quarter note (1 1/2 beats) together with an eighth note (1/2 a beat), the resulting total of two beats could occupy the first or second half of a 4/4 measure. These are extremely common rhythmic combinations, as shown in this sample melody:

Play this eighth-note rhythm pattern and melody using the right hand *C Position*, while counting along. Listen to **track 8** on the CD to "check your work," (did you play it evenly and count correctly?) and then play along.

It's good practice to count *all* of the eighth notes (i.e., 1 & 2 & 3 & 4 &, etc.) in this example as you play it, even though you are not playing on all off these rhythmic subdivisions. That way your rhythm will be correct and even, and when an eighth note comes along (for example, the F in the second measure) you'll be ready for it!

Now it's time for our first song using eighth notes and dotted notes, "Alouette." This time you get to use two hands, though not at the same time (yet!). Each hand is in *C Position* as you've learned in previous chapters, and the song is written on the grand staff (right hand on the upper treble staff, and left hand on the lower bass staff). Make sure to follow the fingering numbers next to each note. This song is not on the CD, so count carefully. It is good practice to write in the counting for all songs you play, especially when you're learning. The first line has been done for you, but you may pencil in the rest. Go on… you can do it!

INTRODUCING TIED NOTES

Now we're ready to look at *tied* notes. When two notes of the same pitch are joined by a curved line, they are tied together. This means that the second note is not played. Instead, the first note lasts for the combined length of both notes.

Listen to **track 9** and play the above eighth-note rhythm pattern while counting along. Notice that the C on the "and" of 4 in the first measure, lasts right up until the start of beat 2 in the second measure. In other words, this tied note lasts for one-and-a-half beats.

The previous example shows the most common situation where a tie is needed in the music: when the note length is longer than the remaining number of beats in the measure. In this case, the last C in the first measure falls on the "and" of 4 (so there is only half a beat left in the measure) and yet we need the note to last for one-and-a-half beats. So, tying across the bar line to the quarter note in the next measure neatly solves this problem.

In the next example, we have a tied note on the "and" of 2, receiving a total duration of one and a half beats. We also have a tied note on beat 4, which lasts for two beats. Remember not to play the second note in tied notes—just hold it!

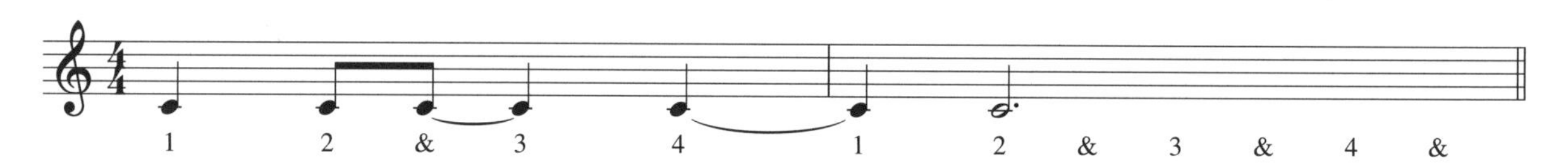

Try playing and counting the above example, and then listen to **track 10** to see if you got it right. Listen one more time while playing along.

"But wait!" I hear you cry, "Why did we need that first tie! Couldn't we have just used a dotted quarter note (which lasts for one-and-a-half beats) starting on the 'and' of 2 in the first measure? There's no bar line anywhere in sight!" Whoa, calm down a minute! The reason we did it this way is to show the start of beat 3. That is to say, whether or not we are actually playing on beat 3, it is very good practice and courtesy to show a note or rest right on the beat when the note begins in between the beat. This greatly aids sight-reading, as we can then quickly scan through the music and pick out beats 1 and 3 (sometimes called the primary beats) in 4/4 time. If you're ever preparing charts for other musicians, maybe to demo or perform your own songs, they will definitely appreciate it if you do this!

THE EIGHTH REST

Back in Chapter 3 we saw how to write rests equal to quarter, half, and whole notes. Now we'll get acquainted with the *eighth rest* (which as you might expect, lasts for half a beat):

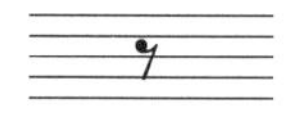

Next we'll look at another melody that includes some eighth notes and rests:

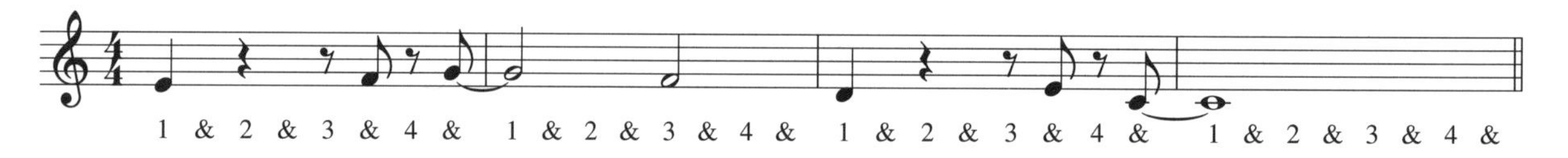

Note the counting under the staff, and the new eighth rests (each lasting for half a beat) in measures 1 and 3.

Play the above example while counting, then listen to **track 11**. As before, make sure that you *don't play* during the rests.

When learning new rhythms, try clapping and counting them first, before you play them on the piano.

EIGHTH-NOTE TRIPLETS

But wait, there's more stuff we can do with eighth notes. We can combine them into "triplets!" This means that, instead of fitting just two eighth notes into the space of one beat, we now squeeze three eighth notes into the same space:

Listen to **track 12** to hear the sound of eighth-note triplets. You'll hear three notes for each metronome tick. Try counting "1 trip-let 2 trip-let" etc., along with this rhythm, as evenly as you can.

Notice that each set of three eighth notes is beamed together, and that the number "3" is shown above each group. The "3" tells you that this note grouping is a triplet, and not just ordinary eighth notes.

"STRAIGHT EIGHTHS" VS. "SWING EIGHTHS"

Next, we have an interesting and useful variation of the previous example. Here we're not playing on the middle (second) part of each triplet, just on the first and third parts:

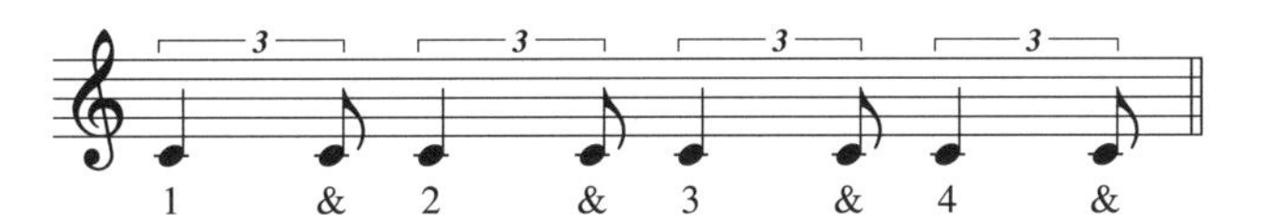

Listen to **track 13** and compare it to **track 12**. It sounds similar, except that the middle note of each triplet is "missing." If you were counting it "1 trip-let, 2 trip-let" etc., like **track 12**, there would be no note falling on the "trip-" syllable.

To simplify the counting, we could count it "1 & 2 & 3 & 4 &" as shown above, but compared to the earlier examples of eighth-note counting in this chapter, each "&" is now later in the beat than before (no longer exactly halfway between the beats). The "&" is now two-thirds of the way through each beat because of the triplet rhythms.

This is where "swing" notation comes into play. When we want this swing style to be played, instead of going through the trouble of writing out two notes with the triplet sign (the "3" inside the bracket) above each time, as in the previous example, we could just write plain old eighth notes and just play them differently. The first eighth gets held longer (like the quarter note under the triplet sign), and the second eighth is shorter (like the second eighth note under the triplet sign).

So, how do we know when to play the "even" eighth notes, and when to play the uneven "swing" eighth notes? If the song is to be played in swing style, it will be indicated with the word(s) "swing" or "swing eighths" above the time signature, where the tempo would be placed. In the next example, we have the same rhythm twice. The first one will be played "straight," with even eighth notes. In the second rhythm, we add the "swing eighths" indication above, telling us that this should be played with uneven eighths, like the triplet rhythms we saw earlier.

Listen to **track 14**, and notice that *Part 1* is played in a straight-eighths style, with each pair of eighth notes dividing the beat exactly in half. In *Part 2* the eighth notes are swung, played as if each pair of eighth notes were a quarter note-eighth note triplet, resulting in all the upbeats or "&'s" falling two-thirds of the way through each beat.

If you're at all interested in playing styles such as pop, rock, and jazz, you need to know this! The swing-eighths feel is present in many styles, and you need to know how to get things swingin' when you see this indication in the music.

Usually, if eighth notes are to be played *straight*, there is no indication of this; you should just assume to play them straight unless you see the "swing eighths" indication. However, occasionally, if you're playing out of a jazz book where most of the music is in swing style, the indication "straight eighths" might be used for a straight tune, to help distinguish it from all the other swinging music.

Also, regardless of how we treat the eighth notes (straight or swing), remember that the downbeats (i.e., beats 1, 2, 3, and 4, in 4/4 time) do not move. We are simply moving the upbeats (or "&s") in between these downbeats.

In addition to the "Swing eighths" indication at the top, sometimes "Shuffle" is used, or we can use this symbol:

This symbol is telling us to play each pair of eighth notes as if it were a quarter note-eighth note triplet," in other words, to divide each beat in a two-thirds/one-third manner (rather than half-and-half). It's very good practice to begin applying straight- and swing- eighths feels to different songs… have fun with this!

INTRODUCING DOTTED EIGHTH NOTES

OK, we're not quite done with eighth notes yet. We can also place a "dot" after them, which as you might expect, adds half as much again to the length of the note (increasing the length to three-quarters of a beat):

We saw earlier that a dotted quarter note often gets together with an eighth note to create a two-beat unit. In a similar way, we can combine a dotted eighth note with a sixteenth note, to create a one-beat unit. "Wait. What is a sixteenth note?" Good question…

INTRODUCING SIXTEENTH NOTES

The sixteenth note lasts for a quarter of a beat and is written with a black (or "filled in") note-head, a long stem attached, and either a double "flag" if the note is by itself, or a double beam if the note is joined to other notes. Sometimes the beams may join a pair of sixteenth notes together, or the beams may join all of the sixteenth notes within one beat.

Now that we're dividing the beat into 4 pieces, we need a different counting method. This new addition to our rhythmic counting includes the three symbols "e," "&," and "a" between each of the beat numbers:

Listen to **track 15** and play the above sixteenth-note rhythm pattern while counting aloud. Now there are four notes for every metronome click. Try to space the notes as evenly as possible between the downbeats.

Just a minute ago we talked about combining sixteenth notes with dotted eighth notes. Here's a melody that does just that:

Listen to **track 16** and play this dotted-eighth–sixteenth-note rhythm pattern and melody using the right hand *C Position*, while counting along.

It's good practice to count all of the sixteenth notes (1 e & a 2 e & a, etc.) in this example as you play it, even though you are not playing on all of these rhythmic subdivisions. This way, everything will be evenly spaced, and when a sixteenth note comes along (i.e., the D in the first measure) you'll be ready for it!

THE SIXTEENTH REST

Next, we'll get acquainted with the *sixteenth rest*, which as you might expect, lasts for a quarter of a beat:

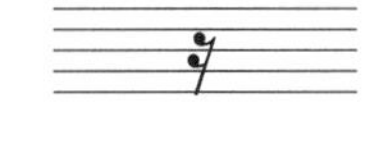

This rest looks like the eighth rest, except that it has two flags instead of one.

Finally, in this chapter, we'll look at a melody that combines quarter notes and quarter rests, eighth notes and eighth rests, and sixteenth notes and sixteenth rests:

Note the counting under the staff and the new sixteenth rests (each lasting for a quarter of a beat) in both measures.

Listen to **track 17** and play the example while counting along. As before, make sure that you don't play during the rests. Have fun!

CHAPTER 7
MAJOR SCALES AND KEYS

What's Ahead:

- The building blocks of scales
- Building major scales
- Playing major scales (with fingerings)
- Key signatures
- Using accidentals

THE BUILDING BLOCKS OF SCALES

In this chapter we're going to learn about the *major scale*, which is the most commonly used scale in Western music. Most famous melodies that you know are constructed from major scales.

A *scale* is a sequence of notes created using a specific set of intervals. Most scales (including the major scale) are created using half-step and whole-step intervals, although some scales contain larger intervals. Back in Chapter 1, we saw that the half step was the interval between any note and the nearest note either above or below on the keyboard. Now we will define the *whole step* as double the size of the half step, as shown below:

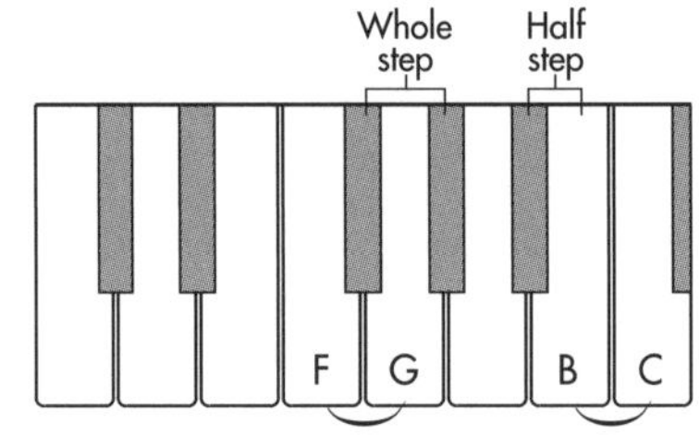

Notice that the whole-step intervals are equivalent to two half steps. For example, the whole step F–G includes two half steps (F–F♯ and F♯–G), and the whole step F♯–G♯ includes two half steps (F♯–G and G–G♯). Two half steps are also shown for comparison (A♯–B and B–C). So now that we have our half steps and whole steps figured out, we can build all of our major scales pretty easily!

BUILDING MAJOR SCALES

We are now going to build a *C major scale*, using a specific sequence of whole steps and half steps:

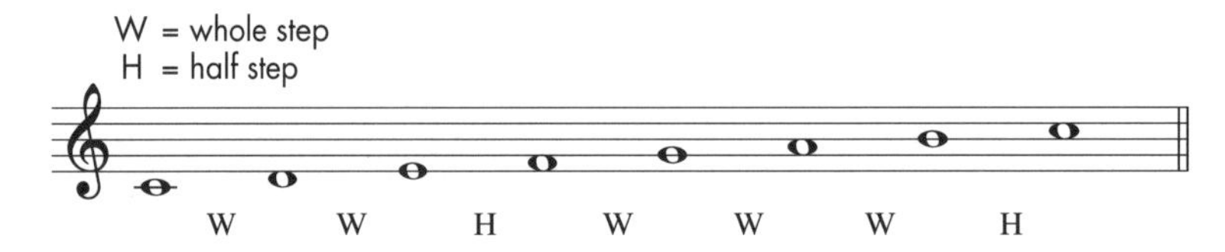

It just so happens that when we construct this pattern of intervals starting on the note C, we use all the remaining white keys on the keyboard. The C major scale is a "white key-only" scale. As we'll see, if we start this pattern of intervals from any other note, we'll end up with a mixture of white and black keys. The major scale is a seven-note scale (i.e., there are seven different pitches), and we have used all the letter names in the music alphabet, consecutively (with no letter name being used more than once).

Play the notes of this scale on your piano, and get the sound "in your ear." Don't worry too much about fingerings for the moment—we'll cover those in just a minute.

The major scale should be a familiar and recognizable sound. My former mentor Dick Grove (one of the greatest American contemporary music educators of the 20th century) was fond of saying that the major scale "came over on a boat from Europe." In other words, it was a pre-determined set of intervals that your "inner ear" already understood, assuming you had some exposure to mainstream tonal music.

Now we'll build this same pattern of whole steps and half steps from F, to create the *F major scale*:

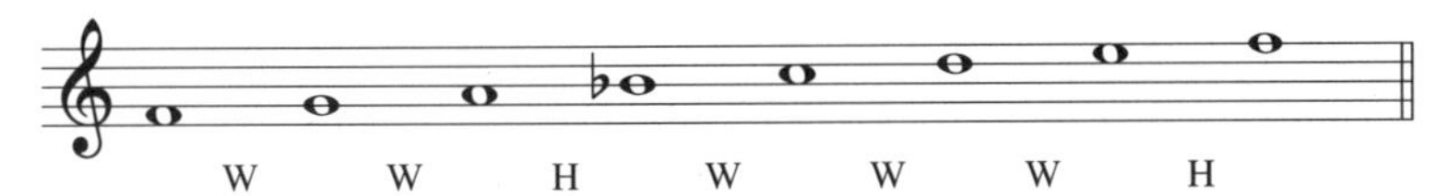

Notice that we now have the note B♭ as the fourth degree of this scale. This is because we need a half step between the third and fourth degrees. B will be the next letter name after A, and thus the black key that we need to get our half step up from A will be called B flat. Next we'll use the same method to build a G major scale:

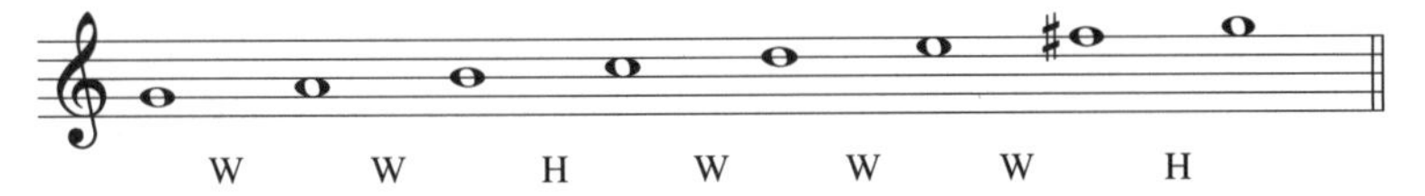

Notice that we now have the note F♯ as the seventh degree of this scale. This is because we need a whole step between the sixth and seventh degrees, therefore, a black key is needed. We also know that the next letter after E is F, and the black key associated with this F should be called F sharp.

There are many more major scales, but for now, these three should get you started. In order to use the scales for playing songs, we first need to learn how to play them with the proper fingering.

Why Do I Need to Play Scales?

Yes, yes, I know… playing scales doesn't seem very exciting, and you might be thinking, "Gee, I just wanna get to the fun stuff!" But wait! Don't turn the page just yet, because knowing and playing the scales will greatly benefit your piano performance, whatever styles you are interested in. So what are the benefits to playing scales, anyway? Several, actually:

- They are great for building technique on the piano. Whether you're playing Beethoven or Jerry Lee Lewis, you're going to need piano technique!
- The *thumb turns* needed to play scales are very good practice for the hand position changes needed when playing songs (coming up very soon).
- A lot of classical pieces and pop songs contain scales or portions of scales in their melodies. Having these sections already "under our fingers" is a great asset—it's like we know that part of the tune already!

Major Scales with Fingerings

The following shows the C major scale, with fingerings.

It's helpful to break the scale fingerings down into *fingering groups*, starting with the thumb: in this case 1-2-3, then 1-2-3-4-5. As you practice this scale with the fingering shown, make sure you keep the back of your hand straight and parallel to the keyboard, with the fingers curved. After the thumb plays C, it right away begins to turn under and cross behind fingers 2 and 3 so it is ready, in place to play F, right after E. As the thumb is playing F, fingers 2, 3, 4, and 5 line up with G, A, B, and C. Executing this thumb turn ahead of time, and lining up the rest of the fingers will help keep the scale "running" smoothly, without pause. To descend back to the starting point, everything runs in reverse. As the thumb is playing F, finger 3 crosses over to land on E, and then fingers 2 and 1 finish up on D and C.

Now it's time to get the left hand involved with the C major scale:

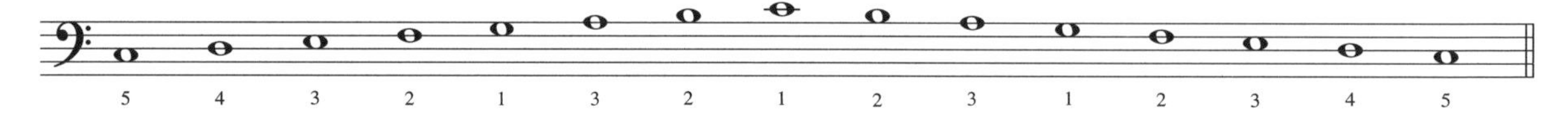

Just like with the right hand, here we can break the fingerings down into *fingering groups:* 5-4-3-2-1, and 3-2-1. Everything here is just like the right hand, but in reverse. With the left hand, we cross finger 3 over on the way up. On the way back down we have our thumb turn under after the first three fingers are played. Remember to get the thumb turning ahead of time to keep the scale running smoothly.

The same fingering works for the G major scale. The only difference is we have to play a black key as we learned a bit earlier. The scale is notated below on the grand staff so you can practice with your right and left hands (separately, for now).

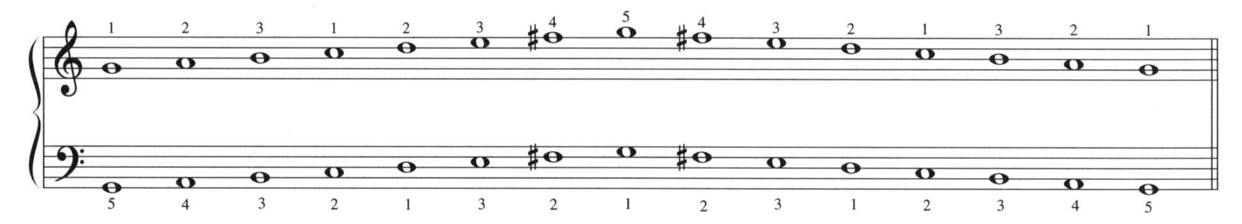

The F major scale uses the same fingering for the left hand, but because of where the black key lies, we have to use a slightly different fingering for the right hand. Instead of the thumb crossing under after the first three fingers, we wait until after the fourth, which plays the black key of B flat. The thumb will then pick things up on C, with the scale ending on the top F with finger 4. Just like the other scales, the reverse fingering is used on the way down. Once you get to the thumb on C, finger 4 crosses over to play B flat, finishing up with 3-2-1 on A, G, and F.

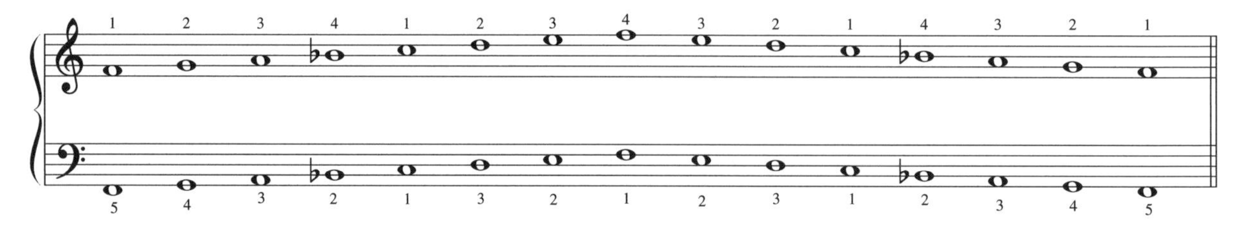

The thumb turn, along with the crossing over of finger 3 (or 4 in the F major scale) is a major part of playing the scales. This technique will also be used in the next chapter as we begin to move the hands around a bit in playing some great songs.

There are many more major scales—you can begin a major scale from every white and black key on the keyboard. We don't have space to show them all here, but you can check out my companion volume, *The Pop Piano Book* (also published by Hal Leonard Corporation) for more information and fingerings for all the major and pentatonic scales.

INTRODUCING KEY SIGNATURES

When we play the C major scale, we can hear that the note C sounds like the "home base" or "tonic" of the scale. If a song uses the C major scale, it is most likely in the *key of C major*.

A *key signature* is a group of sharps or flats at the beginning of the music, which lets you know which key you are in (and which major scale the song is based on). You probably didn't notice any key signatures in the songs we've played so far. That's because all of our songs have used the C major scale up to now, and have, therefore, been in the key of C, and the key signature for C major is "no sharps and no flats."

F major

Let's compare this to the key signature to the right, for *F major*:

G major

Relating this to the F major scale we built earlier, we remember that we needed the note B♭ as the fourth degree of this scale. The key signature is reminding you to play B♭ (instead of B) when playing in the *key of F*. That way we don't need to keep writing flat signs for the B♭ notes that come up in the music. Pretty cool labor-saving device, huh? Now look at the key signature for *G major* (left).

Relating this to the G major scale we built earlier, we remember that we needed the note F♯ as the seventh degree of this scale. So the key signature is reminding you to play F♯ (instead of F) when playing in the *key of G*. That way we don't need to keep writing sharp signs for the F♯ notes that come up in the music.

Here are all of the major key signatures, for your reference:

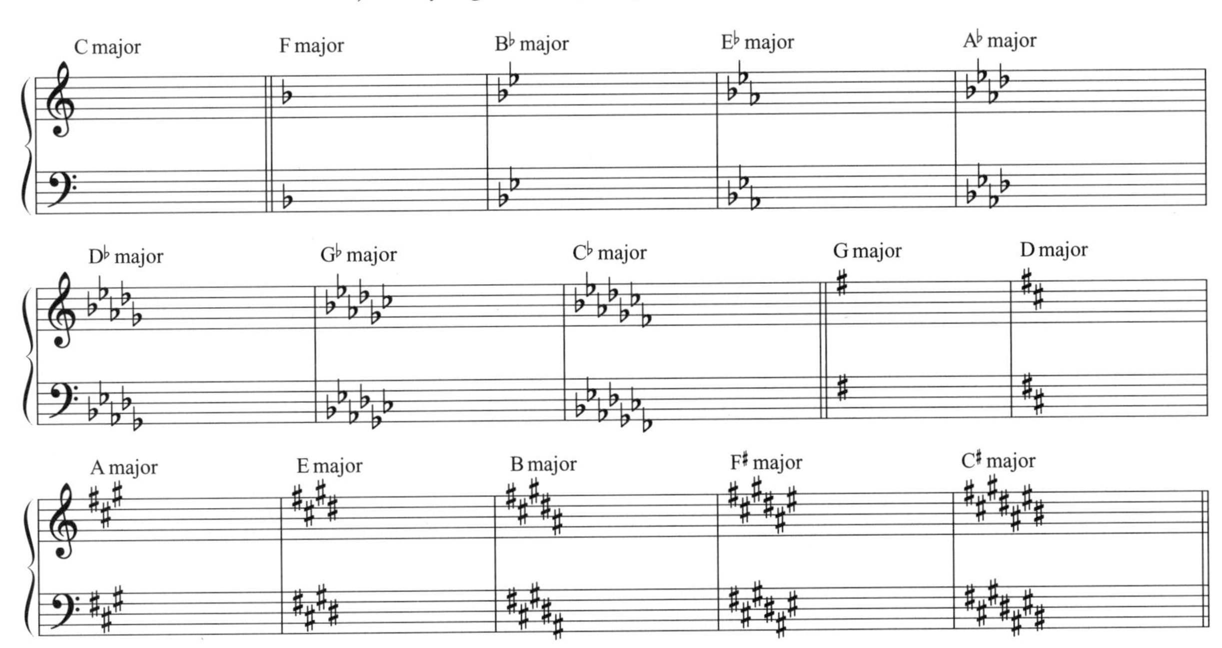

You'll notice that the key signatures consist of either flats or sharps, but not both mixed together. This is because there are no major scales which need both flats and sharps.

Now, if you're reading a piece of music and you see a key signature at the beginning, it's very handy (not to mention, essential!) for you to recognize the key that you're in. That way you'll know what major scale the song is based on, and if you've practiced your major scales, your fingers will *know* what flats or sharps you'll need to play.

When looking at the *flat key signatures* (those containing flats), the second to last flat in the key signature is the key that you're in. For example, looking at the key signature of A♭ major, we see there are four flats. The second to last flat in the key signature is A♭, your key! For *sharp keys*, the last sharp in the key signature is the *seventh degree* of the key that you're in, so you just need to go up a half step from this note (using the next letter name in the music alphabet) to find the key. For example, looking at the key signature of A major, we see there are three sharps. The last sharp in the key signature is G♯, so if we go up a half step from this note (and go to the next letter name) we get to A, our key!

USING ACCIDENTALS

Key signatures are a very convenient way of indicating a major scale restriction for a piece of music. But what happens when we want to go outside that restriction? Then we need to use *accidentals*. These are sharp, flat, or natural signs placed in the music which will contradict the key signature at that point. The *natural sign* cancels a sharp or a flat that would otherwise be required by the key signature. For example, in the key of F (B's are flat), if we wanted to play a plain old B (yes, the white key), we would need a natural sign in front of it. Any other "altered" notes, not normally part of the key would need an accidental in front of them.

Accidentals will be "in force" for the remainder of the measure in which they are introduced, and will then be cancelled out by the next bar line in the music (or beforehand if necessary, by another accidental on the same note, within the measure). Let's now look at an example in the key of F, which uses accidentals:

1. This is the note B♭, as required by the key signature.
2. This is the note B (natural), which contradicts the key signature.
3. This is the note B♭, as required by the key signature. The bar line cancelled out the previous accidental.
4. This is the note B (natural), which contradicts the key signature.
5. This is still the note B (natural). The accidental is still "in force" until the next bar line.
6. This is the note B♭, which needed a flat sign to cancel out the accidental, as we're still in the same measure.

So, watch out for those accidentals, but if you follow these rules, you should do just fine!

CHAPTER 8
SONGS IN EXTENDED F AND G POSITIONS

What's Ahead:

- F Position
- Extending the basic five-finger F Position
- G Position
- Extending the basic five-finger G Position
- Moving hand positions while playing

F POSITION

The next hand position we're going to explore is *F Position*. In the right hand, you'll rest the thumb on the F above middle C, and the pinkie on the C above middle C, with the other fingers evenly spread out on the keys in between (not forgetting to rest the fourth finger on B♭, as required in the key of F):

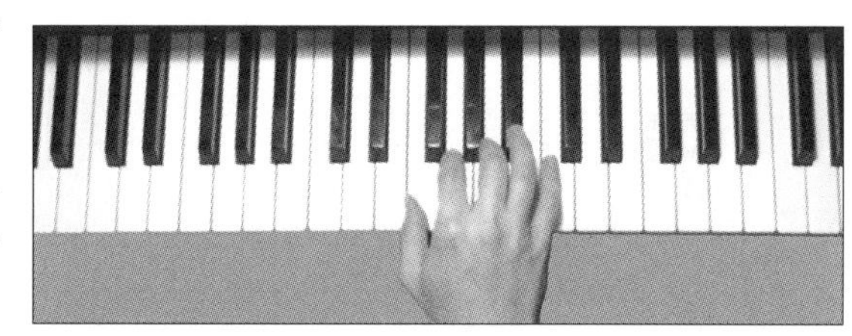

In the left hand, your thumb will go on middle C, and the pinkie on the F below that:

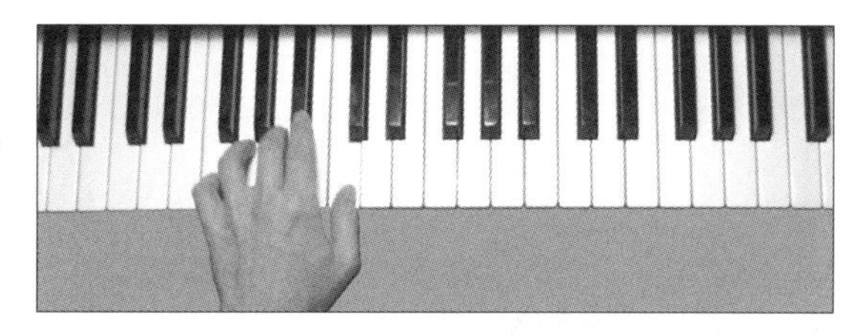

We could play some more tunes which are just contained within this *F Position*, like we did with the *C Position* in Chapter 5… but wait! "Been there, done that!" It's time to move beyond the basic hand position, and extend it so we can access some new notes!

EXTENDING THE BASIC FIVE-FINGER F POSITION

One easy way to extend this basic right-hand position, is to extend the thumb down below the starting note. For example, in the *F Position* the thumb is positioned on F, but you can move it down to E if the song needs you to do so. A similar extension is possible in the left hand. To play the E below the F, simply move finger 5 down one key. Both of these moves are used in our next tune, "Marianne."

Notice that the notes F and E in the melody both have finger number 1 next to them in the right hand, and number 5 in the left hand. As some extra help, the finger numbers have been circled where you have to move them down, "out of position." Give it a try!

audio tracks 18

Did you notice the key signature of F major? If not, and you forgot to play B♭, it probably sounded a little funny. Now have a listen to **track 18** and then play along. Remember those B flats!

G POSITION

I think you're getting the hang of this, and probably know how to find this next position already, but here it is. In right-hand *G Position*, you'll rest your thumb on the G above middle C, and finger 5 on the D above that. The left hand will have the pinkie on the second G below middle C, and the thumb on the D right above that.

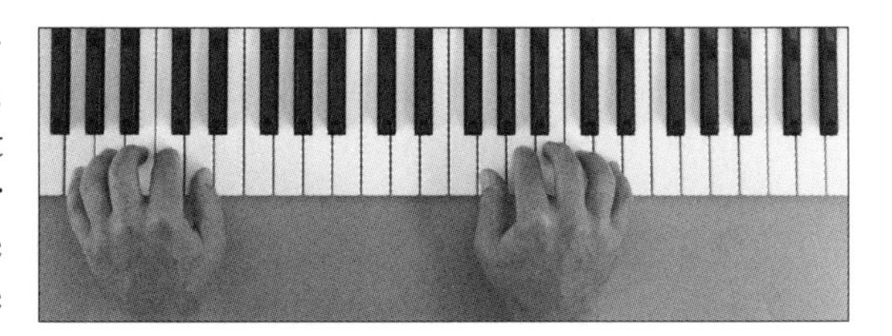

EXTENDING THE BASIC FIVE-FINGER G POSITION

In order to play our next song, we need to extend this *G Position* so that the left hand thumb can reach up to E, and the right-hand pinkie can also reach up to E. If we look at the first measure (after the pickup measure), we see that the note D (which we would normally play with the thumb) is immediately before the E. As it is not good practice to use the same finger on two successive notes, we should play the D with the second finger, saving the thumb for the E. In measure 9, beat three we'll stretch finger 4 of the right hand up to the D in order to place finger 5 on the E.

Our first song in the extended *G Position* is "Michael Row the Boat Ashore." Practice it slowly at first to get those fingers stretched down. When you think you have it, listen to **track 19** and then play along.

Michael Row the Boat Ashore

Traditional Folksong

In "Michael Row the Boat Ashore," notice the key signature of G major (one sharp). You may also notice that there are no F sharps in the song. Although we don't actually play any F sharps in the melody, the key signature is still needed to establish that the song is in G major. This is a common practice in musical notation—a way to help indicate the "home base" of the song.

MOVING HAND POSITIONS WHILE PLAYING

The next stage beyond simple extensions of hand positions is to change to new hand positions entirely, while playing. This will be needed if the music has a greater range (distance between the highest and lowest notes) than the songs we have seen so far. Our first example of this is the famous Beatles' song "All My Loving." Remember playing the scales in Chapter 7? Well, now's your chance to use the thumb turn and other crossing over of the fingers. The fingering for this song follows the fingering for playing the F major scale. The finger numbers have been circled in the places where you need to turn under or cross over.

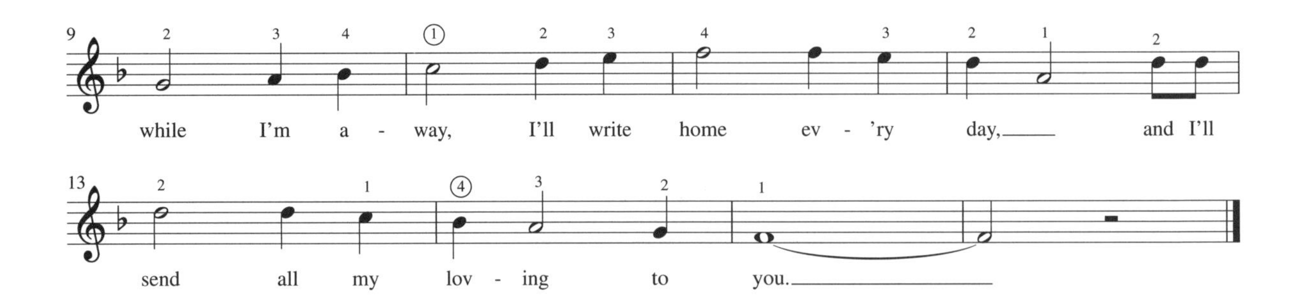

The Beatles

This is the first of several Beatles' songs that we'll be looking at in this book. Beatles' songs are fun to play on the piano, as they have great melodies, interesting chord progressions, and they are generally not too difficult to play.

Here are ten more Beatles' songs you should check out. Get the sheet music, check out the recordings, and have fun playing these classics!

- The Fool on the Hill
- For No One
- Here, There and Everywhere
- Hey Jude
- I Will
- Michelle
- Nowhere Man
- We Can Work It Out
- With a Little Help from My Friends
- You've Got to Hide Your Love Away

Photo courtesy of Photofest, Inc.

The Beatles

When talking about a song like the Beatles' tune "All My Loving," it is useful to make use of the measure numbers shown at the beginning of each staff system, from the second line, onward. In the first line, we have a pickup measure (with just two beats) and then four full measures, which are measure numbers 1 through 4. Then the number "5" is shown at the beginning of the second staff system, reminding us that this line begins with the fifth measure of the song. Next, the number "9" is shown at the beginning of the third line, and so on.

The last song in this chapter is the famous folk tune "Shenandoah," which again requires changes of hand position. The circled finger numbers show places where you need to employ the thumb turn or to cross over a finger. Also be mindful of places where you must stretch your fingers, like the first two notes of the song. Always know *what* the notes are first (i.e., what the letter names are, and what keys on the keyboard need to be played), and then look to the finger numbers to play the notes with the appropriate fingers. If you rely too much on finger numbers alone, you may find that you're using the correct finger, but not playing the correct note. For example, if you're about to play a note, and the number above it is a "2," don't just automatically press down finger 2. Your index finger may not be sitting on the correct key at that moment.

Know what note you need first, and then make sure finger 2 moves to that note and plays it. This is one of the main challenges to playing songs in extended hand positions, and especially in performing tunes where the hand positions change.

Listen to **track 20** and notice the even tempo, without pause. Make sure that when you execute the thumb turns and finger crossings, the music keeps going continuously. Try playing along to help maintain that steady tempo.

CHAPTER 9
MORE TIME SIGNATURES

What's Ahead:

- Alternatives to 4/4 time
- Introducing 3/4 time
- Introducing 6/8 and 12/8 time

ALTERNATIVES TO 4/4 TIME

Back in Chapter 3 we defined what a time signature was. So far we've been working with tunes in 4/4 time, which means that there are four quarter note beats per measure:

The *top* number of the time signature (4 in this case) indicates how many beats there are in the measure. These beats are where you would normally tap your foot! The *bottom* number indicates what rhythmic value is assigned to the beat (in this case, a quarter note).

So now it's time to go beyond the confines of 4/4 time, and play some songs in other time signatures.

INTRODUCING 3/4 TIME

The next most common time signature after 4/4 time is 3/4 time, also referred to as *waltz time* (as the three-beats-per-measure rhythm is needed for waltzing). When we see the 3/4 time signature, we will count: 1, 2, 3, 1, 2, 3, etc. This may take some time to get used to after playing many songs in 4/4, but just remember to leave out that "4" when you count.

The waltz dance form first appeared in the late 18th century, and became very popular in the 19th century, mainly due to the Viennese composers Johann Strauss and Joseph Lanner. Perhaps the most famous waltz from this period is "The Blue Danube" by Strauss, written in 1867.

Note the top number (3) indicating there are three beats in each measure. Many traditional and folk tunes also use 3/4 time, as in the following example, "For He's a Jolly Good Fellow," which uses an extended F position in the right hand, with finger 2 moving to A in measure 9 in order for the pinkie to stretch up to D in the third line. In measure 14, the fingers will stretch again from 3 on B♭ down to finger 2 on G.

For He's a Jolly Good Fellow

Traditional

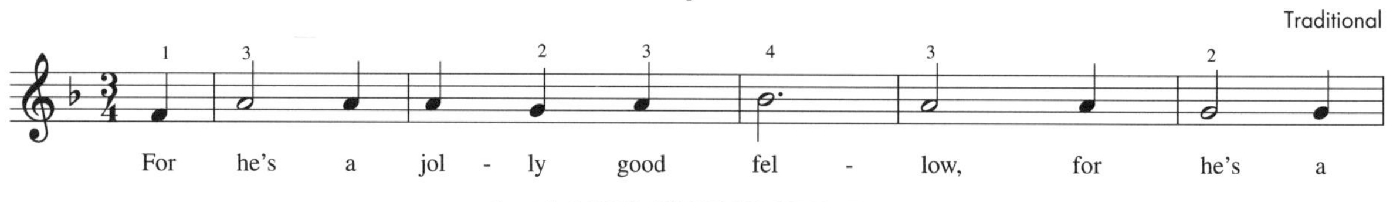

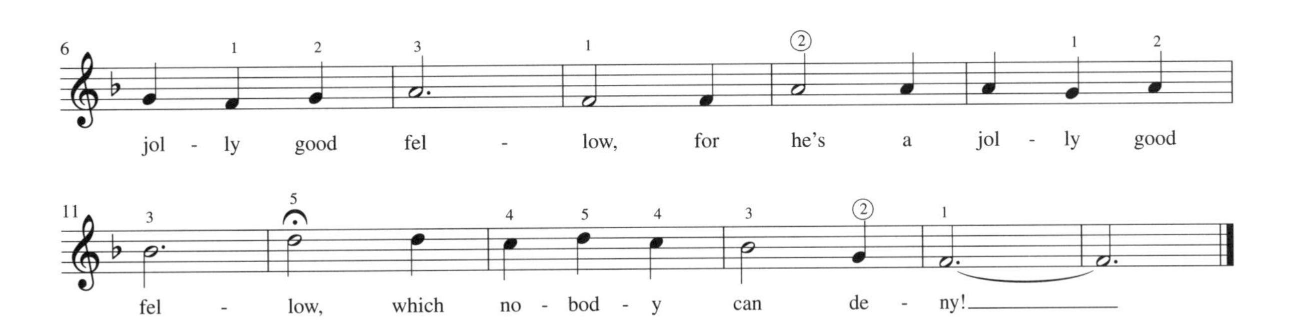

Once you've practiced "For He's a Jolly Good Fellow," and you think you have all the fingerings learned, have a listen to **track 21**. Now play along with the CD, making sure the finger stretches don't hold up the tempo.

Note the *fermata sign*, the bird's eye-looking thing on the first D in measure 12. This indicates to hold the note longer than its normal value. A note under a fermata is a kind of resting place, where the beat stops. When you're ready and satisfied that you've held it long enough, resume with the next note at the regular tempo.

When playing this song, count out each measure (1, 2, 3, 1, 2, 3, etc.) as needed. Notice that we are again starting with a pickup measure, containing only one beat. In 3/4 time, this would then fall on beat 3 (the last beat) of the measure (i.e., we would rest on beats 1 and 2).

On to another traditional tune in 3/4 time, now in the new key of D major. In Chapter 7 we saw that the key signature for D major was two sharps, F♯ and C♯. So these notes need to be sharped whenever they occur. For this song, you can create a *D Position* in the right hand, with the thumb resting on the D above middle C, and your pinkie on the A. In your left hand, the pinkie should sit on the D below middle C and the thumb on the A below middle C. Make sure your third finger is on the black key of F♯ in both hands, as required by the key signature. We also need to extend this hand position to reach the note B, at the end of lines 1 and 3.

Lavender's Blue

English Folk Song

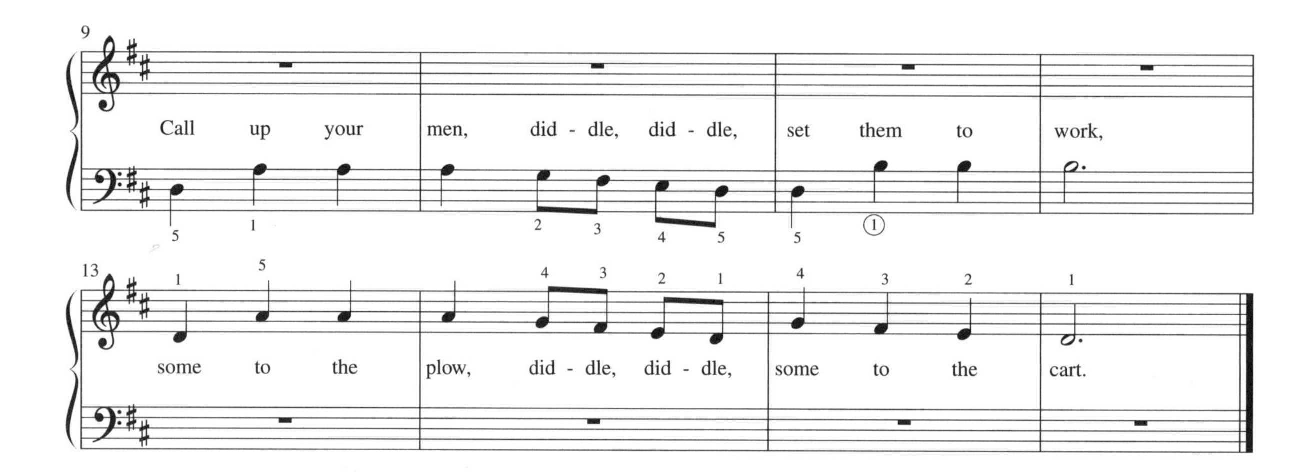

Once you've had some time to practice "Lavender's Blue," listen to **track 22**, and then play along. Were you able to keep the song going while the hands changed from right to left and back to right? Playing with the CD may help you become aware of pauses you weren't aware of when you played the song on your own. After you've played along with the CD a few times, try it again without the CD.

INTRODUCING 6/8 AND 12/8 TIME

So far we've been using time signatures with a "4" on the bottom, meaning that we are counting in quarter-note beats. Now this changes when we introduce the 6/8 and 12/8 time signatures:

In both cases, the eighth note "gets the beat," i.e., we are now counting in eighth notes. In 6/8 time there are six eighth-note beats in each measure, and in 12/8 time there are twelve. So a measure of 12/8 time is equivalent to two measures of 6/8 time, and, in many cases, it's a matter of opinion and preference whether to notate a tune in 6/8 or 12/8.

On to another traditional tune, this one in 6/8 time, and in the new key of B♭ major. In Chapter 7 we saw that the key signature for B♭ major was two flats, B♭ and E♭. So these notes need to be flatted whenever they occur. Note that the range of the song goes from the F (above middle C) up to the D above (excluding the high F in measure 14, for now). So, even though we are in the key of B♭, it would make sense to base the fingering on an F position in the right hand (with the thumb resting on F) and then extending the pinkie up to D as needed. In the last line we also have a thumb turn, so we can reach the F at the top of the staff.

You can count through this song using 1, 2, 3, 4, 5, 6 for each measure, but don't forget that each beat now falls on an eighth note. For example, in measure 5, we would count 1, 2 on the first F, then 3 on the G, then 4, 5 on the A, then 6 on the last F.

Here's a traditional song in 6/8 time, "Hail, Hail, the Gang's All Here." Listen to **track 23** and first count along, without playing. Next, play along, using the fingering numbers provided.

Although we have six eighth-note beats in each measure, in 6/8 time we can actually hear two *big beats* per measure (landing on the 1st and 4th eighth notes). Similarly, in 12/8 time, we can hear four big beats per measure (landing on the 1st, 4th, 7th and 10th eighth notes). When playing this example, try tapping your foot on all the eighth notes, then on the big beats (two per measure). Interesting, huh? In meters with an "8" on the bottom, the beat is essentially the dotted quarter note (equal to three eighth notes). When practicing a song in 6/8, first tap and count each eighth-note beat, slowly. As you get more comfortable, speed it up and begin to feel these "big beats" every three eighth notes or on each dotted quarters. This is actually how meters such as 6/8 and 12/8 are *felt*.

CHAPTER 10
INTERVALS AND CHORDS

What's Ahead:

- Introduction to intervals
- Creating intervals from the major scale
- Using intervals in songs
- Creating three-note chords (triads)
- Diatonic triads and progressions

INTRODUCTION TO INTERVALS

Now it's time for a little more music theory. But don't worry, I'll try to make it as painless as possible! Besides, you're going to need this stuff to build intervals and chords, two very important components of all those cool songs that you'll soon be playing.

An *interval* in music is the distance between two notes. We already got to know some intervals in the earlier chapters, such as the half step and whole step. Now we're going to derive some larger intervals, based on the distance between the notes on the staff. Let's look at the following interval:

The first thing we need to determine is the *interval number*. To do this, we count up from the bottom note (starting at 1), and include all the letter names in between, including the top note. So, if the bottom note (C) is "1," then D (2), E (3), F (4), G (5), and finally, A (6), thus we have a *sixth*. Now be aware that there are different types (qualities) of *sixths*, the most common being major and minor, but we'll learn more about interval quality later.

Use the same technique to find the interval number for any two notes. The simplest is the *second*, which are always adjacent letter names. Skipping one letter name is a *third*, etc. When going from one letter to the same letter up or down is 8 or the *octave*.

Some intervals that go beyond the octave such as 9ths, 10ths, and 11ths are named as such. When we get to an interval such as a twelfth, we can label this as a *fifth plus an octave*, etc.

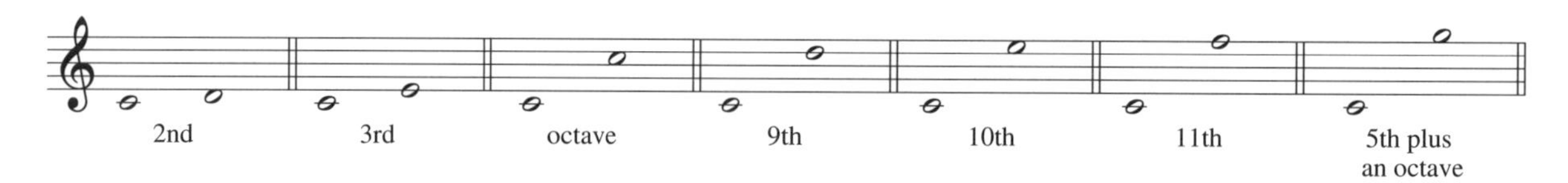

CREATING INTERVALS FROM THE MAJOR SCALE

You remember the C major scale that we built in Chapter 7? Now we'll look at all of the intervals created between the starting note (C) and the other notes in this scale:

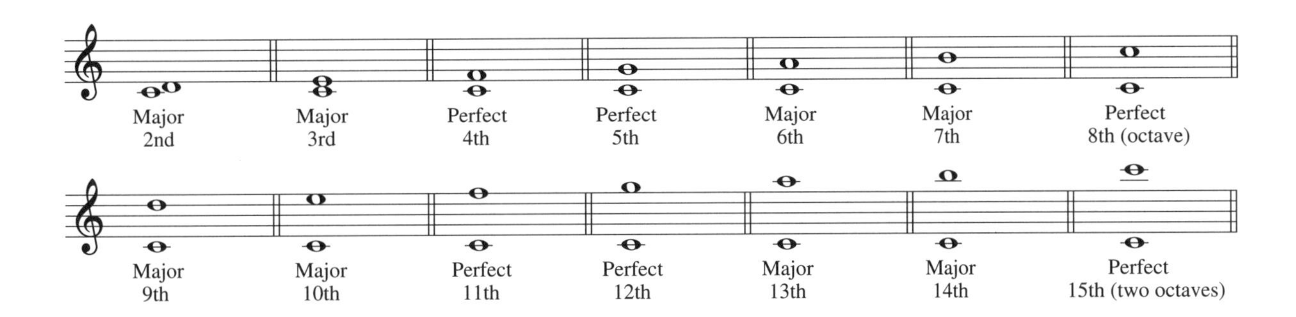

Play each of these intervals on the piano to get the different sounds "in your ear." Since the notes are placed one above the other, or vertically, they get played at the same time (intervals whose pitches are played at the same time are called *harmonic intervals*. More about this soon!) For the second line, you'll want to play one note in each hand.

Notice that the interval numbers are shown with an interval description, which is either *major* or *perfect*. The 4th, 5th and octave (and 11th, 12th and two octaves) are the perfect intervals, and the remaining intervals are major. Again, don't worry too much about these interval descriptions just yet. For now, just remember that from the first note of the major scale to all other notes will produce either major or perfect intervals.

USING INTERVALS IN SONGS

Next, we'll see how some of these intervals are used in famous songs. We'll also see how major intervals reduced by a half step, become *minor* intervals. We'll start out with the 2nd:

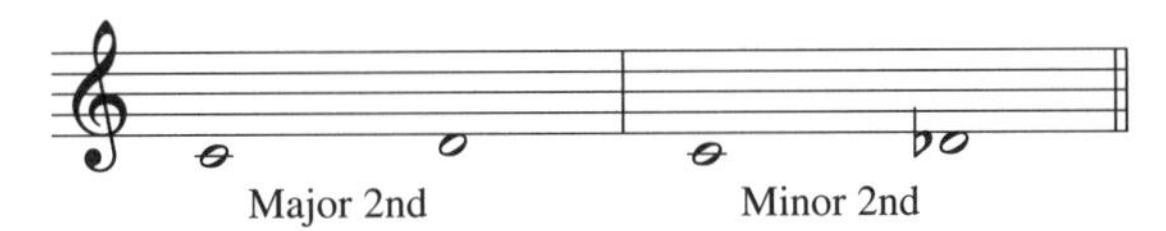

In the first measure we have the major 2nd (C up to D). When this is reduced by a half step, we get a minor 2nd interval (C up to D♭) as is shown in the second measure.

Notice that the major 2nd is equivalent to a whole step, and the minor 2nd is equivalent to a half step.

Because whole steps (major 2nds) and half steps (minor 2nds) are the building blocks of scales, you might expect these intervals to show up very frequently in melodies. Well, you'd be right! Here's our first melody excerpt, containing major and minor 2nds. The intervals are shown above the staff for the first measure (M2=major 2nd, m2=minor 2nd).

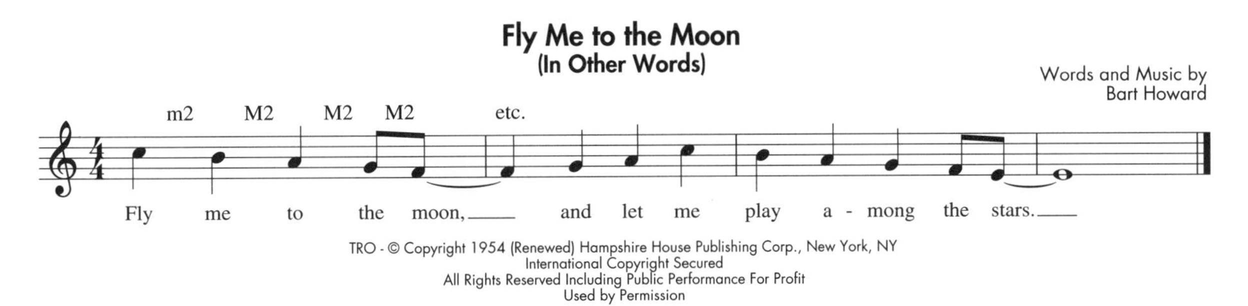

Jazz Standards

"Fly Me to the Moon" is a great example of a jazz standard. Jazz standards are vocal tunes, generally written between the 1920s–1950s, which have very strong and enduring melodies. Successive generations of jazz musicians to this day, always "cut their teeth" on the standards.

Most jazzers will either play the standards from memory, or from a "fake book," showing the melody and chords (more about using fake books in Chapters 14 & 15).

Here are ten more jazz standards that all piano players should be acquainted with. Although pretty much everything else will most likely change over the next 100 years, it's a safe bet that these tunes will still be played by 22nd-century piano players!

- All the Things You Are (Jerome Kern)
- Autumn Leaves (Johnny Mercer)
- Body and Soul (Johnny Green)
- A Foggy Day (George Gershwin)
- On Green Dolphin Street (Kaper/Washington)
- Misty (Erroll Garner)
- My Romance (Richard Rodgers)
- Night and Day (Cole Porter)
- Our Love Is Here to Stay (George Gershwin)
- Stella by Starlight (Victor Young)

Next, we'll spotlight some 3rd intervals (major and minor):

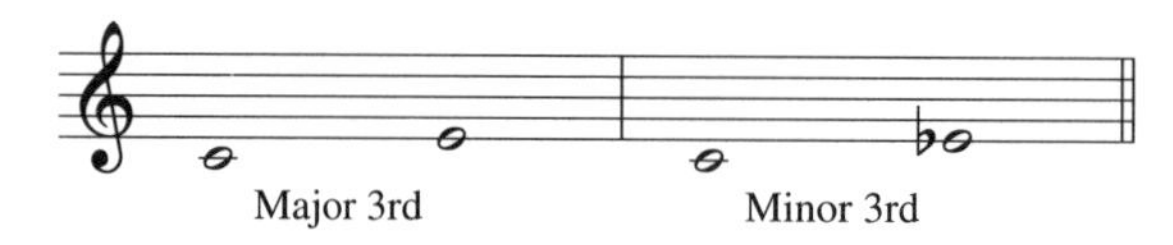

In the first measure we have the major 3rd (C up to E). When this is reduced by a half step, we get a minor 3rd interval (C up to E♭).

Here's our next melody excerpt, one from the classic Four Tops' song "I Can't Help Myself." (I had the pleasure of meeting the co-writer Brian Holland when he visited my home studio in Los Angeles a couple of years ago. He was very down-to-earth, and had a nice dry wit!) This excerpt contains both major and minor 3rds ("M3"=major 3rd, "m3"=minor 3rd):

I Can't Help Myself
(Sugar Pie, Honey Bunch)

Words and Music by Brian Holland, Lamont Dozier and Edward Holland

Next, we'll look at an excerpt of a song which uses perfect 4th intervals. This is "We Are the Champions," one of the most popular and enduring hits from the rock band Queen (written by Freddie Mercury).

We Are the Champions

Words and Music by Freddie Mercury

The previous example contains 2nds and 3rds, as well as 4ths. As you play this excerpt on the piano, try to identify the 2nds and 3rds!

"We Are the Champions" was released in October 1977, and spent ten weeks on the charts, reaching number two and achieving gold status. The song's great melody and triumphant spirit made it a favorite anthem of soccer fans in Great Britain. Queen's classic songs and tremendous showmanship made them one of rock's most important bands of the 1970s and 80s. One of my favorite Freddie Mercury quotes is: "People are apprehensive when they meet me. They think I'm going to eat them. But underneath it all, I'm quite shy."

Photo courtesy of Photofest, Inc.

Queen

Our next song excerpt uses perfect 5th intervals. "Everybody Wants to Rule the World" is one of the best known anthems from the '80s synth-pop band Tears For Fears.

Everybody Wants to Rule the World

Words and Music by Ian Stanley, Roland Orzabal and Chris Hughes

About Tears For Fears

The British pop duo Tears For Fears was one of the most innovative bands to emerge from the 1980s synth-pop era. The band was actually a duo, formed by Roland Orzabal and Curt Smith in the early '80s, after they had both played in a ska revival band called Graduate. The name Tears For Fears was taken from the writings of Arthur Janov, whose "primal scream therapy" influenced much of the band's work, notably their debut album *The Hurting*. This became a major hit in Great Britain, generating three Top-Five singles.

By the mid-1980s, it had become a high priority for the band to have a major success on the U.S. charts. This goal was achieved with the hit single "Everybody Wants to Rule the World," which had a harder-edged, more "American" pop sound.

With its wonderful chorus and innovative guitar work, this song is a classic of the period.

Both this song and the band's other number one U.S. hit "Shout," came from their hugely successful *Songs from the Big Chair* album, which set a new standard for melodic synth-pop.

Photo courtesy of Photofest, Inc.

Tears For Fears

Next, we'll spotlight some 6th intervals (major and minor):

In the first measure we have the *major 6th* (C up to A). When this is reduced by a half step, we get a *minor 6th* as in the second measure (C up to A♭).

Our next melody excerpt is from the song "Where Do I Begin," which was the main theme from the movie *Love Story*. This excerpt contains major and minor 6ths:

CREATING THREE-NOTE CHORDS (TRIADS)

OK, let's take a deep breath and plunge into the fun world of *chords*. A chord is created when three or more notes are played at the same time. A three-note chord is known as a *triad*. Most popular styles are harmonically organized around chords. We'll now use some of the intervals developed in this chapter to "spell" some triads (i.e., figure out what notes we need to build them), starting with the *major triad*.

You'll see that I've measured the intervals (major 3rd and perfect 5th) up from the *root* of the triad in each case. The *root* is the note from which the triad is based. We refer to the middle note as the *third* of the chord, and the top note is called the *fifth*. You'll remember (at least I hope you will!) that these major and perfect intervals are found within the major scale. This triad consists of the first, third and fifth degrees of a C major scale.

Also note the letter C shown above the triad. This is our first example of a *chord symbol*, which tells you the name of the chord; it is placed above the staff.

A chord symbol that consists of a note name with no additional suffix or description indicates a *major triad* built from the note indicated, so the chord symbol C means a *C major* triad.

The major triad is the most basic and fundamental chord, and is used throughout pop and classical styles. So it would be a great idea to learn all of the major triads (i.e., not just C major), don't you think? Well, here they are!

Play through all of these major triads on your piano to learn the sounds and "shapes" of the major triad built upon each of these notes. Use fingers 1, 3, and 5, and try playing the triads with each hand.

Next up, we have the *minor triad*, which we're also going to spell by using intervals as follows:

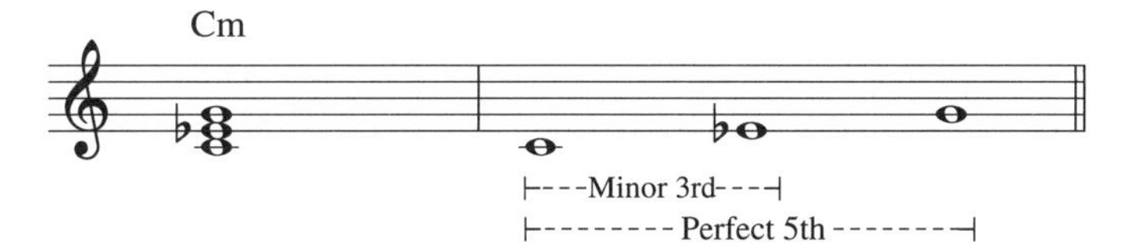

Again, the intervals (this time minor 3rd and perfect 5th) are measured up from the *root* of the triad. When comparing this triad to the major triad, we see that the third interval (between the root and the middle note, or "third" of the chord) is now a *minor 3rd* instead of a major 3rd. So another way this C minor triad can be derived is by taking the previous C major triad and lowering the third by a half step (in this case the note E becomes E♭). This is true of all major triads: take any major triad, lower the third a half step, and you have a minor triad.

The chord symbol above the staff is now *Cm*. There are two components to this chord symbol: the root (C) and the "suffix" or description (m). A chord symbol which consists of a note name followed by the suffix "m," indicates a minor triad built from the note indicated, so the chord symbol of Cm means a C minor triad.

The minor triad is used just about as widely as the major triad, so it's another good candidate for learning in all keys. Note the chord symbols (with the "m" suffix) above each chord:

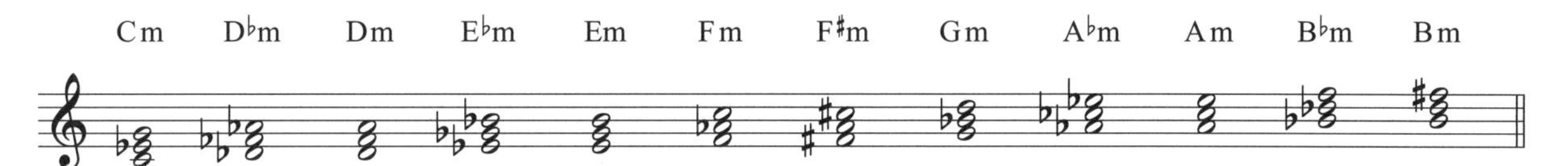

Although the major and minor triads are the most common, there are two more triads that we will sometimes use, the *augmented* and *diminished* triads:

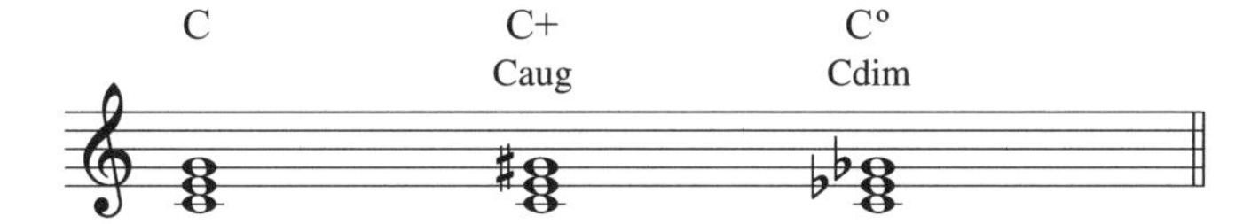

These two new triads are shown above, and we can compare them to the C major triad on the left.

- If we raise the 5th of the C major triad by a half step, we get a *C augmented triad.* Note there are two chord symbols above this chord—both the "+" and "aug" suffixes are commonly used alternatives.
- If we lower the 3rd and 5th of the C major triad by half steps, we get a *C diminished triad.* Note there are two chord symbols above this chord—both the small circle and "dim" suffixes are commonly used alternatives.

Play the C major triad on your piano, and then alter it to create the C minor, C augmented, and C diminished triads. Then try the same exercise, starting with different major triads (i.e., not just C major!).

DIATONIC TRIADS AND PROGRESSIONS

Let's define a couple of terms that will help you understand this section. "Diatonic" means "belonging to the major scale." "Diatonic triads" are therefore triads that are contained within the major scale. Here are all of the triads contained within the C major scale:

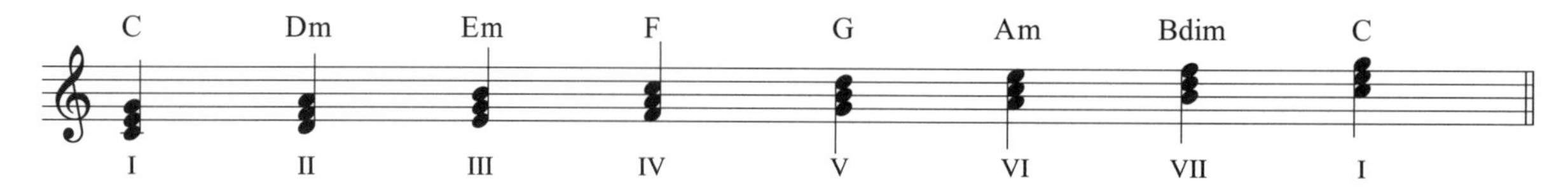

What we're doing here is building a triad from each note in the C major scale, making sure that all notes used are contained with the scale (which in this case means they are all white keys… pretty easy huh?). This gives us the various triad "qualities" shown here, from left to right (major, minor, minor, major, major, minor, diminished, major).

The Roman numeral under the staff indicates chord *function*. Each chord within a key has different tendencies in terms of what kinds of chords they lead to, what kinds of chords they follow, and other tendencies within the context of a piece of music. These Roman numerals actually serve as symbols for chords that have particular functions, or different roles within a key. For more on the specifics of chord function, please see my book *Contemporary Music Theory*, Level 2, published by Hal Leonard Corporation. For now, all you need to know is that within the key of C, a C major triad is a "I" chord; a D minor triad is a "II" chord, and so on, based on scale degrees.

Now we'll start looking at *triad progressions*. These are simply sequences of chords used in songs. Our first example is the chord progression used in "Mr. Jones," a hit for the rock band Counting Crows in the 1990s. This will also be our introduction to repeat signs in the music.

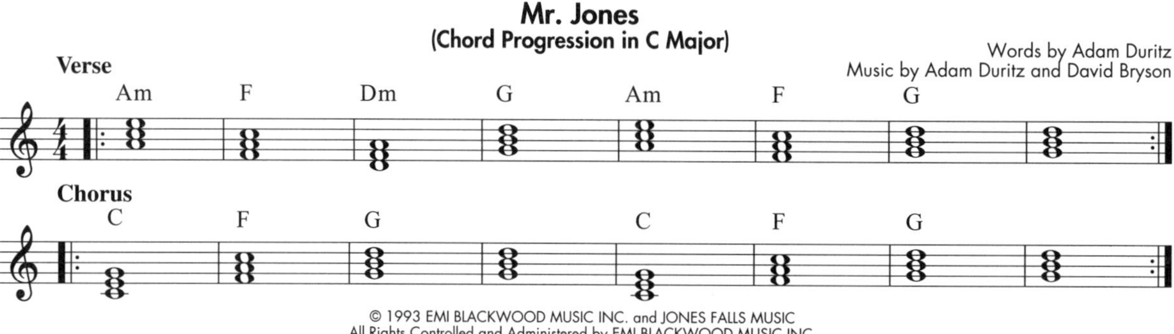

A repeat sign is made up of a thin bar line and a thick bar line, like that of the end of a song. The addition of two dots around the middle line completes this sign, which means to repeat back either to the beginning, or to a previous repeat sign with the dots to the right of the pair of barlines.

Each measure in this song contains a whole-note triad, with a chord symbol above the staff. The key signature of "no flats and no sharps" tells us we are in the key of C major, and all of the chord symbols are diatonic triads from the C major scale (check the previous diatonic triad example as needed). The first line is the verse of the song, and the repeat signs around measures 1–8 tell us to play this line twice (i.e., 16 measures total). Then the next line is the chorus of the song, which is also repeated.

It's a good exercise to figure out the function (i.e., Roman numeral) of each chord in this song by comparing it to the diatonic triads in the key of C. For example, the first triad is Am (which is a VI in C), the next triad is F (which is a IV in C) and so on. The chords for many simpler songs can be analyzed this way, which helps when you're communicating with other players, as in, "Hey Nigel, the chorus is a I -IV-V in C!"

Photo courtesy of Photofest, Inc.

Counting Crows

Play through the triads of this "Mr. Jones" to get a feel for the progression, and have a listen to the original song if you can. Although it's a great tune, the chord progression is very simple and basic!

Of course, we can have diatonic triads in any key, not just in C major! So now we'll derive the triads within a couple more keys, and look at some songs using these triads. Next up are the diatonic triads within F major:

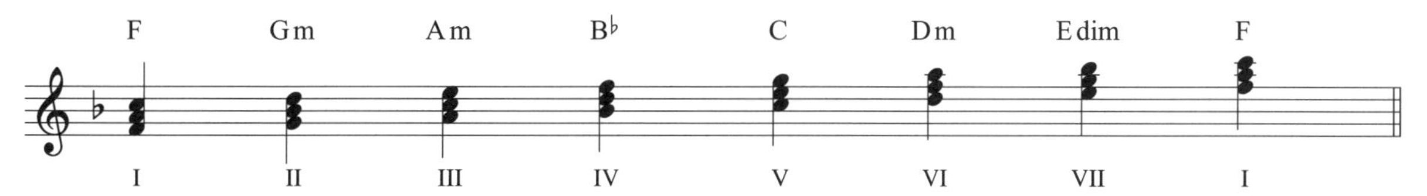

Again, note the chord qualities above the staff, and the Roman numerals underneath. The famous Beatles' song "Hey Jude" was written in the key of F, and here's an excerpt from the chord progression from this song:

Hey Jude
(Chord Progression in F Major)

Words and Music by
John Lennon and Paul McCartney

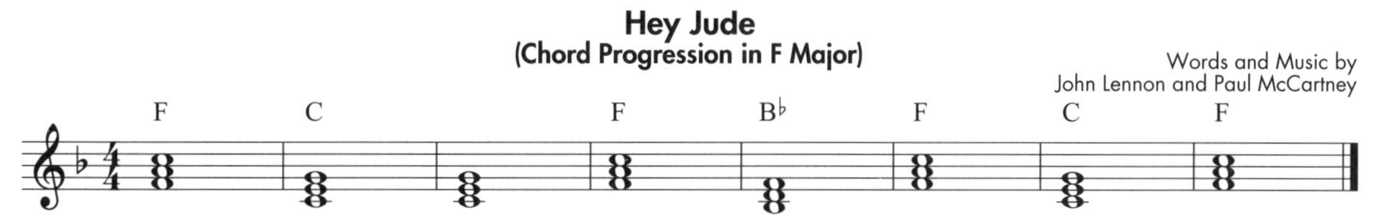

Again, try to analyze the function (I, V, etc.) of each chord in the key of F. Also play through the triads of this song. Many songs use this simple I- IV-V progression, although there are few examples better than "Hey Jude"!

A lot of simpler pop, rock, and country songs use diatonic triads exclusively for their chords. So you get a lot of "bang for the buck" from these. Learn them in as many keys as you can!

CHAPTER 11

COMBINING THE LEFT AND RIGHT HANDS

What's Ahead:

- Playing the melody with both hands
- Adding single notes below the melody, in the left hand
- Adding triads (chords) below the melody, in the left hand
- Using the damper (sustain) pedal

PLAYING THE MELODY WITH BOTH HANDS

OK, take a deep breath… now it's time to combine the two hands while playing! You've had some experience using both hands in a song, but not at the same time. An easy way to get started with this is to play the melody of the song in both hands (sometimes referred to as "doubling" the melody). This means that you'll be playing the same notes in both hands, separated by one or more octaves. Let's see how this works on a well-known Christmas carol (just pretend it's Christmas, OK?… even if you are reading this in April!). Notice that both hands are using the *C Position*.

Our first "hands together" song is "Jingle Bells." Once you've run through the song, listen to **track 24** and play along.

As you practice this song, try playing through it "hands separately" first, figuring out where the notes are within the hand positions. Then play each hand's part using a metronome to help you keep time. You can begin by playing slowly, increasing the tempo as you become more comfortable. Then when you combine the hands, you'll have a head start on coordinating the hands correctly. This is a good practice technique for all of the songs we'll be working on, from now onwards!

For extra practice, go back in the book and try "doubling" in all the songs: add the left hand to right-hand-only songs, and vice-versa. This is good practice to get the hands working together.

ADDING SINGLE NOTES IN THE LEFT HAND

Next, we're going to work on a couple of important areas that will make your performances sound more professional. Both hands will play together, but now with more independent parts. Most often in piano music, the right hand will play the melody, while the left hand plays the *accompaniment*. Accompaniment parts are usually simpler than the melody, and range in a variety of styles. This part can play a simple *bass line*, a *counter melody* (another melody to help support and add interest to the main melody), *chords*, or a combination of all three.

We will begin with "Ode to Joy," a tune that includes a very simple *bass line* consisting of single notes. Watch out for the finger crossing in measure 11 in the left hand. Practice this part separately first, and then put the hands together.

When you feel you have this song up to tempo, give a listen to **track 25** and try playing along.

Now you can pretend that it's New Year's Eve! Here's the famous party song "Auld Lang Syne," with the right hand playing the melody, and the left hand playing single notes below it. The left hand is playing in an extended *G Position*, and is a bit more adventurous than our accompaniment part for "Ode to Joy." Notice the chord symbols above the staff. Our left hand part simply plays the roots of these chords. To make matters even more interesting, the right hand moves around quite a bit. Since it is not confined to one position, it is important that you spend a considerable amount of time practicing the right hand by itself before combining both hands. We'll get into the details of how to tackle a song like this after you take a look at the tune.

A great way to practice a challenging song like this is to break it up into small groups. These groups may consist of phrases that coincide with the lyrics. For example, the first phrase ends in measure 4 with the lyric "mind." Practice this part first, several times in a row. First, make sure you find all the correct notes on the keyboard, and play them with the fingerings given. Pay attention to where fingers have to stretch, cross, or turn, as well as places where the whole hand has to move. As we have seen before, it is a good idea to circle the finger numbers in these spots.

Once you have the first phrase learned, move on to the second. When you are comfortable with the second phrase, try playing the first two phrases together, without stopping. Continue this process until you have the whole right-hand part learned. You may work similarly on the left hand, then use the same process again when you put the hands together. Practice this way with all songs, from now on.

If you're getting stuck as you practice, have a listen to **track 26** for some guidance. Once you've done all that hard (and fun) work learning the hands separately, try playing along with the CD, one hand at a time. Next, continue working on the hands together, and when you think you're ready, try playing along with the CD, this time using both hands.

Have you ever wondered what "Auld Lang Syne" means? It translates as "times gone by." The song is adapted from a traditional Scottish folk song dating back to the 18th century. The Scottish poet Robert Burns is credited with first publishing it in the mid-1790s. The song recalls the days gone by, and says we will always remember them. Guy Lombardo is credited with turning the song into a New Year's Eve tradition. He first heard the song in his youth, sung by Scottish immigrants in his hometown of London, Ontario. For nearly fifty years, Guy Lombardo and his orchestra performed "Auld Lang Syne" on radio broadcasts on New Year's Eve.

ADDING TRIADS IN THE LEFT HAND

Next we're going to play triads (three-note chords) in the left hand, below the melody in the right hand. So instead of just playing the root of each chord (as we did in the previous example), now we're playing the whole chord (review major and minor triad spelling in the last chapter as needed).

In "Buffalo Gals," the left hand plays all of the triads with a 5-3-1 fingering. The first chord is an F major triad, and then in measure 3, the left hand must move down to place the pinkie on C to play the C major triad. In the following measure, the hand moves back up to the F chord. This back and forth movement continues throughout the song. Practice this hand move by itself a few times to get used to it. With the right hand, find the notes on the keyboard first, and then play them with the indicated fingers. Break up the song into phrases for practice as we did previously.

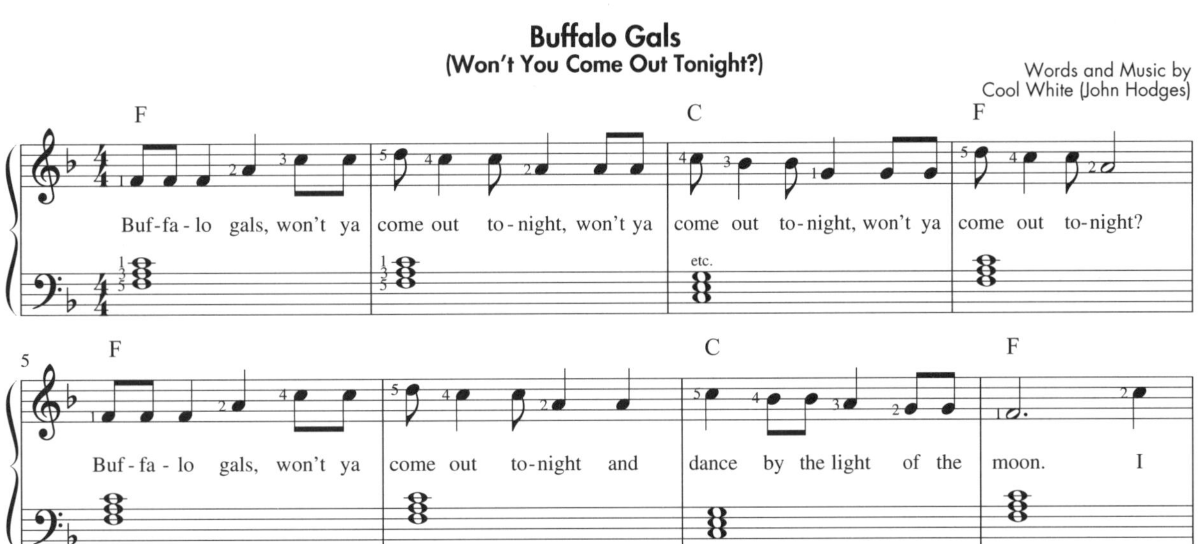

Now listen to **track 27** for some extra guidance, and then play along, hands separately first, then together.

The triads used in this song can be referred to as *root position* triads, as the root of each chord is on the bottom (for example, in the first F major triad in the left hand, the lowest note is F). Soon, we'll see how to rearrange the notes of a triad using "inversions." For now, be aware that the song is in the key of F major, and we are using two chords in the accompaniment: the F chord (I) and the C chord (V).

Next, we'll try one more song using root-position triads in the left hand. Look at the tune and plan out where and when your left hand will need to move. The song is in the key of C major, and thus we see the common I (C), IV (F), and V (G) chords, plus a few others. What function (Roman numeral) are these "others"? There is also a "Gsus4" chord. The "sus" stands for suspended, and what is being suspended is the third of the chord. Instead of the note B, it as if a C is hanging on from the previous C chord, delaying the complete G chord until beat 3. On the third beat, the C moves to a B as if resolving itself. The term "suspended" is usually used when the third of a chord is delayed, with a 2nd or 4th in its place. In the case of our G chord here, it is the 4th (C) that represents the suspension.

Beauty and the Beast

from Walt Disney's ***BEAUTY AND THE BEAST***

Lyrics by Howard Ashman
Music by Alan Menken

This version using left hand chords is similar to our earlier arrangement of "Buffalo Gals," except that we now have minor and suspended chords as well as major chords.

USING THE DAMPER PEDAL

Back in Chapter 1 we saw that this pedal *disables* the dampers which would otherwise stop a note from sounding after you release the note. So when you depress the pedal, the notes you play will mix together, even after you have physically released them. This is ideal for slow ballad-type songs, as the notes of the chord can continue sounding together, adding to the expressive character of the tune.

Well, not really dangerous, but kind of annoying! Be careful not to "smear chords together" when using the sustain pedal. This happens when the chord changes (like in the last song, when we went from an C major triad to a Gsus4 triad), and the pedal is depressed while the chords change. The resulting harmonic "mess" is not pleasant for you or your audience (unless you're going for a particular avant-garde effect!). The secret to avoiding this problem is to release the pedal exactly at the point of chord change (this is normally on beat 1 of the measure, with the new chord symbol). You must then depress the pedal just after you play the next chord, that you want to be sustained.

Play "Beauty and the Beast" once more, but this time, use the sustain pedal. *Change* the pedal each time there is a new chord symbol and listen to the difference in sound as compared to when you played it without pedal.

SECTION 3

Playing, Part 2

CHAPTER 12
MORE CHORDS AND INVERSIONS

What's Ahead:

- What are inversions and why do we use them?
- Inverting major and minor triads
- Voice leading between inversions
- Introducing "slash chord" symbols
- Four-part (seventh) chords and inversions
- Diatonic four-part chords and progressions

WHAT ARE INVERSIONS AND WHY DO WE USE THEM?

So far all of the chords we have developed have been in *root position*, meaning that the root of the chord has been on the bottom—this is the simplest way to spell the chord. However, this is not necessarily the easiest way to play chords, nor does it always *sound* the best. As we develop musically, we need to start using chord *inversions*. This means having a note other than the root on the bottom. So instead of playing a triad "root-3rd-5th" (from bottom to top), we might instead use "3rd-5th-root" or "5th-root-3rd." So why would we want to do this? Well actually, there are a few good reasons to use chord inversions:

- Inverting chords can promote less moving around of the hands when going from chord to chord.
- Less moving around helps us to *voice lead*, or allow for a more smoothly connected sound between chords.
- Inverted chords can be placed below a melody as a way to harmonize (or "flesh out") your arrangement.

INVERTING MAJOR TRIADS

Let's start with our good friend the C major triad, and see what happens when we *invert* it. The notes of the C major chord are C, E, and G, so no matter what order or position we place these three notes in, as long as we have these three, it will always be a C major triad.

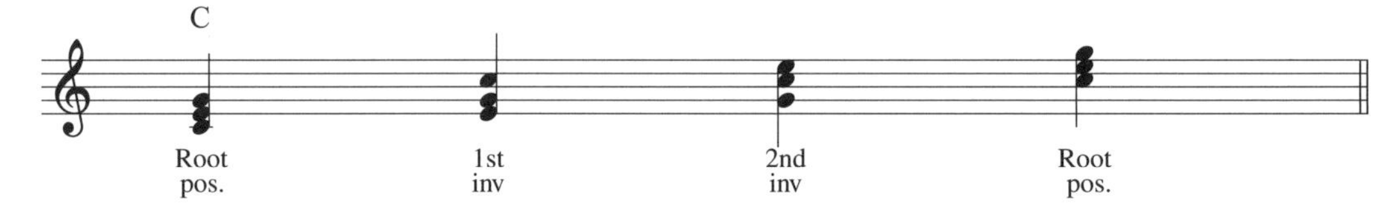

We'll define the different inversions of the C major triad as follows:

- the first triad is in *root position* (with the root on the bottom)
- the second triad is in *first inversion* (with the third on the bottom)
- the third triad is in *second inversion* (with the fifth on the bottom)
- the last triad is in *root position*, an octave higher than the first.

Back in Chapter 10 we showed the (root position) major triads in all keys. Now it's time to introduce the inversions of all these, starting with the *first inversions*:

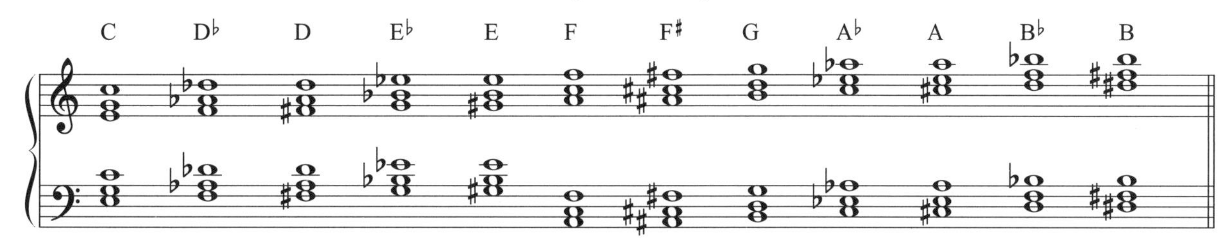

Play through each of these first-inversion triads on the piano, starting with the C triad, hands separately. As there is now a larger interval on top, use a 1-2-5 fingering for each right-hand chord, but still use fingers 5, 3, and 1 for the left hand. Notice the different combinations of black and white keys as you play through all the first inversions.

And now… for the *second inversions* of the major triads:

C D♭ D E♭ E F F♯ G A♭ A B♭ B

Play through each of these second inversions, again starting with the C triad. The larger interval is now on the bottom, so either a 1-3-5 or 1-2-4 fingering will work fine in the right hand. Use a 5-2-1 fingering for the left hand. Again be aware of the different black and white key combinations as you play.

INVERTING MINOR TRIADS

Now we'll go through the same process for minor triads, starting with the C minor triad:

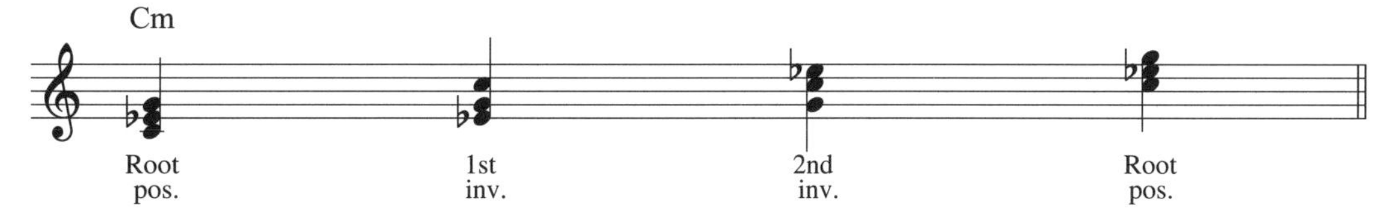

Similar to the major triad inversions at the beginning of the chapter, here we have minor triads in root position, first inversion, second inversion, and finally root position again, from left to right.

Remember how to change a major triad into a minor triad? In case you forgot, just lower the third a half step. Now take all the minor triads and try inverting each one; we won't spell them all out for you.

Get a sheet of staff paper and write out the minor triads in first inversion and second inversion, in both hands. Use the previous examples of major triads to help you. Writing music yourself is a great way to learn.

VOICE LEADING BETWEEN INVERSIONS

Voice leading is a term used to describe the melodic lines created as one "voice" of a chord leads to the next chord. For example, when going from a C chord to an F chord, to a G chord (chords using only three notes each), the "line" created by the middle voice of each chord is a kind of melody in itself. How the middle voice in one chord leads to the middle voice in the next chord is what voice leading is all about. This is just one example, but the line does not always have to be connecting only the middle voices of chords (especially with larger chords that have multiple "middle" voices). "Proper" voice leading will help chord progressions sound smooth and continuous. This is largely achieved when the melodic lines travel mostly by steps, without "jumping around" all over the place. Using inversions helps to promote proper voice leading for a smooth flowing sound. In working through some voice leading examples, we'll revisit "Beauty and the Beast" from the last chapter.

This is the same song as in Chapter 11, but now some of the left hand chords have been inverted. Isn't this easier to play? Doesn't it sound better—more *smooth*? We'll point out a few of these inversions so you know where they came from. In measure 2, the Gsus4 chord is made up of the notes G, C, and D. We simply took the C and D from the top (as in the Chapter 11 version)

and moved these two notes an octave lower. Now, when coming from the C chord in measure 1, the hand does not have to move at all. The E in the middle of the C chord simply moves to a D…sounds much more logical, right? Inversions were applied to all chords other than the C chords in order to make hand movement as small as possible. This also promotes proper voice leading as the left hand sounds more like three smooth melodic lines rather than separate chords that jump around.

Next, we'll look at a triad progression in the left hand, to see more closely how a progression can benefit from inversions and voice leading.

Listen to **track 28** to hear a series of left-hand triads in root position:

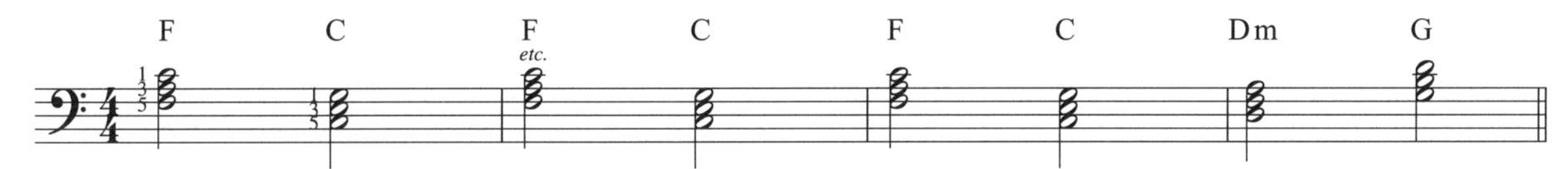

Notice how this sounds rather "disjointed" because we are jumping around in root position. Now with the use of inversions, this left-hand part sounds smoother and more musical.

Listen to **track 29** on the CD to hear inversions and voice leading applied to these left-hand triads:

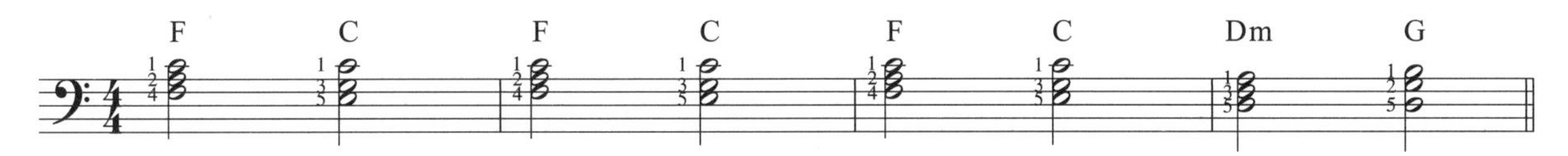

Next, we will take these inverted triads and use them to harmonize an excerpt from the famous Disney song "Can You Feel the Love Tonight," written by Elton John:

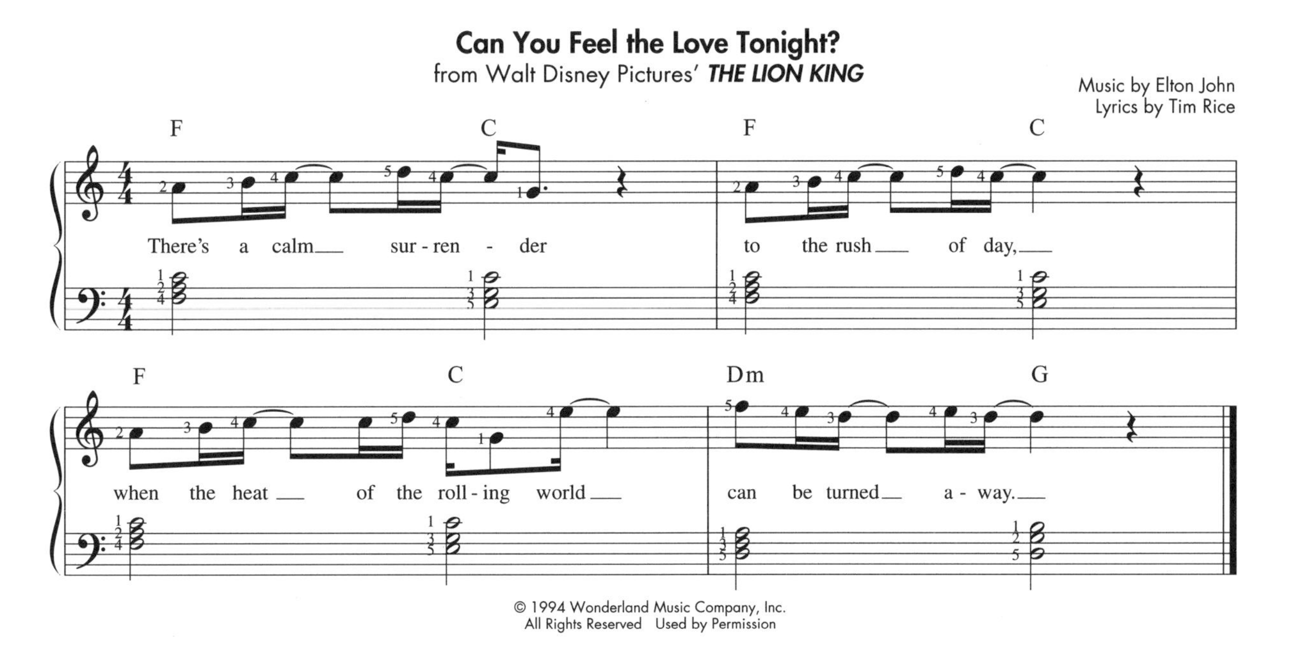

Count through the melody, which is our first example using 16th-note rhythms (review the 16th-note counting in Chapter 6 as needed), then work through it and apply the fingerings shown. When the right-hand melody is familiar, add the inverted triads in the left hand!

Elton John is one of the most important pianists and songwriters of the late 20th century, hitting his peak of pop superstardom in the '70s and '80s. (More about Elton later on in Section 10 – Who's Who.)

In 1994, Elton co-wrote "Can You Feel the Love Tonight" with lyricist Tim Rice for Disney's animated feature *The Lion King*. It won the Academy Award that year for Best Original Song. Here are ten more Elton John songs you should check out:

- Candle in the Wind
- Crocodile Rock
- Daniel
- Don't Let the Sun Go Down on Me
- Goodbye Yellow Brick Road
- Honky Cat
- I Guess That's Why They Call It the Blues
- Kiss the Bride
- Rocket Man
- Your Song

Photo courtesy of Photofest, Inc.

Elton John

INTRODUCING "SLASH CHORD" SYMBOLS

When we took the left hand triads in the previous example and applied inversions and voice leading to them, notice that one effect of this was to change the bottom note on some of the chords. For example, the C major triads in the first three measures now have the note E on the bottom instead of C.

In popular styles we will frequently see *slash* chord symbols used to indicate that a chord tone other than the root is to be placed on the bottom. For example, the symbol "C/E" means "play a C major chord, but use E as the bottom note." A simple way to achieve this is to use left-hand triad inversions as in the previous example. (Later, we will see some other ways to do this, with different voicings and patterns). We will see slash chords in some of the great songs you'll be playing later in the book.

In a "slash chord" symbol, the note to the left of the slash is the name of the overall chord, and the symbol to the right of the slash is the bottom or lowest note ("bass note"). I often see beginning players get the two halves of a slash chord symbol "switched around," so be careful with these!

MAJOR SEVENTH CHORDS AND INVERSIONS

Now it's time to go beyond triads, into the world of four-part chords called *seventh chords*. When we add a fourth note to a triad, it is often the 7th of the chord, as the triad already contains the root, 3rd, and 5th. That is why four-part chords are sometimes referred to as "seventh" chords. The first four-part chord we will look at is the *major seventh chord*:

As with the triads in Chapter 10, the intervals from the root have been indicated (major 3rd, perfect 5th, and major 7th). These major and perfect intervals are found within the major scale, so you may think of this chord as the first, third, fifth, and seventh degrees of a C major scale.

The chord symbol above the staff is now Cmaj7. There are two components to this chord symbol: the root (C) and the *suffix* or description (maj7).

Like the triads, these four-part chords can also be inverted. Here are the inversions of a C major 7th chord:

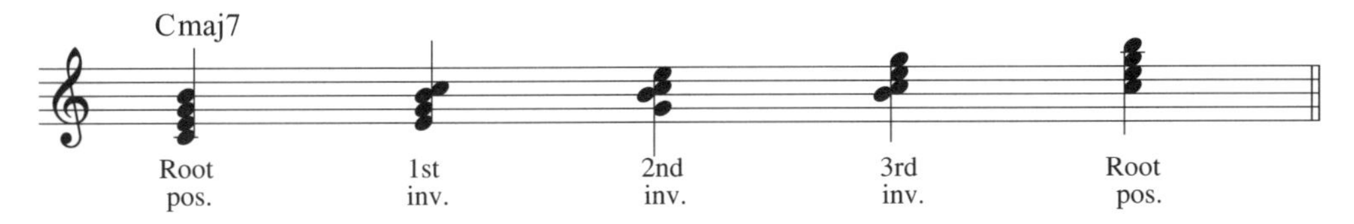

We'll define these different inversions of the C major seventh chord as follows:

- the first chord is in *root position* (with the root on the bottom)
- the second chord is in *first inversion* (with the third on the bottom)
- the third chord is in *second inversion* (with the fifth on the bottom)
- the fourth chord is in *third inversion* (with the seventh on the bottom)
- the last chord is in root position, an octave higher than the first.

MINOR SEVENTH CHORDS AND INVERSIONS

Next, we'll go through the same process for some more commonly used four-part chords, starting with the *minor 7th chord.*

We can also invert the C minor 7th chord, as follows:

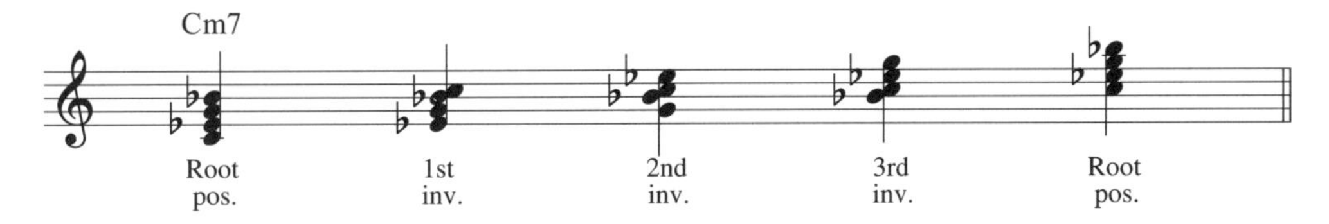

MINOR SEVENTH (WITH FLATTED 5TH) CHORDS AND INVERSIONS

If we *flat the 5th* of the minor 7th chord, we get another useful chord, which is called… you guessed it… a minor 7♭5 chord:

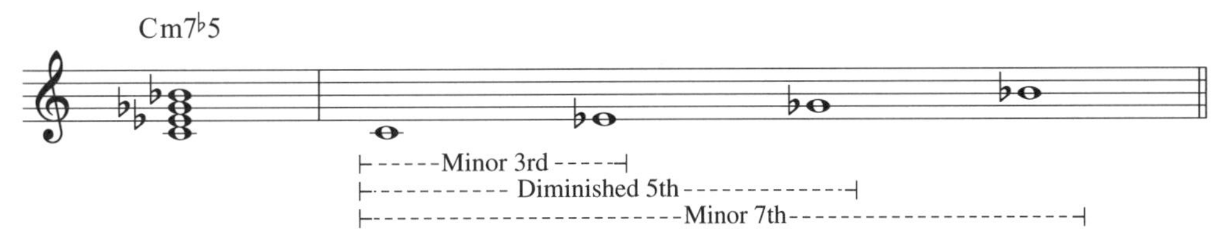

Note the new *diminished 5th* interval description on the previous page. When we take a perfect interval (such as a 5th) and reduce it by a half step, we get a diminished interval.

The "minor 7th ♭5" chord is also referred to as a *half diminished* or *half diminished 7th* chord.

We can invert the C minor 7th ♭5 chord, as follows:

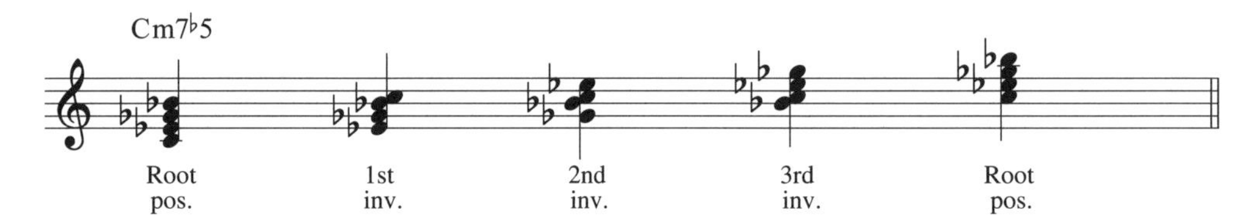

DOMINANT SEVENTH CHORDS AND INVERSIONS

The last four-part chord we will look at in this section is the *dominant 7th chord*, which is built as follows:

We do not use a specific symbol to indicate the word or function *dominant*. A chord symbol which consists of a note name followed only by the suffix 7 indicates a dominant 7th chord.

OK, you know what comes next… this dominant 7th chord can then be inverted, as follows:

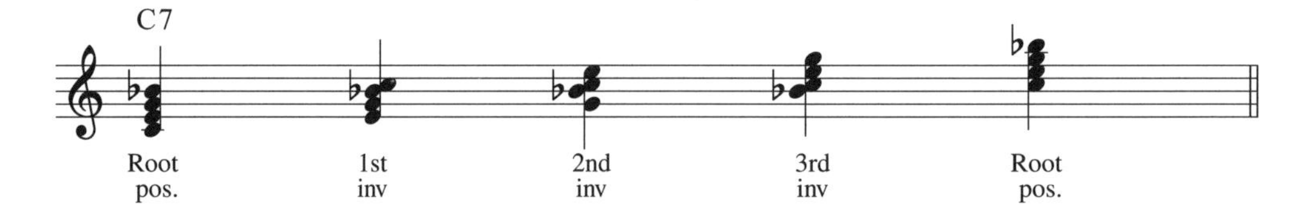

Play through all of these four-part chords (and their inversions) in the right hand, and then try playing them in the left hand (one octave lower). Then, try to become familiar with these chords built from all roots (i.e., D7, E7, F7, etc.).

DIATONIC FOUR-PART CHORDS AND PROGRESSIONS

Now it's time to see how these various four-part chords fit into different keys. Do you remember when we found out about the triads that lived within major keys (the *diatonic* triads in Chapter

10)? Well, now we're about to do the same thing with these new four-part chords. Here are the diatonic four-part chords contained within a C major scale:

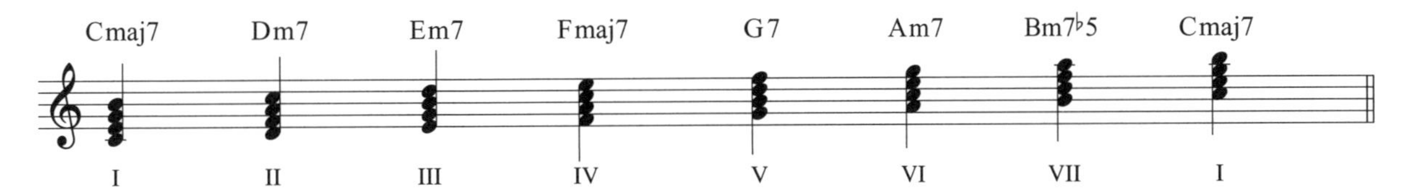

What we're doing here is building a four-part chord from each note in the C major scale, making sure that all notes used are contained with the scale (which, in the key of C means we are only using the white keys again). This gives us the various chord *qualities* shown here from left to right (major 7th, minor 7th, minor 7th, major 7th, dominant 7th, minor 7th, and minor 7th with flatted 5th, in that order). Just like we said for the diatonic triads, a lot of songs are written using these diatonic four-part chords!

As with the triads we demonstrated earlier, the Roman numeral under the staff indicates the chord *function*.

Of course, we can have diatonic four-part chords in any key, not just in C major! So now we'll derive the four-part chords within a couple more keys, starting with F major:

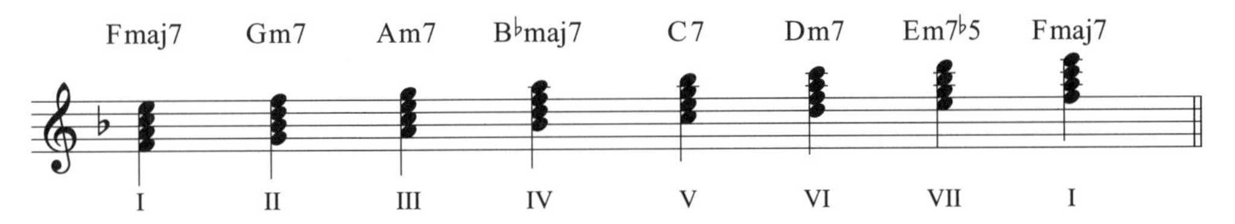

Next, we'll look at a diatonic four-part chord progression in the left hand, and see how it benefits from inversions and voice leading.

Listen to **track 30** to hear a series of left-hand four-part chords in root position. These are all diatonic to the key of F:

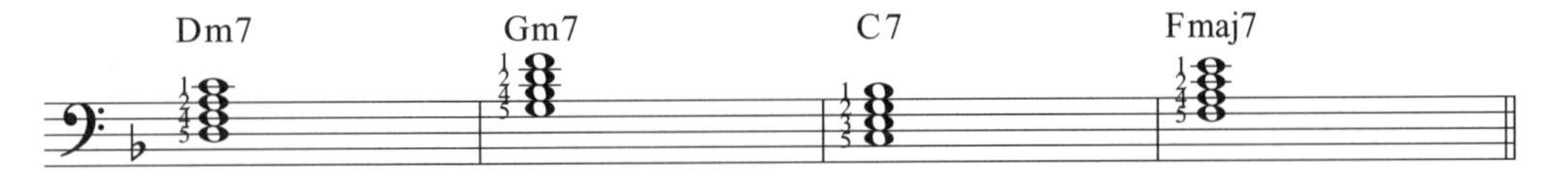

Notice how this sounds rather "disjointed" because we are jumping around in root position. Now with the use of inversions, this left-hand part sounds smoother and more musical.

Listen to **track 31** on the CD to hear inversions and voice leading applied to the previous progression of four-part chords:

We will next use these inverted triads to harmonize an excerpt from the famous R&B/pop song "Killing Me Softly with His Song."

Count through the melody (review the eighth-note counting in Chapter 6 as needed), then work through it and apply the fingerings shown. When the right-hand melody is familiar, add the inverted four-part chords in the left hand!

Finally, in this chapter we'll examine the diatonic four-part chords in G major, as follows:

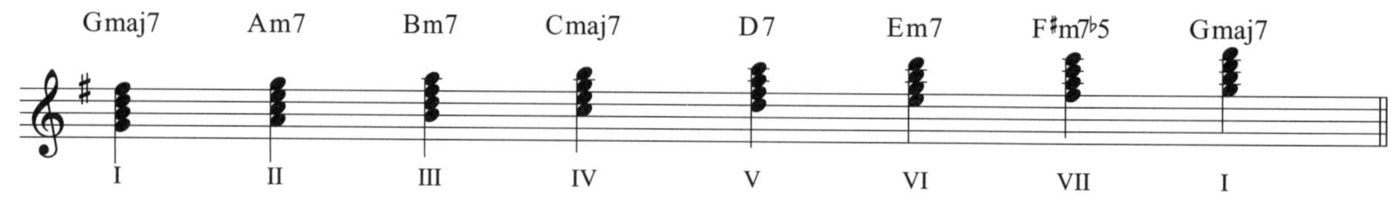

Now we'll take a look at the accompaniment (comping) figure from the classic Santana song "Oye Como Va." Note that it alternates between two chords: Am7 and D7 (II and V of G major, as shown above). The Am7 chord is voiced in second inversion, to lead smoothly into the D7 chord in root position:

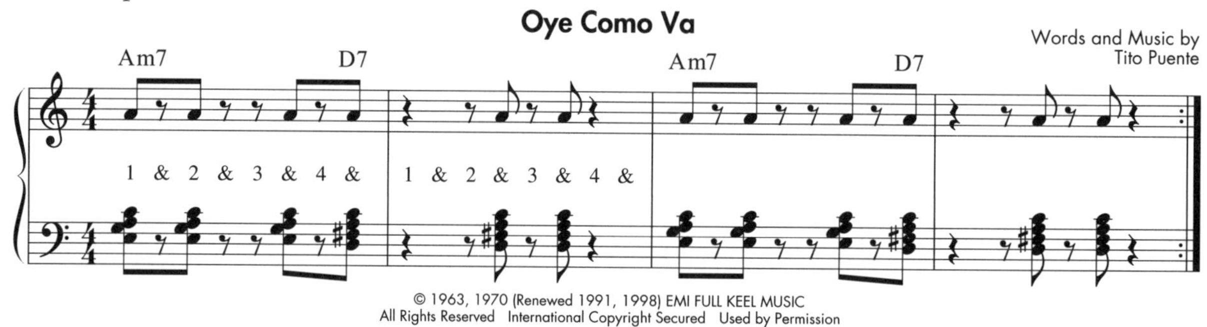

The counting has been written in the first two measures to help you with this syncopated rhythm. Count carefully with all these eighth notes and eighth rests.

A lot of pop and R&B songs are written using diatonic four-part chords, so you should learn them in as many keys (and inversions) as you can!

The song "Oye Como Va" was originally written by Tito Puente, one of the world's best-known salsa musicians. Santana added some rock elements to their version of the tune, which was included on their groundbreaking *Abraxas* album, released in 1970. An eclectic mix of rock, blues, salsa, and jazz, this record is a good example of the experimental spirit underpinning the West Coast rock scene in the late '60s and '70s.

CHAPTER 13
ADVANCED PLAYING—BEYOND HAND POSITIONS

What's Ahead:

- Moving your hands to the notes as needed
- Pop and classical tunes
- Arpeggios
- Dynamics, slurs, and articulations

MOVING YOUR HANDS TO THE NOTES AS NEEDED

So far in this book we've seen a lot of music examples with fingerings notated. We started out using basic five-finger positions, then we extended these positions, and then we started to use thumb turns and position changes to get to the larger melodic ranges needed. This has all been preparation for a kind of "free hand-motion," where your hands will often be moving to the notes as needed, no longer remaining (for too long) in one five-finger position. The more you practice this, the more it will become second nature to you. You've already done this a bit, but here we go for some more! Here are some pointers to bear in mind along the way:

- Always look ahead in the music. That way you can anticipate register changes (the music going higher or lower), among other things.
- During ascending or descending passages, thumb turns may be needed.
- Most music is organized in *phrases* or sections. Each phrase might require a new hand position to access all of the notes needed in the phrase. Again, try to see these ahead of time.
- Try to be aware of the *melodic range* (lowest and highest notes) needed in a phrase or section. This will help you position your hands and fingers correctly.

When I'm playing music, it's rare for me to consciously think about each individual finger. At first, you'll probably need to be conscious of this. But soon it will gradually become more automatic, and your hands will just go where they are needed. The more you play and apply these principles, the faster this will occur! One of the most important things needed to achieve this is to really *know* the notes on the staff and keyboard.

In this chapter, most of the fingerings are still shown in the music examples. However, pretty soon we'll be working on pieces with no fingerings marked, so if you are still fuzzy on your note recognition, keep working at it, using some of the methods discussed earlier.

POP AND CLASSICAL TUNES

In this next section we'll be doing a lot of stuff—most importantly, playing some real tunes! We'll learn about arpeggios and apply more triad voicings to a couple of classic pop songs: "Wonderful Tonight" and "Walk of Life." Then we'll look at two famous classical pieces by Clementi and Satie, and discover that the chords and scales that we have learned so far are also found in classical music… who knew?

First up, we have a great pop song from the 1970s, "Wonderful Tonight." We'll get familiar with the melody, and then add some basic triads in the left hand. Then we'll learn about arpeggios and develop some new patterns from the left-hand triads. Note that there's an 8-measure intro melody before the verse begins:

Wonderful Tonight

Words and Music by
Eric Clapton

Remember those slash chords we talked about in the last chapter? Well, we have several D/F♯ chord symbols in this song. This means that we need to place the D major triad with F♯ as the lowest note. So you'll notice that in these measures we have used the D major triad in first inversion, so that the F♯ is on the bottom. For all of the other chords, the root is placed on the bottom (i.e., the triads are in root position).

ARPEGGIOS

An *arpeggio* is simply a *broken chord*. Instead of playing all of the notes in a chord together, we play them one at a time, in succession. We'll try a new version of "Wonderful Tonight," this time with the chords in the left hand "broken up" into arpeggios. All the notes and fingerings are the same as in the previous version, but now we play the notes of the chords one at a time, in an even eighth-note pattern.

First, practice the hands individually, particularly as we're introducing a new pattern in the left hand. Again, use a metronome while practicing to keep on track. You can start around 50 beats per minute, and gradually work up to 80–85.

This is a pop ballad that will greatly benefit from use of the damper pedal! This pedal is especially effective when playing arpeggios in an expressive style. Review the damper pedal techniques in Chapter 11 as needed, and make sure you release the pedal exactly when the chords change… no "smearing" please!

The song "Wonderful Tonight" comes from one of Eric Clapton's most critically acclaimed albums, *Slowhand*, which was released in November, 1977 and sold over a million copies. The song was inspired by his then-wife Patti, as he was (impatiently!) waiting for her to get ready for an evening out. Nonetheless, it is known as one of the most emotional and touching love ballads of the modern era.

Photo courtesy of Photofest, Inc.
Eric Clapton

Our next song is a very fun pop-rock tune from Dire Straits called "Walk of Life." Although the keyboard part on the record is actually played by the organ, the music can easily be adapted for the piano. This excerpt of the song is the instrumental melody used for the intro.

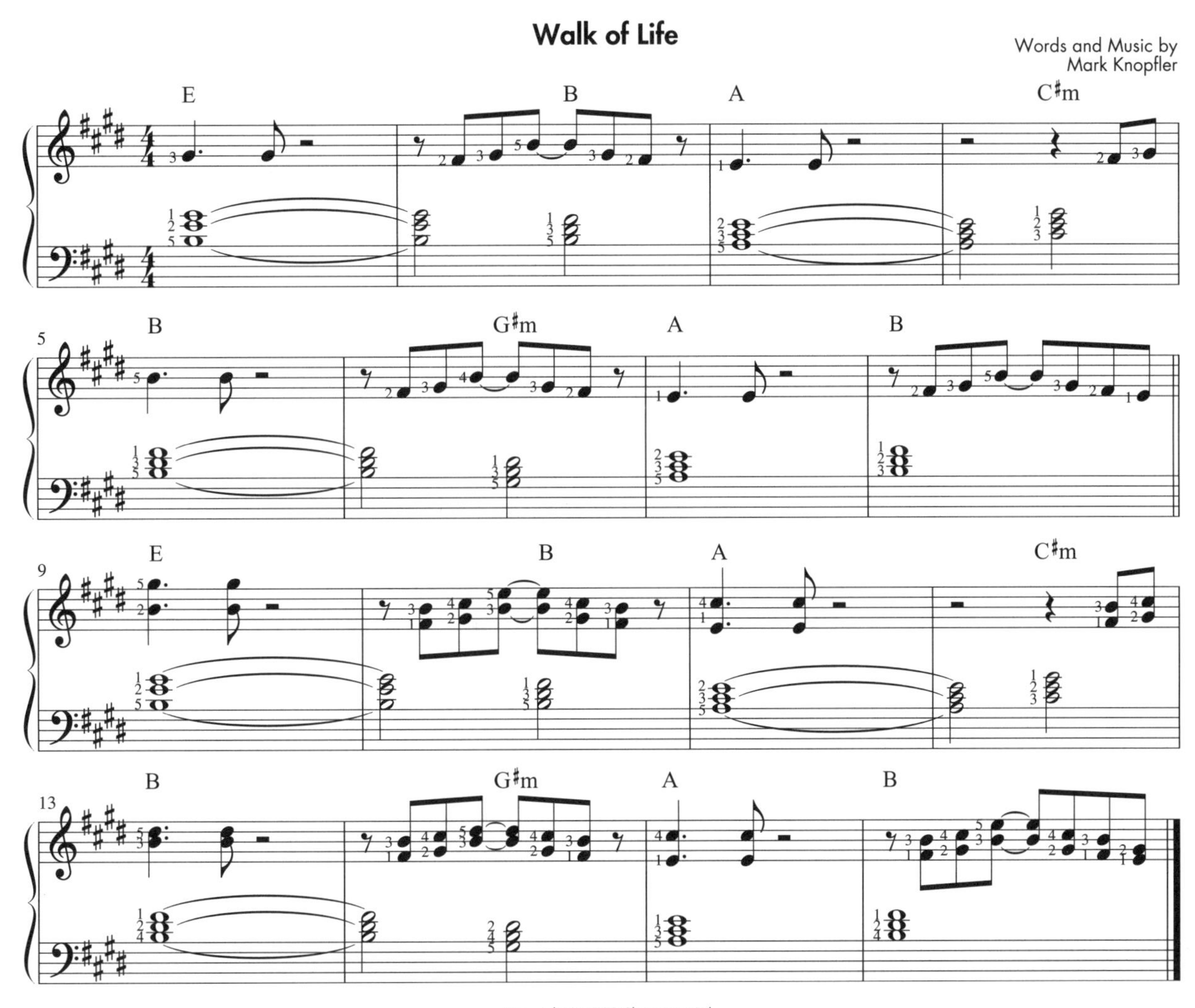

Make sure you notice the key signature. What key is this? What are the four notes that are to be played as sharp? Also pay attention to the fingerings and hand position needed for the 4th intervals in measures 10, 14, and 16. This type of figure occurs in a lot of rock and funk songs!

As you play songs in new and/or unfamiliar key signatures, it may help to go through and circle all notes affected by the key signature (i.e., all notes to be played sharp in "Walk of Life") in a red pencil. This will not only serve as a reminder to play the proper notes, but the act of circling them can also help you get to know the key signature a little better.

The song "Walk of Life" came from the Dire Straits' album *Brothers in Arms*, released in 1985. This record was a big success in the U.S., selling over nine million copies. Dire Straits was essentially a vehicle for the writing, vocal, and guitar talents of Mark Knopfler, who also became an accomplished film composer (with scores for *Local Hero* and *Wag the Dog*, among others). Pianist Guy Fletcher was an essential part of the Dire Straits sound from the mid-'80s.

OK, let's straighten our bow ties now as we head into the classical realm (or as my jazz musician friends might say, "the legit stuff"!). In Clementi's "Sonatina in C Major," (I know you'll recognize this one!), you really get to put your scale practicing to good use (review Chapter 7 if you've been lax in that area). Just by looking at the piece, you can probably recognize the scalar patterns throughout in the right hand. The left hand fills things in with single notes, and a few arpeggios. Practice the hands separately to get a preview, and then we'll discuss a few more items about the piece before you get back into the practicing.

DYNAMICS, SLURS, AND ARTICULATIONS

Listen to **track 32** to hear an excerpt from "Sonatina in C Major" by Muzio Clementi. Notice *how* the notes are played: sometimes they are smooth and connected and sometimes short and separate. Also notice the changes in volume which are called *dynamics*. Once you're done listening and looking at the music, we'll discuss some of these items below, and then give the piece a try.

Now let's go over some of those things we mentioned earlier as well as some other new and important items in this piece.

- Look at the time signature. It looks like the "C" used for *common time* (equivalent to 4/4), except there's now a vertical line running through it. This tells you we are in *cut time*, equivalent to *2/2 time* (meaning two half-note beats per measure). Notice that a cut-time measure still contains the same number of quarter notes (4) that a 4/4 measure does. The difference is that we just feel two main pulses per measure (on 1 and 3), instead of four.

- Notice the ***f*** in measures 1 and 8, and the ***p*** in measure 5. These are *dynamic markings*, which tell you how loud or soft to play. The ***p*** stands for *piano*, which means soft. The ***f*** stands for *forte*, which means loud. Like most musical terms, these are borrowed from the Italian language.
- There are also some long curved lines above some of the notes throughout the piece. These are called *slurs* and mean to play smooth and connected, or *legato* (another one of those Italian words!)
- By contrast, some notes have dots either above or below them (for example, the G's in measure 1, the C in measure 6, etc.). These are to be played short, so as to leave a gap between one note and the next. This is known as *staccato*, and is the opposite of legato (…we'll have you fluent in Italian in no time at all!). Play staccato as if the keys are a hot stove—bounce your hand a bit for a short and detached sound.

Ok, now it's time to get back to practicing.

As usual, work through this piece with hands separately first, using the fingerings shown. Watch out for the dynamics (loud or soft) and the articulation (*legato* or *staccato*). Start at a slow tempo, and gradually increase when you get comfortable. When you're ready, put the hands together.

When using a metronome with this piece, start with the click on the quarter note (as usual). But then, as you get more familiar with it, try playing it with the click on the half note. This is consistent with the cut time signature we discussed earlier, in that we really have two half-note beats per measure.

Toward the end of the 18th century, the new *pianoforte* instrument was introduced, and it quickly began to overtake the harpsichord (the dominant keyboard instrument up to that time) in popularity. Muzio Clementi was a key figure in that transition, writing sonatas and studies that used the potential of this new instrument, and influencing the technique of many pianists. He also wrote many exercises for young pianists and students, and co-founded a music publishing and piano manufacturing company.

Muzio Clementi

Finally, in this chapter, we'll take a look at "Gymnopédie No. 1" by Erik Satie, one of the most popular and enduring pieces in the modern classical repertoire.

Listen to **track 33**, "Gymnopédie No. 1," for a "preview" of all the interesting musical things going on in terms of *dynamics* (volume changes) and *phrasing* (how the notes and measures are grouped together by slurs, producing musical sentences).

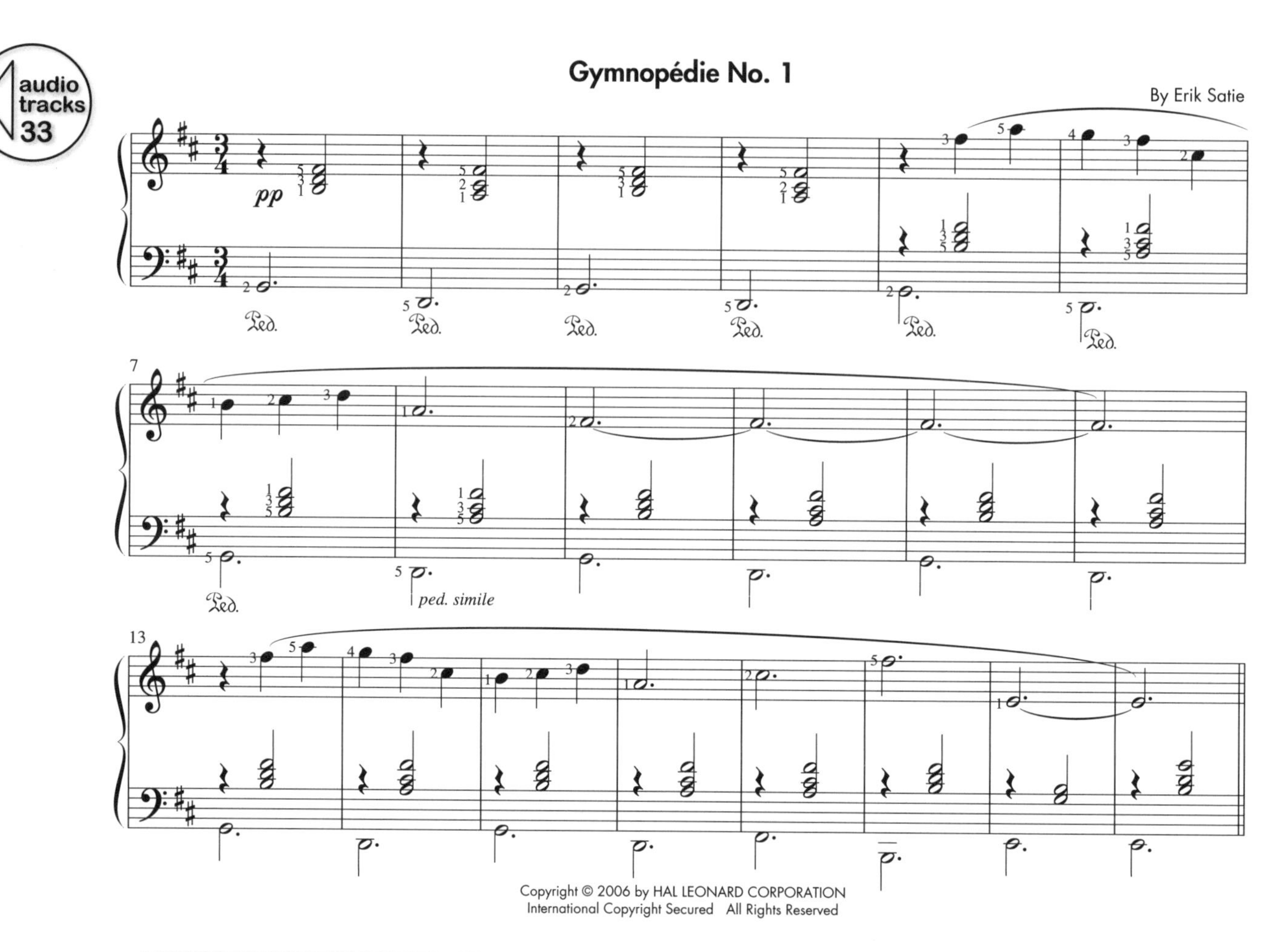

This is our first piece to mix slurs and ties together.

They are visually similar, but have a completely different function. A quick review:

- Ties extend the duration of a note, and connect only two notes of the same pitch.
- Slurs tell us to play the phrase *legato* (smooth and connected), like in the right-hand phrase during measures 5–12. Slurs can connect many notes together (more than just two, like the tie).

You may also notice there are a lot of triads in this piece. For example, in the right hand, in measures 1 and 3, we have root position B minor triads, and, in measure 2 and 4, we have first inversion F♯ minor triads. These same triads are then played by the left hand, starting in measure 5.

Looking at the first measure, you'll see there is a G in the bass clef, below the B minor triad in the treble clef. Remember those major 7th four-part chords we met in the last chapter? Well, it so happens that if we think of the G in the left hand combined with the triad in the right hand as all one chord, we come up with a G major 7th chord (the notes G–B–D–F♯). In playing and "figuring out" chords, it may be helpful to think of notes in the right hand and left hand separately. This type of "upper structure triad voicing" is used extensively in popular styles, as we'll see very soon! However, the overall sound and, therefore, harmony is actually a combination of what is being played in both hands. Cool, huh?!

CHAPTER 14
"COMPING" FROM A FAKE BOOK

What's Ahead:

- What is "comping" from a fake book?
- The two stages to "faking it"
- Introduction to "upper structure" voicings
- Applying the techniques to songs

WHAT IS "COMPING" FROM A FAKE BOOK?

Well, there are two terms we need to explain in this sentence: *comping* and *fake book*. So here we go.

- *Comping* is a colloquial music term for "accompaniment." If you are singing a song and playing an instrument at the same time (i.e., piano or guitar), most likely you're using the instrument to accompany yourself while singing. This normally involves playing the chords of the song in a way that is rhythmically suited to the style and supportive of the melody.
- A *fake book* is a book containing *charts* of tunes (rather than fully written-out arrangements). "So what's a chart?" I hear you ask. Well, a *chart* (also known as a lead sheet) normally just has the treble staff (rather than a grand staff), and shows only the melody, lyrics, and chord symbols for a song. You then have to "fake" (or improvise) a piano arrangement based on this information.

Some charts don't even show the melody of the song. They just have chord symbols and "slashes" showing the beats in each measure. This type of chart is sometimes referred to as a *chord chart* or *slash chart*. You don't normally find this type of chart in fake books, but they are often used in band and rehearsal situations, where one of the players might prepare a chord chart to give everybody a quick "road map" of the song.

When improvising an arrangement from a chart, you will either be comping (if you are accompanying yourself singing, or accompanying another singer or instrumentalist) or you will be playing the melody (if you are playing solo piano, for example). If you want to play the melody, it would need to be shown on the chart, of course (i.e., not just a chord chart). In this chapter, we'll focus on comping using chord charts as a simple way to get started. In the next chapter, we'll look at how to play the melody from a fake book.

If you're at all interested in playing popular music, there are great advantages to being able to work from fake books and charts. When you go to the music store and buy the sheet music for a popular song, what you are actually buying is somebody's arrangement of that song for the piano. So, no matter how well you read and play it, your performance can only be as good as "someone else's arrangement." If you're at all familiar with sheet music and folios of popular songs, you'll know that the quality of arrangements out there is rather variable, to say the least. So an experienced player with a good understanding of harmony and styles will very often be able to improvise or "fake" a better arrangement, working from a fake book chart.

The individual charts in fake books are normally no longer than two pages (and frequently are just one or even half a page), which makes them easy to use "on the gig" (or when practicing at home), and means that each book can contain many different songs!

THE TWO STAGES TO "FAKING IT"

Now we're going to begin the fun process of "faking it," making up our own piano arrangement in response to a chart of a song. Whether we're working from a chord chart, or a chart which also shows the melody, the method of creating a comping arrangement is essentially the same: you're using the chord symbols to generate the comping part. Let's start with our first progression, which is presented as a simple chord chart:

This is a typical example of a chord chart. We have a chord symbol over beat 1 in each measure, and four slashes in each measure (one for each beat). If one of your band mates throws this on top of your keyboard during a rehearsal, it's basically telling you to comp according to your understanding of the style, over these chord changes.

Assuming we are in the key of C here, do you know how the chords are functioning in this key (in other words, what scale degree of the key they are built from)? Well, we saw in Chapter 10 that the F major and G major triads are the IV and V chords in the key of C major, so this progression may be labeled as I–IV–V–I. This type of progression is used for a lot of basic pop, rock, and country songs!

It's very common for chord changes to fall on beat 1 of the measure, as in this example. If there is more than one chord in the measure, the second chord will most likely fall on beat 3. If you don't see a chord symbol over a measure, this means that the previous chord symbol is still in effect.

In order to "fake" our comping arrangement, the *two stages* we need to go through are:

1) Create a voicing for each chord, and then invert it as needed to voice lead smoothly between chords.
2) Apply a rhythmic pattern to these voicings, suitable for the style.

"But wait! What's a voicing?" Good question… well, a voicing is actually an interpretation of a chord symbol. At this beginning stage, we can think of a voicing as a distribution of notes between the hands. In other words, once we figure out which notes are in the chord, we then decide which notes of the chord we play in the left hand, and which notes we play in the right hand.

Listen to **track 34** to hear *Stage 1* applied to this chord progression. Here we're using triad voicings suitable for a wide range of contemporary pop styles.

Let's make sure we understood how *Stage 1* was applied to this progression:

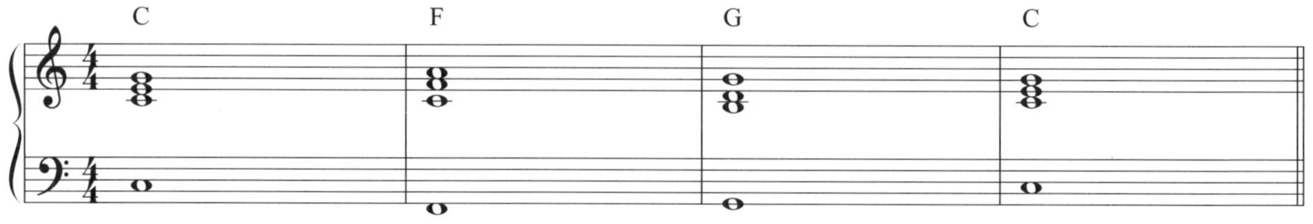

- We made a *voicing* decision which works for triad progressions in many simpler styles: we'll play the root of the triad in the left hand, and all three notes (i.e., root, 3rd, and 5th) of the triad in the right hand. You can spell each of the triads in our head if necessary, i.e., the C major triad is C–E–G, and the F major triad is F–A–C, and so on. (Review Chapter 10 for the triad spelling, if needed).
- We then inverted the triads to promote good voice leading. The inversion used for the first chord is an arbitrary decision, but you'll normally want to start in the midrange (i.e., not too high and not too low). In this case, we started with the C major triad in root position, so rather than jump up to the F major triad in root position (which would be poor voice leading), we went to the F major triad in second inversion, which was much closer. Similarly, the G major triad in first inversion, followed by the C major triad in root position results in good voice leading each time. In general, the goal is to keep the *top-note movement* down to a whole step or less, if possible, and we've done that.

Going through these steps will be helpful, especially if you have not yet worked very much with chord progressions. However, what will make this substantially faster is to get all of these triads and inversions into your muscle memory, so that you don't have to "spell" the triads out each time in order to find or construct them. With chords memorized, the voice leading between inversions will become more automatic. So make sure you have the triads and inversions in Chapters 10 and 12 "under your fingers."

OK, let's take a deep breath and move on to *Stage 2* (…drums roll…) This is where we make it sound like music, rather than just a bunch of chords with no rhythm! First of all, we'll apply a rhythmic style suitable for a simple pop ballad.

Listen to **track 35** to hear *Stage 2* applied to this chord progression, using a pop ballad rhythmic pattern.

It's important to understand that your hands are in exactly the same position, and playing exactly the same notes, as in *Stage 1*. All we're doing is applying a "rhythmic template" to these voicings, as described below.

Instead of playing just whole-note triads, the right hand is *alternating* between playing the top two notes of each triad on the downbeats (i.e., 1, 2, 3, and 4), and the bottom note of each triad on the upbeats (i.e., all of the "&'s" in between the downbeats). This is a classic pop ballad pattern used on many famous songs. Meanwhile, the left hand is still playing the root of each chord, this time using half notes instead of whole notes. This style will also sound more authentic if you use the sustain pedal for the duration of each chord (again, don't forget to release the pedal when the chords change!).

Next, we'll apply a rhythmic style suitable for a more driving pop/rock groove.

Listen to **track 36** to hear *Stage 2* applied to this chord progression, this time using a pop/rock rhythmic pattern.

To give this more drive in a rock style, the right hand is now playing the triads in a two-measure rhythmic pattern that includes playing some chords on the off beats. This type of "kick" to the rhythm is common across a range of pop styles. Again, we're playing exactly the same notes as in **track 34**, but with a rhythmic pattern applied. Meanwhile, the left hand is providing a steady eighth-note pulse, repeating the root of each chord.

INTRODUCTION TO "UPPER STRUCTURE" TRIAD VOICINGS

Before looking at our next chord progression example, we need to learn about some "upper structure" voicings. An *upper structure* is a chord in the right hand, played "over" a bass note in the left hand. The simplest upper structures occur when one of the four-part chords we derived in Chapter 12 is "split" so that the root is played in the left hand, and the rest of the chord (the 3rd, 5th, and 7th, which themselves form a triad) is played in the right hand. Thinking in *upper structures* is a quicker and easier way to figure out and play bigger (4-part and larger) chords. Our next chord chart example consists of four-part or seventh chord symbols.

Assuming we are in the key of C major here, let's think about how the chords are functioning. We saw in Chapter 12 that the Am7 and Fmaj7 chords are the VI and IV chords in the key of C major. This progression may be labeled as I–VI–IV–I, with all chords being four-part/seventh chords. This is a typical chord progression in pop/R&B styles.

Next, we'll review how to spell these chords, using the rules we learned in Chapter 12.

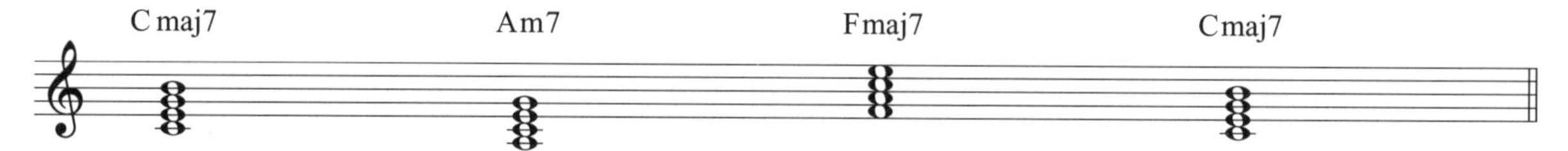

OK, just in case you need a quick review of how we built these chords:

- The *major 7th* chords are built using major 3rd, perfect 5th, and major 7th intervals up from the root.
- The *minor 7th* chords are built using minor 3rd, perfect 5th, and minor 7th intervals up from the root.

To begin *Stage 1* of our comping process, we'll voice the chords with upper structures by separating the root (placing it "alone" in the left hand) from the other chord tones.

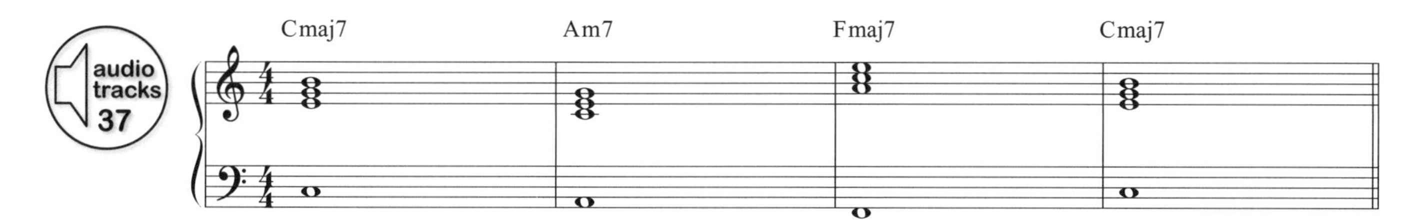

Listen to **track 37** to hear upper structures applied to this four-part chord progression (*Stage 1*). We can compare this to the chords shown on the previous page, as follows:

- On the *Cmaj7* chords, the upper three notes (E,G,B) are in the treble clef, and the root (C) is in the bass clef. To find and play a Cmaj7 chord more easily, you can think of it as an E minor chord over a C in the bass.
- On the *Am7* chord, the upper three notes (C,E,G) are in the treble clef, and the root (A) is in the bass clef. This chord may be thought of as a C major chord over an A in the bass.
- On the *Fmaj7* chord, the upper three notes (A,C,E) are in the treble clef, and the root (F) is in the bass clef. This chord consists of an A minor chord over an F in the bass.

We're not quite done with *Stage 1* yet, as we still need to use inversions for better voice leading. These inversions will be applied as follows:

- On the Cmaj7 chords, the upper E minor triad is in root position.
- On the Am7 chord, the upper C major triad is in first inversion.
- On the Fmaj7 chord, the upper A minor triad is second inversion.

Listen to **track 38** to hear how inversions promote better voice leading.

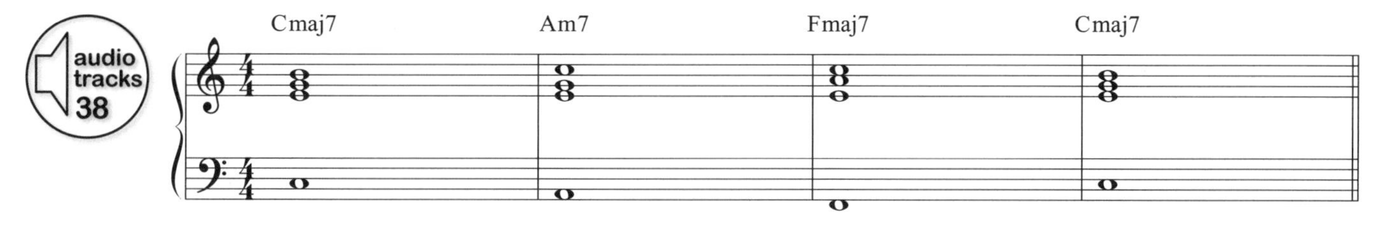

Stage 1 is now completed on this progression, as all the chords are now properly voiced. Next, we'll move on to *Stage 2* and apply some rhythmic interest to these voicings.

Listen to **track 39** to hear *Stage 2* applied to this chord progression, using an R&B ballad-type rhythmic pattern.

The "star-like" signs in the same line as the pedal symbols underneath the staff indicate places to release the pedal.

Just like with the first chord progression, note that your hands are in exactly the same position, and playing exactly the same notes, as in *Stage 1*. We're just applying a rhythmic style to make it sound like music!

So now, instead of playing just whole-note triads, the right hand is playing a quarter-note triad on beat 1, and then arpeggiating the triad during beat 2, ending on the last sixteenth note of beat 2 (which is then a sixteenth-note anticipation of beat 3—a classic R&B ballad device). During beat 4, the triad is "split", with the outer two notes falling on beat 4, and the middle note falling on the "and" of 4. Meanwhile, the left hand is still playing the root of each chord, gently rocking back and forth using octaves. This style will also require the use of the damper pedal for the duration of each chord. Congratulations… you just played an excerpt from an R&B ballad working only from the chord symbols… wasn't too tough, was it?

Though we carefully analyzed how we applied rhythm and arpeggios to the previous chord progression, eventually you will not need to make such analytical decisions for every little thing you play, and will just "play by feel" like a pro—play what sounds good to you!

Next, we'll apply a rhythmic style suitable for a more up-tempo R&B/funk groove.

Listen to **track 40** to hear *Stage 2* applied to this chord progression, this time using an R&B/funk rhythmic pattern.

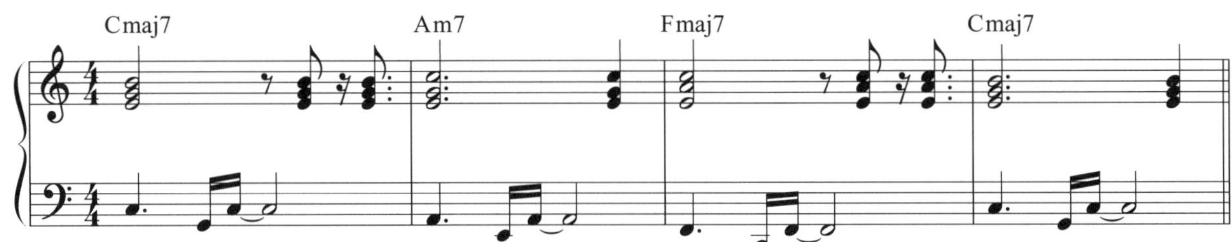

In this version, the right hand is playing the triads in a two-measure rhythmic pattern. The first measure of the pattern features syncopation in the chords as they are played in places other than on the beat. The triads on the second sixteenth note of beat 4 impart a strong rhythmic "kick," helping to emphasize the syncopated nature.

The left hand is playing the root of each chord on beat 1, and then the 5th of each chord on the "and" of 2, returning to the root on the last sixteenth note of beat 2. This last bass note, therefore, anticipates beat 3 by a sixteenth note—a very common sound in funk styles.

When playing these R&B/funk patterns, articulate everything cleanly and be sure to observe the rests, as this helps to bring out the syncopated figures.

APPLYING THE TECHNIQUES TO SONGS

Next, we'll see some comping techniques at work on a number of different songs. In each case, we'll look at how the chord symbols have been voiced, and how the rhythms have been applied. We'll start out with the piano comping figure from one of the Beatles' most famous songs, "Let It Be."

Let It Be

Words and Music by
John Lennon and Paul McCartney

C G Am Fmaj7 F6 C G F C

If you play this on the piano, it will be instantly recognized by everyone in the room (unless they've been living in a cave for the last 40 years!) Let's take a closer look at this pattern.

- In the right hand, some *octave doubling* is being used i.e., doubling the top note of a triad an octave lower. Most of the voicings are simple triads derived from the chord symbol, but the Fmaj7 is voiced with an upper structure: an A minor triad over F in the left hand. Also, the A-C-D on beat 4 of measure 2 is the upper part of an F major 6th (or F6) chord. This may be considered as a variation of the four-part major 7th chord, but with a 6th instead of a 7th.
- The left hand is playing the root of each chord in octaves, landing on beats 1 and 3 (the points of chord change), and then playing on the upbeats in between the right-hand triads, creating a very effective *combined rhythm* between the hands.

Try applying this very cool ballad pattern to some other chord progressions. Get those fake books out, and go for it!

Everything You've Ever Wanted to Know About "Let It Be"...

The song "Let It Be" was released in 1970 and became a Number One hit single. Although it was credited (like virtually all off the Beatles' songs) to Lennon and McCartney, it was written by Paul McCartney alone. The song has a spiritual, gospel-like quality, due to the uplifting nature of the lyrics, and also the piano part which has something of a gospel flavor. On the mix used for the single, the gospel feel is further enhanced by the "church-like" organ used for the solo section. On the album version, however, this was less obvious, as Phil Spector added a raunchy rock guitar solo on the top, sparking an eternal debate among Beatles' fans about which was the "better" mix. Have a listen to them both and see what you think!

The song (along with the rest of the *Let It Be* album) was actually recorded in early 1969, but the recordings weren't released for over a year, as the band wasn't sure what to do with them. The album was finally released in 1970, and the song hit Number One on the charts in the same week that the Beatles broke up, in April of that year. The fact that *Let It Be* was the last Beatles' album to be released, reinforced the impression that the song was unofficially the band's "epitaph."

Numerous other artists have covered the song, and many of these versions are rather forgettable. One notable exception is a version by Aretha Franklin, which was recorded in 1969, but not released until the Beatles' version came out. Some have said that this was because the Beatles decided to make it a single themselves, after they had originally given the song to Aretha Franklin to cover.

Photo courtesy of Photofest, Inc.

Paul McCartney

Next up is a comping figure from the famous Carole King song "It's Too Late." This actually consists of two separate parts: on the record, one was played on an acoustic piano, the other on a Wurlitzer electric piano.

It's Too Late

Words and Music by
Carole King and Toni Stern

Am7 D6 Am7 D6

This tune uses another very recognizable pattern, which we'll now take a closer look at:

- Although this pattern uses some sixteenth notes, they are really just used as ornamentation—the song still has an eighth-note "feel" overall. This tune is typical of an older pop/rock style.
- The right hand of the acoustic piano part is playing complete four-part chords (the Am7 and D6), interspersed with single-note figures towards the end of measures 2 and 4. Each of the D6 chords lands on the "and" of 4, and anticipates beat 1 of measures 2 and 4.

The single-note figures or riffs in between the full chords are actually built from an A minor pentatonic scale, which consists of the notes A–C–D–E–G. This is a commonly used scale across a range of pop and rock styles.

- The left hand of the acoustic piano part is playing the root of each chord, on beat 1 for the Am7 chords, and on the "and" of 4 (anticipating beat 1) for the D6 chords.
- The right hand of the electric piano part is using the same four-part chords, but in different inversions. On the Am7 chords, the electric piano adds some extra rhythm, landing on the "and" of 3 in measures 1 and 3. This adds extra rhythmic energy to the arrangement.

The hit song "It's Too Late" came from Carole King's 1971 album *Tapestry*, one of the most successful pop music albums ever. At that time, she had already earned a reputation as a great songwriter, with songs covered by many artists including the Beatles; Aretha Franklin; James Taylor; the Byrds; and Blood, Sweat and Tears. *Tapestry* was the ultimate singer/songwriter album of the period—a reflective and thoughtful work that prominently featured her influential pop piano stylings.

It's time to put your Stetson on. Next, we'll check out a country ballad comping example.

Listen to **track 41** to hear "Let Somebody Love You," a tune reminiscent of ballads by country-rock bands such as the Eagles. **Track 42** has a full band accompaniment so you can jam along with the entire group!

- The pattern uses eighth-note subdivisions overall, at a slow tempo. This is typical of an older country ballad style.
- The right hand is playing triads and four-part chords in a pattern similar to the pop ballad comping we developed for the first chord chart in this chapter. The difference here is that instead of the *alternating* eighth-note figure (playing the upper notes of the chord on the downbeat, and the lowest note on the upbeat) occurring throughout the measure, we are now just "alternating" within beats 2 and 4.
- The left hand is playing the root of each chord on beats 1 and 3 (the points of chord change), and then repeating the root on the "and" of 2 (leading into beat 3), and/or the "and" of 4 (leading into beat 1 of the next measure). This type of left-hand eighth-note *pickup* is common across a range of pop, rock, and country styles.

This example also has some new chord symbols!

- The Dm/G in measures 1 and 5 is a new upper structure. It's simply a D minor triad with a G in the bass.
- The Cm6 in measures 2 and 6 is a new four-part chord symbol. You can think of it as a minor triad with a (major) 6th interval added.
- In measure 7, the G/D is a major triad inverted over the 5th in the bass, and the B7/D♯ is a dominant 7th four-part chord inverted over its 3rd. These inversions enable the smooth bass movement to occur using successive half steps in measure 7.

Now it's time to rock 'n' roll! We're going to look at the intro from the Bon Jovi classic "Runaway." This is a single-staff keyboard part (just written in treble clef).

Runaway

Words and Music by
Jon Bon Jovi and George Karakoglou

Am Asus2 Dm/A Am Asus2 Am

Gsus4 G Gsus2 G Gsus4 G Gsus2

This was originally recorded using a synthesizer, so fire up your synth to play it if you have one—if not, playing it on piano will work fine. This type of driving eighth-note *ostinato* or repeated figure is common in '80s and '90s rock styles. The part consists of different triads and suspensions. The Asus chord in measures 1 and 2 is a variation on the normal suspension, with the added B, which may be thought of as the 2nd or 9th (a kind of *double suspension*).The Dm/A chord in measure 1 is a minor triad in second inversion.

The signature keyboard part on "Runaway" was played by Roy Bittan, a member of Bruce Springsteen's E Street band and a session ace on many other hit recordings. The song is the first track on their debut album *Bon Jovi*, released in January, 1984. Although the band could definitely be classed as "arena rock," keyboards have always played a prominent part in their sound, as played by the band's regular keyboardist, David Bryan.

Photo by David Redferns/Redferns Music Picture Library

David Bryan

It's time to look at one more country comping example. This one is in more of an up-tempo, country-rock vein.

Listen to **track 43** to hear the piano-only version of "You Can't Hide," a tune reminiscent of country-rock bands such as the Eagles, Poco, and the Byrds. **Track 44** has a full band accompaniment so you can "join the band."

You Can't Hide

By Mark Harrison

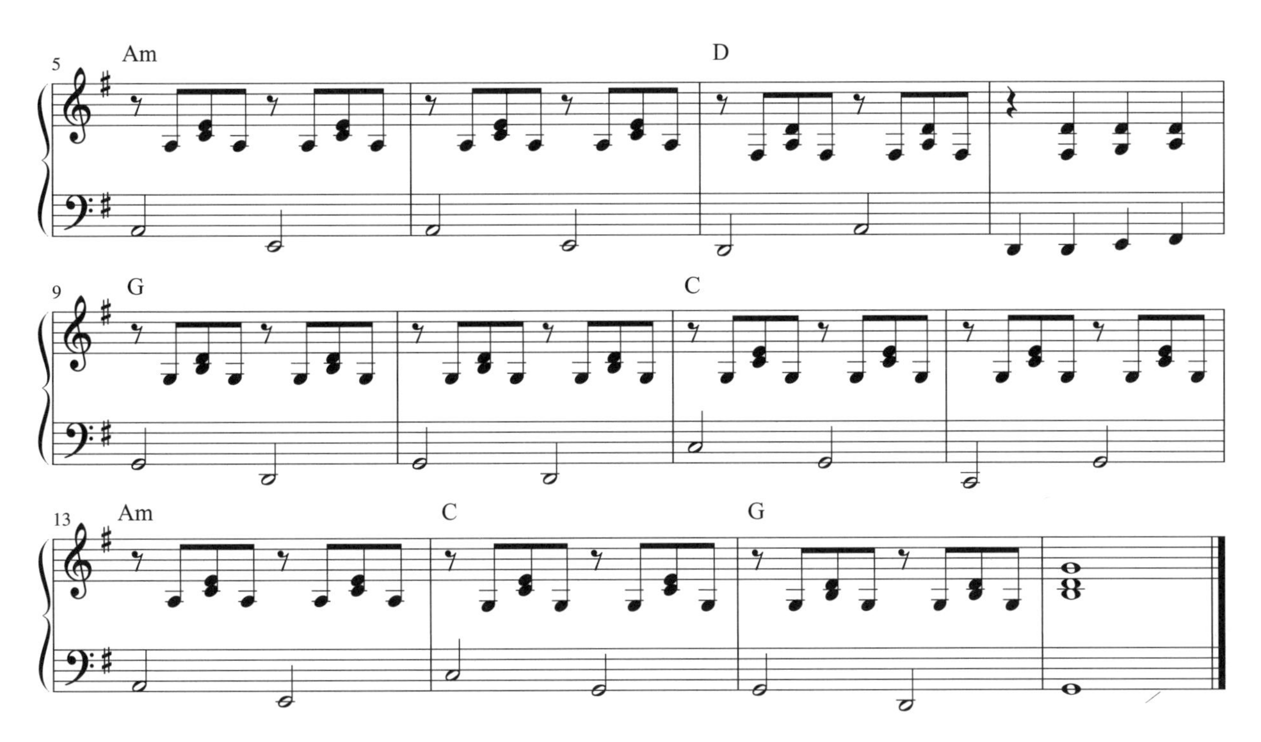

- This pattern uses eighth-note subdivisions at a medium-to-fast tempo. This is typical of mainstream country and country-rock, from the 1970s, onward.
- The right hand is playing a similar ("alternating" eighth-note) pattern to the pop ballad example on **track 35**, but with an important difference: there is now an eighth-note rest on beats 1 and 3. This extra space in the right-hand part helps to give us that authentic "country feel." The voicings are simply major or minor triads, with the C major chords in second inversion (in the right hand part) for smooth voice leading.
- The left hand is playing the root of each chord on beat 1, followed by the 5th of the chord on beat 3. This is a very common "bass pattern" in simpler country (as well as pop and rock) styles.

This is a great pattern that you can apply to many country and country-rock songs. Find some Eagles' tunes in your fake books ("Lyin' Eyes", "Take It Easy", "Peaceful Easy Feeling," etc.) and "fake" your way through the chord changes!

Finally, we'll end the chapter with another famous comping example, "Imagine," by John Lennon.

This is our first example showing two bass-clef staffs, instead of the normal treble and bass clefs. The right hand still plays the top staff, and the left hand plays the bottom staff. We notated it this way because the right hand is playing in a low register (below middle C), and to write this in treble clef would require quite a few ledger lines. It's much more readable to write this part in the bass clef!

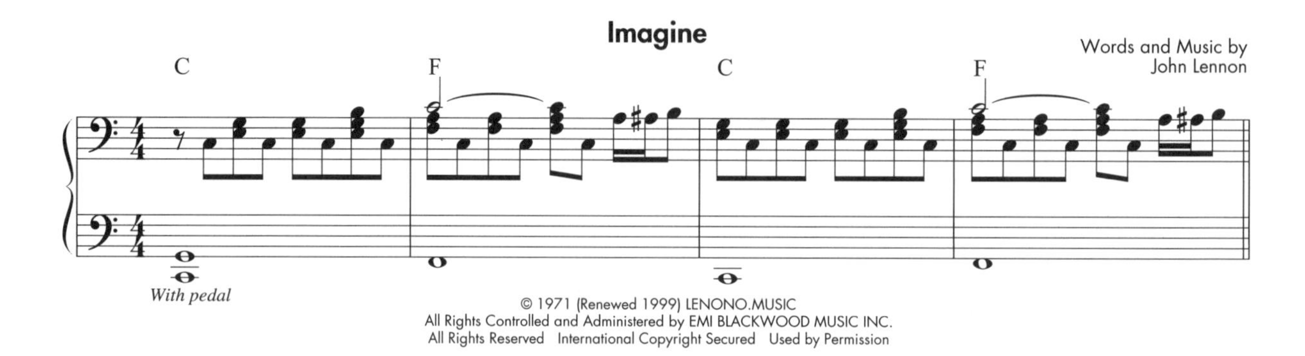

- The right hand adds the 7th of the C major chord on beat 4 of measures 1 and 3. This "upgrades" the chord to a Cmaj7 (with an "upper structure" E minor triad) overall. Also, the 5th of the F major chords (C) is being added on top in measures 2 and 4, resulting in "octave doubling" (C's are on the top and bottom of this triad figure). Then during beat 4 of measures 2 and 4, there is a "signature" melodic phrase using ascending half steps: A–A♯–B.
- The left-hand part is playing just the roots of the chords, except for the "root-5th" interval (C up to G) that is played on the first C major chord.

Everything You've Ever Wanted To Know About "Imagine"...

"Imagine" is John Lennon's best-known song from his career as a solo artist. He wrote the song in 1971, after his first solo album *John Lennon/Plastic Ono Band* was released. During this period, his political views and concerns were increasingly apparent in his songwriting, and the lyrics to "Imagine" include criticisms of capitalism and religion. However, the song had such a great melody and uplifting spirit that it became universally popular, even with people who presumably did not share Lennon's views on these subjects.

Lennon composed the song at the piano, inspired by the poetry book *Grapefruit*, written by his wife Yoko Ono. He said that the message of the song was "sugarcoated" compared to "Working Class Hero," another of his classic songs which had a decidedly more bitter flavor and mood. "Imagine" was the title track on his second album, which was released in 1971 and went gold, topping the charts in the U.S. The song was also a hit single in the U.S. in the same year, and was released three times as a single in the U.K.: in 1975, 1980 (following Lennon's assassination, when it hit Number One), and 1999.

"Imagine" has been covered and recorded by dozens of well-known artists over the years, including:

- Diana Ross
- Andy Williams
- Average White Band
- Chet Atkins
- Liza Minnelli
- Henry Mancini
- Ben E. King
- Randy Crawford
- Richie Havens
- Ray Conniff
- Joan Baez
- Blues Traveler
- Roger Whittaker
- Gerry and the Pacemakers

Photo by Tom Hanley/Redferns Music Picture Library
John Lennon and Yoko Ono

These subtle enhancements show how a simple comping pattern can be turned into something unique and identifiable. Practice adding your own subtle enhancements to all your comping parts to develop your own special playing style.

The examples we went through in this chapter show what kind of *comping* parts are possible from various chord progressions in a few different styles of music. After studying and playing them, it is up to you to go to your fake books and try creating your own comping parts. At first, pick tunes with very simple chord progressions (i.e., triads, and 3 or 4 chords only), then work your way up to more complex tunes. Comping parts are also great to sing along with (actually, that's one of the main purposes of comping), so try your hand (voice) at some singing along with what you're playing, once you get the parts solidly under your fingers.

Have fun!

CHAPTER 15
PLAYING THE MELODY FROM A FAKE BOOK

What's Ahead:

- More advanced left-hand patterns with arpeggios
- Using intervals below the melody
- Forming triads below the melody
- Using right-hand triads with single notes in the left hand
- Using the 7th and 3rd of the chord below the melody

MORE ADVANCED LEFT-HAND PATTERNS WITH ARPEGGIOS

Before we go on to various ways of playing the melody (in the right hand) from a fake book, we'll look at some interesting ways the left hand can use the chord symbols to play what will accompany the melody.

Do you remember learning about arpeggios back in Chapter 13? These were the *broken chords* we applied to "Wonderful Tonight." We're now going to expand our playing of arpeggios by using open triads, which will be very useful when playing left-hand accompaniment parts.

An open triad is a triad in which the notes have been spread out, encompassing a space larger than an octave. One way to create an open triad is by moving the middle note up by one octave.

Listen to **track 45** to hear the sound of open triad arpeggios on both F major and F minor chords:

So let's make sure we understand how these open triads are created. As you know, we would normally spell an F major triad (in root position) with the notes F–A–C, from bottom to top. In the first measure above, we have taken the middle note (or 3rd of the chord) A, and moved it up an octave.

Similarly, we would spell an F minor (in root position) with the notes F–A♭–C from bottom to top. In the second measure, the middle note of the chord (A♭) has been moved up an octave.

When you are comfortable with this pattern, you should then try it on as many different major and minor triads as you can (ideally in all keys), as it will be very useful on many songs! As you *transpose* the pattern for different chords, try not to play it too low (it will sound "muddy") or too high (too much above the middle C area—it may get in the way of the right hand playing melody).

Next, we will explore some variations on these patterns. In the last chapter, we saw examples of chords "inverted over" (or placed over) the 3rd or the 5th in the bass. For example, the chord symbol F/A means "take an F major chord and place it over the note A in the bass." Now we will create open triad patterns for these types of chords.

Listen to **track 46** to hear the sound of open triad arpeggios for F major and F minor chords in first inversion.

This pattern is created by taking a first inversion triad and then moving the middle note (this time the fifth of the chord, C) up by one octave. Similarly, an F minor triad in first inversion is spelled A♭–C–F from bottom to top. So, in the second measure above, we have again taken the middle note C and moved it up an octave.

Listen to **track 47** to hear the sound of open triad arpeggios for an F major chord in second inversion (F/C), and an F minor chord in second inversion (Fm/C).

Again, this pattern is created by taking a second inversion triad and then moving the middle note (the root, this time) up by one octave. Thus, the F in both the major and minor triads gets moved up.

Again when you are comfortable with these *inverted* patterns, you should then try them on as many different major and minor triads as you can (ideally in all keys)!

Next, we're going to look at some more patterns, this time for various four-part chords. These all involve playing the 7th of the chord immediately following the root. You can still use the 5–2–1 fingering, and although the larger intervals look more awkward, don't forget that you don't have to *stretch* the fingers for these larger intervals—you'll have the sustain pedal depressed, so you can just "skip" between the notes as needed, letting go of finger 5 and moving your hand up.

Listen to **track 48** to hear the sound of open arpeggios for the G7sus, G7, and Gm7 chords. Each of these patterns starts out with the root, then the 7th of the chord (in each case G up to F), followed by another chord tone as the highest note.

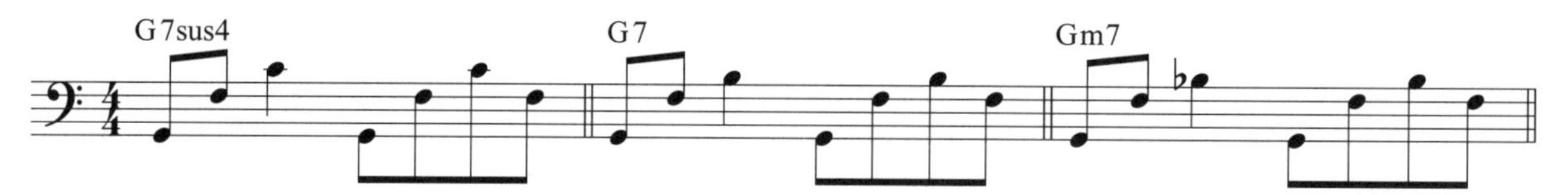

- The G7sus is a suspended dominant 7th chord, where the 4th (C) has replaced the 3rd (B). The highest note in the pattern is C.
- The G7 is a dominant 7th chord, and the highest note in the pattern is the 3rd (B).
- The Gm7 is a minor 7th chord, and the highest note in the pattern is the 3rd (B♭).

Now let's put these new patterns to work to help us play a pop ballad melody, working from a fake book. You'll remember from the last chapter that a fake book chart only contains the melody and chord symbols, and it's up to us to do the rest! Here's a chart for a pop ballad called "Easy Going," which we're going to play a few different ways in this chapter.

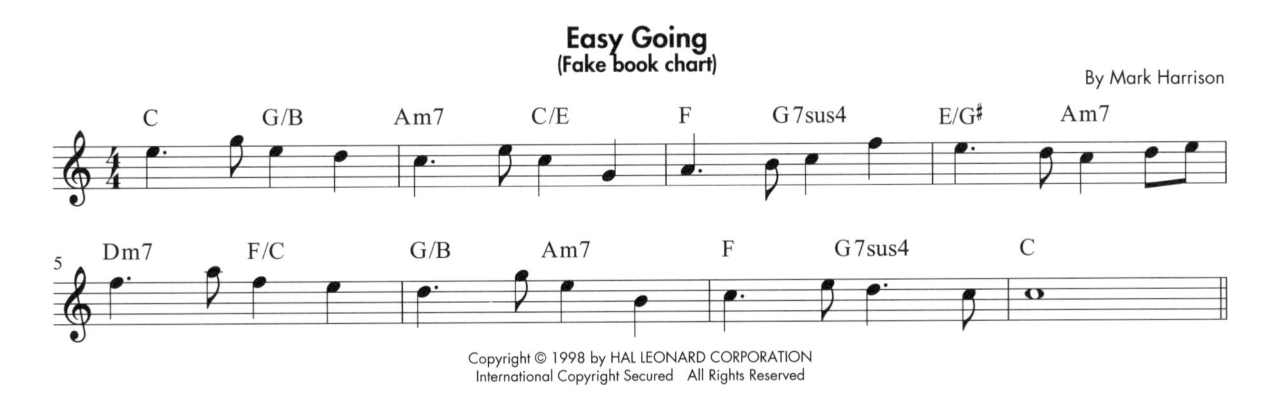

One easy way to improvise a professional-sounding melody arrangement from a pop ballad chart is to play the melody as written on the chart with the right hand. The left hand can play simple open arpeggio patterns derived from the chord symbols.

Sounds pretty easy, huh? Well, actually it *is* fairly easy, if you have the left-hand patterns under your fingers, and you can keep up with the melody! As with all piano music, practice the hands separately first.

Listen to **track 49** as you follow along with the music to hear a melody treatment for "Easy Going," with left-hand open arpeggios below the right-hand melody.

OK, so playing the right-hand part was easy enough. We just played it as written in the chart. So where did we get the left-hand patterns? Glad you asked… First of all, we divide the chord symbols into two groups: those without a slash in the chord symbol, and those with a slash in the chord symbol. If the symbol doesn't have a slash, then the root of the chord will also be the bottom note in the open arpeggio pattern (like on **tracks 45** and **48**). If the symbol does have a slash, then we probably have an inverted chord (like on **tracks 46** and **47**). Also notice that these left-hand patterns use an eighth–eighth–quarter-note rhythm, rather than continuous eighth notes.

With this in mind, we can comment on the individual pattern choices as follows:

- On the major chords in root position (C in measure 1, and F in measures 3 and 7), we have a root–5th–3rd open arpeggio.

- On the minor chords (Am7 in measures 2, 4, and 6, and Dm7 in measure 5), we again have root-5th-3rd open arpeggios.
- On the suspended dominant 7th chords (G7sus in measures 3 and 7), we have a root-7th-4th open arpeggio.
- On the major triads inverted over their 3rds (G/B in measures 1 and 6, C/E in measure 2, and E/G♯ in measure 4) we have a 3rd-root-5th open arpeggio.
- On the major triad inverted over its 5th (F/C in measure 5), we have a 5th-3rd-root open arpeggio.

So, on the slash chord symbols, you have to figure out whether the note to the right of the slash is the 3rd or 5th (or sometimes, neither) of the chord to the left of the slash, in order to apply the correct pattern. If you have all of your major and minor triads learned from Chapter 10, you should be able to do this! Otherwise, take your time and figure it out—*knowing* all of your triads takes time, and playing tunes from a fake book like you're doing now is one method of gradually learning/memorizing more and more chords.

Next, we'll apply this new left-hand technique to the classic 1990s pop ballad, "Tears in Heaven." Notice that we have quite a few inverted chord symbols (slash chords).

Start by practicing the right-hand melody by itself. Next, play the melody along with a simple version of the left hand: only play the bass note on each chord change and hold it. This would involve playing half notes only on beats 1 and 3 of each measure (i.e., in measure 1, C on beat 1, then B on beat 3). This gets you started with the hands together. When this feels comfortable, start adding the arpeggio patterns. You can use this practice technique with all of your fake book playing.

Now that you're getting the hang of this, look at "Tears in Heaven" and try to determine how the left-hand part was created. You can do this!

"Tears in Heaven" is one of Eric Clapton's best-loved songs, and was written following the death of his son, Conor. The beautiful melody is complemented by the poignant lyric, expressing sadness and loss. The studio version appears on the *Rush* movie soundtrack, but it wasn't until a live acoustic version appeared on Clapton's 1992 *Unplugged* album, that the song became world-famous. This album was a refreshing contrast to the more "produced" sound from his '80s records, and sold over seven million copies in the U.S.

USING INTERVALS BELOW THE MELODY

So far we've been playing only the melody in the right hand, which is a great way to get started. Now we're going to add some more notes in the right-hand part, which will help to create a "fuller" arrangement. If we add just one note below the melody in the right hand, we create an interval below the melody. The most common intervals used for this in popular styles are *6ths* and *3rds*, due to their warm consonant characteristics.

With the exception of some country and rock 'n' roll styles, any notes added in the right hand will be below (not above) the melody. This is because the ear will tend to be "attracted" to the highest pitch being played, so we may obscure the melody if we put extra notes above it.

Sometimes, when you play a 6th below the melody, it may sound a bit too "tense" with the chord, or with the bass note in the left hand. In this case, reducing the interval to a 5th can often solve the problem. Similarly, 3rds can be increased to 4ths if these problems occur. Let your ears be the judge!

When adding notes below the melody, we will normally stay within the key of the song, except in cases where the chord symbol is not contained within the key. For example, the tune "Easy Going" is in the key of C, yet we have an E/G♯ chord on beat 1 of measure 4 in the following example. When creating the interval below the melody, the chord "wins out" over the key, so the note G♯ has been added below the E. G♯ is the 3rd of an E major triad, and yet is *chromatic* (i.e., is not contained within) to the key of C.

Listen to **track 50** to hear a melody treatment for "Easy Going" using intervals below the melody. The initial approach would be to add 6ths below all of the melody notes, and this could work in this tune. However, in this example we reduced some of the 6ths to 5ths (indicated with a double-asterisk in the music) to reduce the tension on the chord, creating a simpler harmonic sound. For variety, we even have a 4th below the D in the melody on beat 4 of measure 4. This sets up a nice *contrary motion* effect with the following 6th interval. The left hand is playing the same open triad patterns as in our earlier example of this tune.

All of the notes added below the melody are within the key of C major, except the G♯ below the E in measure 4, beat 1. We can check some of the places where 5ths were used instead of 6ths (indicated by the double-asterisk) to hear what difference this made to the sound. For example, in measure 1, we used a C (the root of the C major chord) below the G in the melody on the "and" of 2, rather than the B (which would have been the 7th of the chord). Although 7ths are commonly used on major chords, this sound can still be too *dissonant* (an unresolved sound, sometimes "clashing") for simpler pop styles. Similarly, on beat 4 we used a G below the D in the melody, rather than the F (which would have been the 7th of the chord). Adding the F would have implied a G7/B, which again imparts a more sophisticated sound. These are judgment calls which you can make *by ear* as you become more experienced. If your choice sounds "funny," go with a note that is part of the chord.

Next, we'll apply these new right-hand interval techniques to the classic 1960s Beatles' ballad, "Yesterday."

In the right hand, we added 6ths below the melody within the key of F major, with the following exceptions:

- As a variation we did not place any notes below the A and B in the melody in measure 2 (beat 2).
- We "reduced" the 6th to a 5th on the C/E chord in measure 5 (beat 4). This C is, of course, a member of the C chord, and sounds "better" than playing a B.
- As another variation, we placed 3rds below the melody (again within the key of F), from measure 6 (beat 4) until measure 7 (beat 2).

Meanwhile, the left hand is playing root–5th–3rd on all of the chords, except:

- On the A7 in measure 2 (beats 3–4), we have a root–7th–3rd pattern.
- In measure 5 beat 4, the left hand plays an E to support the C/E chord falling on beat 4.
- In measures 6 and 7, we are using a root-5th-root pattern (no 3rds of the chords) on the G and B♭ chords, so that the left hand pattern does not collide with the right hand.

Get out your fake book and try this melody technique on some pop ballads. You can mix 6ths and 3rds together in the right hand (as we did in "Yesterday"), and don't forget to adjust the intervals (i.e., reducing 6ths to 5ths, and increasing 3rds to 4ths) as needed to work with the chords. Trust your ears, and have fun!

Everything You've Ever Wanted to Know About "Yesterday"...

"Yesterday" has become one of the most frequently performed pop standards of the 20th century, and has been covered by more artists than any other Beatles' song. When the song was released in 1965, it had a wholly fresh and original sound, with a timeless melody, a poignant lyric, and a very imaginative arrangement from producer George Martin. Although it was put out as a Beatles' record, it was in fact a Paul McCartney solo recording: his vocal and guitar was augmented by a sparse string quartet. The understated elegance of Martin's string arrangement was in stark contrast to the heavy-handed string parts which Phil Spector added to McCartney's "The Long and Winding Road," five years later on the *Let It Be* album.

In the U.K., the song was not even released as a single. It was just an album track on the *Help!* album, and wasn't even on the *Help!* movie soundtrack. However, in the U.S., it was released as a single by Capitol Records in late 1965, and immediately topped the charts, remaining there for a month. One reason why so many cover versions were recorded (apart from the fact that it was such a great song) is that it was suitable for a lot of pop and "easy listening"-type artists, perhaps more so than most other Beatles' songs. For example, the British middle-of-the-road ballad singer Matt Munro released a rather forgettable rendition of the song in late 1965, which became a Top Ten hit. A more interesting "soul" version was put out by Ray Charles in 1967, which got into the Top 30 in the U.S. However, it was reported that John Lennon did not care for Ray Charles' version of the song.

"Yesterday" (along with another Paul McCartney classic, "Michelle") even made it into *The Real Book*, the best-known and most widely used fake book in working musician circles.

FORMING TRIADS BELOW THE MELODY

Our next "melody treatment" technique will be to form triads below the melody in the right hand. These might be basic triads derived from the chord symbol, or they could be "upper structure" triads that work *on* the chord.

Think about what triad you would use if you were simply "comping" on the chord (as we did in the last chapter), then add two chord tones below the melody note. For example, if the melody note is E, and you have a C chord symbol, the two notes "missing" from the full C chord are C and G. Find the closest C and G below the melody note E, and play those two notes underneath the melody (see the next example of "Easy Going," the first measure, beat 1).

In most cases, the melody notes at the points of chord change are within these triads, so it's just a matter of adding the two missing notes. If the melody note is not part of the chord indicated, then we still just select two chord tones underneath the melody note. In the first measure of "Easy Going," beat 3, the melody note is E, yet E is not part of a G/B chord. The G/B chord is made up of the notes G, B, and D, and so we must pick which two to be added underneath the melody. Part of choosing which notes to add will be considerations of voice leading. Since we have a G already in the bottom voice from the previous chord, why not keep that? The other voice from beat 1 is a C which could either go up to D or down to B. Since the melody eventually goes down to D on beat 4, B is the better choice for the other note to add.

Listen to **track 51** to hear this melody treatment for "Easy Going" that forms triads along with the melody. The melody is now notated using "upward" stems, and the remaining triad tones added below the melody are notated with downward stems.

You generally want to add the triads below the melody only at the point of chord change, which in this case is on beats 1 and 3 of each measure. Playing full chords on every melody note would be too "heavy" and a bit cumbersome to play. Also, as a variation, you do not have to complete full triads at every chord change point. Sometimes, for better flow, you may add just one note (like the adding of intervals we previously discussed) at the chord changes instead of completing the whole triad. In our most recent version of "Easy Going," we've added just 3rds below the melody on beat 4 of measures 2 and 6.

The "oddball" chord in this tune is the G7sus. Though technically the notes of this chord are G, C, D, and F, a common way to voice this chord is by thinking of it as an "upper structure" triad—a major triad built from the seventh. This gives us the same pitches, but with an A put into the mix. As you can see, in measures 3 and 5, we've added the F and C below the melody notes under the G7sus chords.

The left hand is playing the same open triad patterns as before, but again, when you put the hands together for the first time, try just playing half notes in the left hand (the notes on beats 1 and 3) to start out.

Next, we'll apply these new right-hand triad techniques to the theme song from the movie *Titanic*, "My Heart Will Go On."

In this simple ballad style, we are completing basic major and minor triads below the melody at the points of chord change.

Notice that on the last eighth note of measures 3 and 11, the melody note A and the rest of the D major triad placed below it, are all anticipating (landing an eighth note earlier than) the following downbeats. This is an effective rhythmic variation, but don't overdo it on slower-tempo ballads.

Most of the melody notes are part of the indicated chords, with the following exceptions:

- On the C chord in measures 3 and 11, the melody note is a D, which is not part the C major triad. *Voice leading*—where the melody is coming from and where it is going to—helps us decide to use the E and G from the C chord below the melody note.
- On the C chord in measure 15, the melody note is an F♯, which is again not part of the C major triad.

So you know what comes next, right? You guessed it: try forming triads below the melody on your favorite fake book songs. This is a common technique that will work in a lot of situations—go for it!

The 1997 release of "My Heart Will Go On" was a huge smash hit for Celine Dion, who was already one of the biggest female pop singers of the 1990s. The popularity of the movie *Titanic* ensured that the song remained near the top of the charts for over a year.

USING RIGHT-HAND TRIADS WITH SINGLE NOTES IN THE LEFT HAND

Next, we'll look at an arrangement of the classic Sarah McLachlan gospel ballad "Angel." This is in 3/4 time and uses triads with the melody in the right hand, over a static left-hand part playing mainly the roots of the chords, with some "walkdowns" (descending scale passages) added.

This example also has some new chord symbols, so I need to tell you about these!

Dm F C Fmaj7/A G
25
trac - tion oh beau - ti - ful re - lease. Mem - o - ry seep from my veins.
Dm7 F C
32
Let me be emp - ty oh and weight - less and may - be I'll find some
Am7 G Em7 Dm7 C C6
38
peace to - night in the arms of the an - gel.
F♯m7♭5 C/F Em F(add9)
44
Fly a - way from here, from this dark, cold ho -
C Am G Em G/D
51
tel room and the end - less - ness that you fear. You are
C Cmaj7 C6 F♯m7♭5 C/F Em
57
pulled from the wreck - age of your si - lent rev - er -

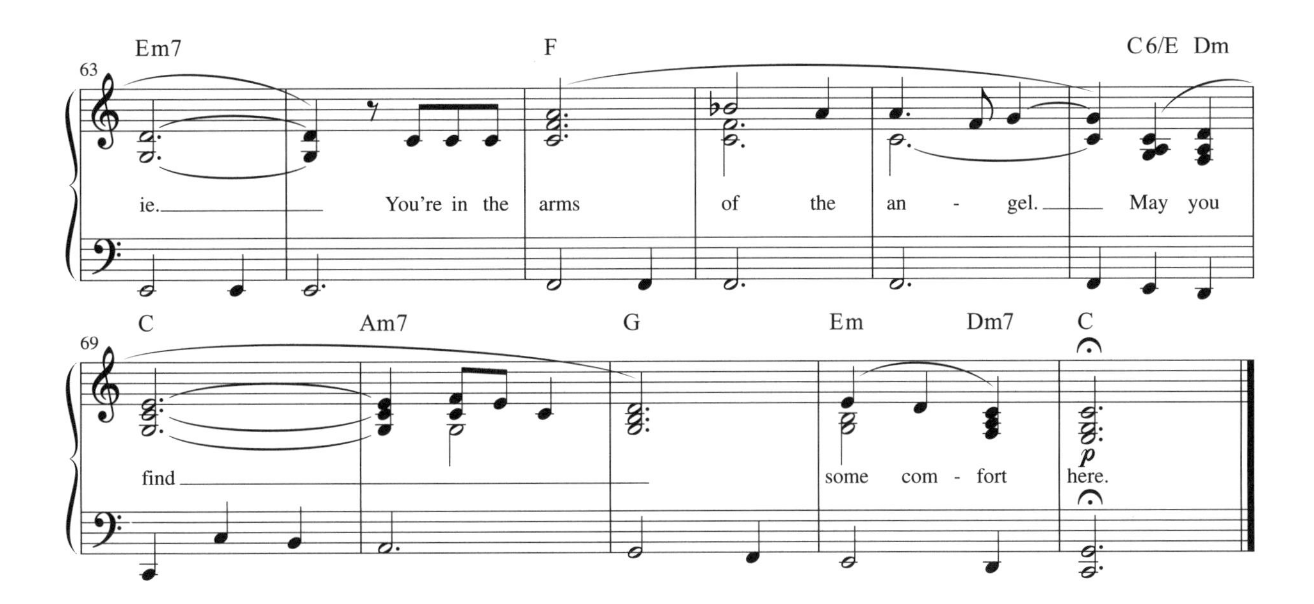

Let's look at some of the new chords used in this song.

- The (*add9*) suffix after a major or minor triad, means "add the 9th" to the triad.
  A 9th interval is an octave plus a 2nd, so you can think of the 9th as a 2nd above the root. For example, on the F(add9) chord in measure 49, the 9th (G) has been added. We also have an F(add9)/C chord in measures 3 and 7; this is an F(add9) chord inverted over C in the bass.
- We've already seen several examples of triads in first and second inversion, and now we have some four-part chords that are inverted, i.e., the Fmaj7/A chords in measures 14 and 30.
- The C/F chords in measures 44 and 60 are just C chords with F in the bass. If you look at the bass line in these measures, you'll see how it's moving down smoothly by half steps. Putting the root of the C chord would interrupt this flowing line.

The right-hand part mostly forms triads below the melody at the points of chord change, adding some 3rd intervals and "counter lines" in the spaces between the melody. Use this interesting arrangement as a springboard for your own melody treatment ideas!

USING THE 7TH AND THE 3RD OF THE CHORD BELOW THE MELODY

Our last "melody treatment" technique in this chapter will be to add the 7th and 3rd of the chord below the melody. The melody and supporting "7–3" voices may all be played in the right hand, or the 7th and 3rd may be "split" between the hands (often played by the thumb of each hand in this case). Using "7–3" voicings is a staple technique when playing jazz tunes and standards, as demonstrated on the following excerpt from "All the Things You Are."

Let's look at some of these voicings to see what is happening and how we can use them!

- On the Fm7 in measure 1, A♭ is the third of the chord, and the 7th of the chord is E♭. We can then fit these two notes below the melody, all in the right hand. In the left hand, we have a root-7th interval, which is always a desirable support to the right-hand voicings in jazz styles.
- Exactly the same process is at work on the B♭m7 chord in measure 2: the 7th and 3rd of the chord are A♭ and D♭, which are placed below the melody note D♭. Again, the left hand is playing a root-7th interval.

Notice that when the melody gets down to the middle C area, and is already a 3rd or 7th, we might just place the 7th below the 3rd in the melody (like in measure 9 on the Cm7 chord), or the 3rd below the 7th (like in measure 12 on the E♭maj7 chord)—in other words, we're just placing one note below the melody in the right hand, instead of two.

This "7–3" voicing technique is the most important foundation for my beginning-level jazz piano students. You need to know how to spell your four-part chords in order to easily access the 7ths and 3rds. Try these voicings out on as many jazz standards as you can, and make sure you have a large "tip jar" on top of your piano!

SECTION 4

Styles

CHAPTER 16
BOOGIE-WOOGIE

What's Ahead:

- Introduction to boogie-woogie styles
- "Baby Look at You" (Pete Johnson/Joe Turner)
- "Chicago Breakup"—play along with the CD!

INTRODUCTION TO BOOGIE-WOOGIE STYLES

Boogie-woogie piano styles emerged in the early 20th century, and featured fast tempos and "driving" left-hand patterns. As with most blues-related styles, your left hand literally is "the band," as it propels the rhythm while defining the chord progression. This style is very percussive, and the right hand is most often playing either single-note lines or chordal syncopations. The eighth notes are almost always treated as "swing eighths."

Noted boogie-woogie pianists from the 1930s include Albert Ammons, Pete Johnson, Meade Lux Lewis, and Cow Cow Davenport. Boogie-woogie (and in particular, the driving left-hand patterns) also influenced later blues styles, notably Chicago blues as performed by Roosevelt Sykes and Big Maceo Merriweather.

So now we'll take a look at a great boogie-woogie tune written by Pete Johnson and Joe Turner. (Turner was a key figure in the transition from boogie-woogie into the 1940s "jump blues" period.) The left-hand pattern for "Baby Look at You" uses two-note intervals (*dyads*), playing the root of each chord on the bottom, combined with the 5th, 6th, or 3rd above. The right-hand part uses mostly single notes, with some third and sixth intervals (outlining the chords of the 12-bar blues progression), as well as some half-step neighbor tones and grace notes.

Photo courtesy of Photofest, Inc.

Pete Johnson

Baby Look at You

By Pete Johnson
and Joe Turner

The other tune we'll look at in this chapter is written in the style of Big Maceo Merriweather, whose boogie-woogie stylings were a big influence on Chicago blues. This song is again based on a 12-bar blues progression (this time in G), and uses ascending and descending octaves in the left hand—an immediately recognizable boogie-woogie pattern. This left-hand pattern is also considerably more difficult than the pattern you played on the last tune, so make sure you put in some good practice time on this part separately! The right-hand part is now mostly using dyads and triads, with some arpeggios starting in the 4th chorus. Note the chord progression in measures 47–48—a commonly used ending in boogie and blues styles.

Grace notes are the small notes with the slashes through them (measures 14, 16, 18, 20, 33, 35, 38, 40, 44, and 46), which function as "ornaments" to the notes that follow them. They are not part of the meter and take up no real time value, but are played immediately before the note they ornament. *Tremolo* is used in measures 29 and 30 in the right hand. Indicated by the three lines between the two whole notes, this tells you to alternate quickly back and forth between the two notes over the course of the 4 beats.

Listen to **track 52** (slow tempo) and **track 53** (full speed) to hear "Chicago Breakup." This tune is recorded with a rhythm section on the left channel, and the piano part (left and right hands) on the right channel; so, to jam along with the band, just turn down the right channel! Also listen carefully for how the grace notes and tremolo are played. When first practicing the song, try the right-hand part without the grace notes, then add them later.

audio tracks 52
audio tracks 53
Chicago Breakup
By Mark Harrison
Fast ♩ = 150 Swing 8ths
G7
C7
G7
D7
G7

18
G7
21
D7
G7
24
3rd Chorus
27
C7
30
G7
33
D7
G7

36
39
C7
42
G7
45
D7
C6
C#o7
G/D
A♭9
G9

CHAPTER 17
ROCK 'N' ROLL

What's Ahead:

- Introduction to rock 'n' roll styles
- "Lawdy Miss Clawdy" (Little Richard)
- "Rock My Soul" - play along with the CD!

INTRODUCTION TO ROCK 'N' ROLL STYLES

Rock 'n' roll emerged with a bang onto the American music scene in the 1950s, and popular music has never been the same since. Rock 'n' roll took elements of the blues, R&B, country, and gospel music, and fused them in a new way to create a highly rhythmic and danceable style. Although this was greatly assisted by the invention of the electric guitar in 1948, there is no doubt that the piano also played a vital part in the development of rock 'n' roll.

Important rock 'n' roll pianists from the 1950s include Little Richard, Jerry Lee Lewis, and Johnnie Johnson (Chuck Berry's piano player during the '50s and '60s). These pianists all developed a highly energetic playing style, with repeated right-hand eighth notes, often in a very high register on the piano, as well as an emphasis on showmanship. The rock 'n' roll piano styles from this period have also greatly influenced later generations of rock pianists, including Nicky Hopkins (The Who), Jools Holland (Squeeze), and Chuck Leavell (Rolling Stones).

Photo courtesy of Photofest, Inc.

Jerry Lee Lewis

Our first music example is the actual piano "comping" part used by Little Richard on the song "Lawdy Miss Clawdy." The right-hand part consists entirely of triads, in a "shuffle" rhythm at first, and then going into an "eighth-note triplet feel" towards the end of the first 12-bar chorus. Then, in the second chorus, the right-hand triads are played an octave higher, adding to the energy and excitement. Meanwhile, the left hand plays a steady root–5th and root–6th pattern on all of the chords, a '50s rock 'n' roll staple.

Our other tune in this chapter is a more "soulful" rock 'n' roll example, one in the style of Wilson Pickett, whose 1960s Memphis soul sound had a significant rock 'n' roll (and blues) influence. This mid-tempo groove has a straight-eighths feel, and again uses root-5th and root-6th intervals in the left hand, this time in a steady eighth-note pattern. In the right hand, we are using triads and dyads derived from Mixolydian modes. A *Mixolydian mode* is simply a major scale displaced to start on its 5th degree, so an F major scale displaced to start on C would be called "C Mixolydian" (C, D, E, F, G, A, and B♭). This works great over dominant chords in blues and rock styles. In measures 1–4, on the C7 chord, all of the right-hand figures (except for the grace notes and ♭3rd–3rd movements) come from C Mixolydian. Similarly, the pattern in measures 5–6 and the descending triads in measure 10 come from F Mixolydian (a B♭ major scale, displaced to start on F), and so on. Cool, huh?!

Listen to **track 54** to hear "Rock My Soul." This tune is recorded with a rhythm section on the left channel, and the piano part on the right channel; so you can play along with the band by turning down the right channel!

audio tracks 54

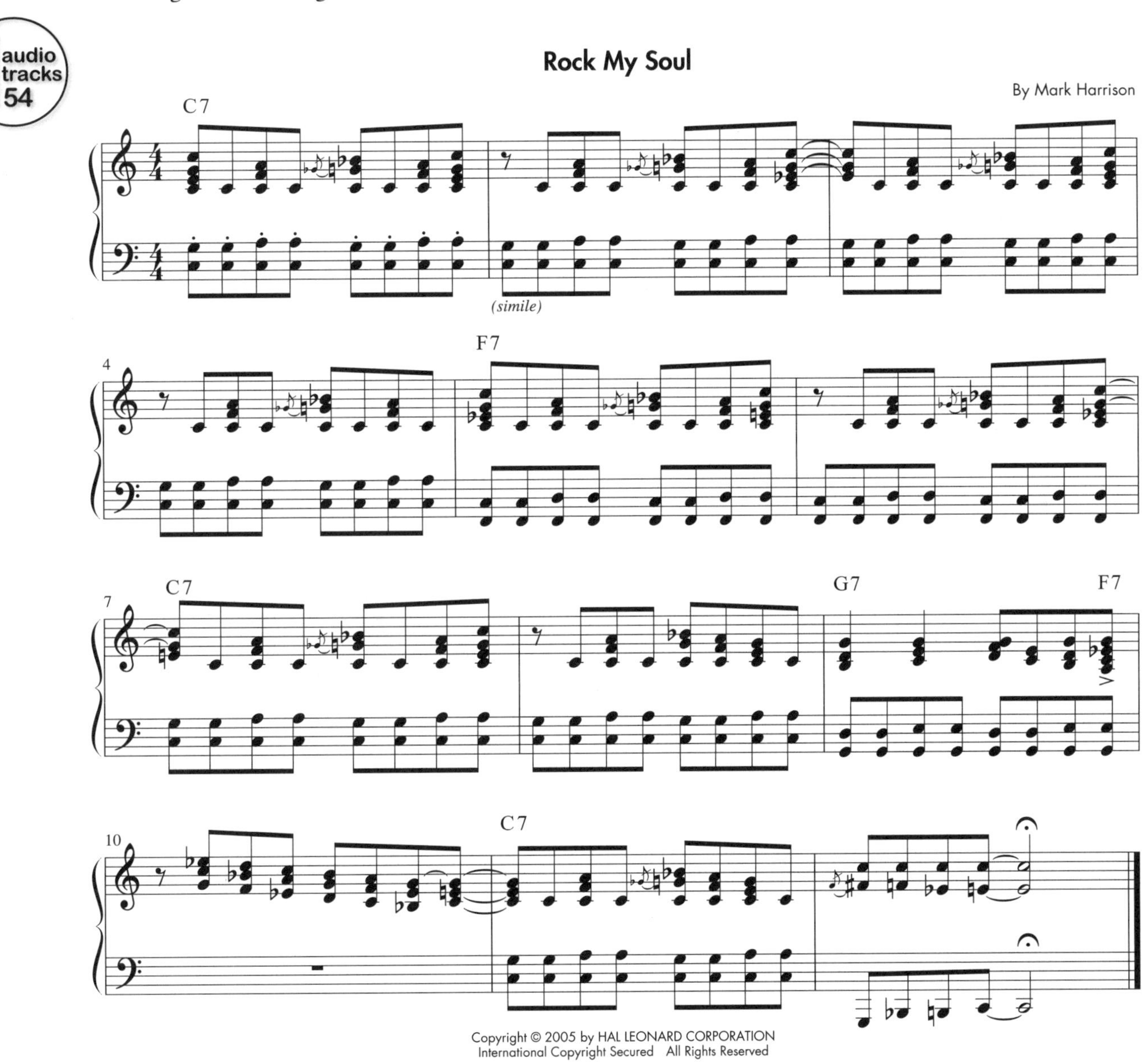

CHAPTER 18
BLUES

What's Ahead:

- Introduction to blues styles
- "C-Jam Blues" (Duke Ellington)
- "Every Night I Have the Blues" – play along with the CD!
- "Blue Bop" - play along with the CD!

INTRODUCTION TO BLUES STYLES

Blues is an indigenous American music that emerged in the late 19th century, flourished and developed in the 20th century, and laid the foundations for modern-day R&B and rock 'n' roll styles. The blues also has strong connections to other music styles, notably gospel, country, and jazz. Many blues singers got their vocal training in church, and some early blues artists performed both blues and gospel tunes. The heartfelt emotions in traditional country lyrics form a strong link to the blues, and more contemporary country music connects to the blues through its similarities to rock 'n' roll styles. Jazz and blues have always been intertwined to varying degrees, and the term *jazz-blues* is used to describe music which significantly combines these elements (for example, taking a blues tune with a 12-bar form and interpreting it with jazz rhythms and harmonies).

As blues developed in the 20th century, a number of regional blues styles emerged. The best known is probably *Chicago blues*, personified by the Muddy Waters and Howlin' Wolf bands of the late '40s and early '50s. This style amplified the blues and created the now-classic small-band lineup of guitar, piano, bass, drums, harmonica, and saxophone. Noted Chicago blues pianists include Otis Spann (a pivotal member of Muddy Waters' band), Lafayette Leake, and Memphis Slim. Another very important regional style is New Orleans blues, which is a melting pot for different influences: African and Caribbean rhythms, variations on the 12-bar blues form, and a "laid-back" yet danceable feel. Noted New Orleans pianists include Fats Domino (who spanned the period from New Orleans blues and R&B to rock 'n' roll), Professor Longhair, Huey 'Piano' Smith, Allen Toussaint, and Dr. John. Other regional blues styles include St. Louis, Kansas City, Texas, and the West Coast.

Photo by David Redferns/Redferns Music Picture Library

Otis Spann

First, we'll check out a classic jazz-blues tune, "C-Jam Blues" by Duke Ellington. This is a good example of a blues from the "Swing/Big Band era" of the 1930s and '40s. Swing bands from this period would often play 12-bar blues tunes, but in a jazz swing style. In the first 12-bar chorus, the two hands are often playing the same rhythms, giving a syncopated effect to the voicings. In the second chorus, the left hand is playing a "walking bass line" under the right-hand syncopated chords. These are all typical jazz-blues devices.

C-Jam Blues
Medium Swing
By Duke Ellington
C9
F7
mf
With pedal
Dm7/G
G7
G7♯5
Gm7
C7
B9
B♭9
A9
Dm7
E♭7
C

Seven Great Blues "Crossover" Licks You Should Know...

A *crossover* or *resolving* lick is a descending right-hand phrase (normally an arpeggio) which requires the fingers of the right hand to cross over the thumb, on the way to the lower notes in the phrase. *Resolving* refers to the fact that these licks normally end with a half-step resolution into the 3rd of the chord. All of the following examples work over a C7 chord.

Learn these in as many keys as possible, and drop them into your favorite blues song. It'll make your audience pay attention!

Our next song is written in the style of Memphis Slim, an important Chicago blues pianist. Notice the classic "Chicago blues" left-hand pattern, moving from the ♭3rd to the major 3rd of the chord during beat 2 of each measure. The tune also has a 4-bar intro before the first 12-bar chorus begins. The right-hand part has a lot of rhythmic syncopations (i.e., in the first 12-bar chorus), and so it will help to get the left hand as much on "auto-pilot" as possible! Starting in the second chorus, the right hand uses a lot of blues scale intervals and phrases. Also see if you can spot some of the crossover licks we just saw in the last sidebar!

Listen to **track 56** (slow tempo) and **track 57** (full speed) to hear "Every Night I Have the Blues." This tune is recorded with a rhythm section on the left channel, and the piano part on the right channel; so, to jam along with the band, just turn down the right channel!

Photo courtesy of Photofest, Inc.

Memphis Slim

G7
F7
C7
G7
2nd Chorus
C7
F7
C7
F7
C7
G7
F7
C7
G7
3rd Chorus
C7

Our last tune in this chapter is a "bop blues" in the style of jazz piano icon Thelonious Monk. Jazz musicians from the bebop era often played blues tunes, adding more sophisticated chords and embellishments. There are a lot of half-step melodic movements and "neighbor tones" in the right-hand part, again typical of bebop styles. Also notice the 7–3 voicings (using sevenths and thirds of the chords) that we saw at the end of Chapter 15. In the solo choruses, the left hand is using syncopated "root–7th" and "root–3rd" intervals on the chords as a rhythmic counterpoint to the solo phrases. This rather "stark" playing style is typical of Thelonious Monk.

Listen to **track 58** (slow tempo) and **track 59** (full speed) to hear "Blue Bop." This tune is recorded with a rhythm section on the left channel, and the piano part on the right channel; so, to jam along with the band, just turn down the right channel!

audio tracks 58

audio tracks 59

5
E♭7
Edim7
B♭7
F7♯9
B♭7
9
F7♯9
E♭7
B♭7
G7♯9
C7♯9♯5
F7♯9
13
B♭7
E♭7
B♭7
17
E♭7
Edim7
B♭7
G7♯9
21
C7♭9
F7♯9
B♭7
G7♯9
24
C7♯9♯5
F7
B♭7
E♭7

27
B♭7
E♭7
Edim7
30
B♭7
G7♭9
C7
34
F7♭9
B♭7
G7♯9♯5
C7♯9♯5
F7♯9
B♭7
38
E♭7
B♭7
F7♯9
B♭7
E♭7
42
Edim7
B♭7
F7♯9
B♭7
F7♯9
E♭7
46
B♭7
G7♯9
C7♯9♯5
F7♯9
B♭7

CHAPTER 19
JAZZ

What's Ahead:

- Introduction to jazz styles
- "Satin Doll" (Ellington/Mercer/Strayhorn)
- "Bird of Prey" - play along with the CD!
- "Hand Prints" - play along with the CD!
- "Linus and Lucy" (Vince Guaraldi)

INTRODUCTION TO JAZZ STYLES

Jazz music has similar historical origins to the blues in that it emerged in the late 19th century and then flourished in the 20th century. *New Orleans* and *Dixieland* jazz styles first developed in the 1910s and '20s, featuring solo and group improvisation. This was then followed by the *Swing* era in the 1930s, which emphasized big bands and danceable arrangements. Then, in the 1940s, many younger musicians broke away from the swing styles to create *Bebop* or *Bop*, a less danceable small-group style with more advanced harmonies and rhythms. This was in turn followed in the 1950s by the more mellow *Cool Jazz*, and the extended improvisation of the *Post Bop* styles. Then, in the 1960s and 70s, the *Fusion* movement began, combining jazz elements with modern styles such as rock and R&B. All of the *Contemporary Jazz* styles of the late 20th and early 21st centuries are descended from this period. Today, all of these jazz styles (modern and traditional) co-exist, and are performed and recorded around the world.

Throughout the 20th century, many piano players emerged who were hugely influential in creating the various jazz styles. Jelly Roll Morton was at the forefront of the early New Orleans movement, and immodestly called himself the "inventor of jazz." Art Tatum and Teddy Wilson were giants of the Swing era, followed by Bud Powell and Thelonious Monk, trailblazers in the Bebop period. The Post Bop harmonic style of Bill Evans was a major influence on both fusion and mainstream jazz pianists from the 1970s onwards, including Chick Corea, Herbie Hancock, Joe Zawinul, and Keith Jarrett.

Photo by David Redferns/Redferns Music Picture Library

Bill Evans

Our first example is the tune "Satin Doll" by Duke Ellington, Johnny Mercer, and Billy Strayhorn, a true jazz standard. The *A section* is made up of an 8-bar phrase that repeats itself for a total of 16 bars. The *B section* is half as long, at 8 bars followed by a return to the *A section* for the final 8 bars of the tune. Both sections are similar in that they begin with a minor II chord going to a V in the first 2 bars, and then repeat the same progression, transposed up one step: Dm–G7, then Em–A7 in the A section, and Gm7–C then Am7–D7 (with an F chord in between) in the B section. Play this in a lazy swing style, with a slight feeling of being "behind the beat" in the right hand.

Satin Doll

from ***SOPHISTICATED LADIES***

Words by Johnny Mercer and Billy Strayhorn
Music by Duke Ellington

Next, we're going to look at a piano comping example from the bebop era, a tune in the style of pianists such as Bud Powell and Erroll Garner. This piece is actually made up of two 12-bar blues choruses, but with lots of extra chord changes. Bebop musicians would typically "jazz up" the blues by using colorful chords (those with more extensions such as 9ths, 11ths, and 13ths), and by substituting chords that share a few of the same pitches, but add bite by borrowing notes from different keys (other than the key of the song). For example, considering that this tune is in the key of F major, the blues would utilize the I, IV, and V chords. But in measure 2, instead of going to a V7 chord, the Em7♭5 and A7♭9 chords are used, which are borrowed from the key of D minor. In the first chorus, the left hand is playing the roots of the chord, often within root-7th or root-3rd intervals, and the right hand is playing triads or four-part chords on top. Then, in the second chorus, the right hand moves up an octave to allow the left hand to play some three-note voicings around the middle C area. The rhythmic syncopations throughout are typical of bebop and mainstream jazz styles, generally.

Photo courtesy of Photofest, Inc.

Duke Ellington

Listen to **track 60** to hear "Bird of Prey." This tune is recorded with a rhythm section on the left channel, and the piano part on the right channel; so you can play along with the band by turning down the right channel!

Bird of Prey
By Mark Harrison
audio tracks 60
1st Chorus
Swing 8ths
Fmaj7 Em7♭5 A7♭9 Dm7 G7 Cm7 F7
B♭7 B♭m7 E♭7 Am7 D7 A♭m7 D♭7
Gm7 C7 Fmaj7 Dm7 Gm7 C7
2nd Chorus
Fmaj7 Em7♭5 A7♭9 Dm7 G7 Cm7 F7
B♭7 B♭m7 E♭7 Am7 D7 A♭m7 D♭7
Gm7 C7 Fmaj7 Dm7 Gm7 C7 Fmaj7

Now we're going to look at a more modern jazz-blues waltz which uses a piano voicing style pioneered by Bill Evans. This tune again has a blues form; this time with 24 bars (double the normal 12), which is normal for a "waltz" in 3/4 time. Notice the very "open" and transparent voicing style, with fourth intervals being used in both hands in the first chorus, and the left hand voicings supporting the right hand fills and solo in the second chorus. This is all very typical of the more "modern" jazz styles which originated in the 1950s and '60s.

Listen to **track 61** (slow tempo) and **track 62** (full speed) to hear "Hand Prints." This tune is recorded with an electric piano sound to help with the style, so if you have an electric piano, punch in one of these sounds to enhance your playing. It is also recorded with a rhythm section on the left channel, and the piano part on the right channel; so, to jam along with the band, just turn down the right channel!

Our last jazz example in this chapter is an excerpt from the Vince Guaraldi tune "Linus and Lucy," beloved by Peanuts fans everywhere! Although this song comes under the general heading of "jazz," it also includes some other style elements. For example, the driving left-hand part in the intro, A, and C sections is reminiscent of some blues and boogie-woogie styles, while the right-hand fills in the B section have a country flavor. I suggest you practice the left hand part separately first, and make sure it is steady and secure before adding the right hand. Have fun!

C
22
A♭
A♭6
A♭
25
A♭6
A♭
A♭6
A♭
29
A♭6
C♭
C♭6
A♭
33
A♭6
C♭
A♭
A♭
A♭6

CHAPTER 20
POP/ROCK

What's Ahead:

- Introduction to pop/rock styles
- "Goodbye Yellow Brick Road" (Elton John)
- "Walking in Memphis" (Marc Cohn)
- "A Thousand Miles" (Vanessa Carlton)
- "Before I Get Old" - play along with the CD!

INTRODUCTION TO POP/ROCK STYLES

Pop/rock emerged in the late 1970s, hit its peak during the '80s, and continued in various forms into the '90s and beyond. The more "rock" style combines the commercial, melodic "hooks" of pop music, with the hard driving energy of rock music. Many pop/rock artists also wrote pop ballads, songs at slow tempos and softer dynamics. A large number of artists fall into the pop/rock category, from solo superstars like Billy Joel and Elton John, to bands such as Toto (David Paich on keys), Journey (Jonathan Cain on keys), Doobie Brothers (Michael McDonald on keys), and Bon Jovi (David Bryan on keys), to name just a few.

Piano and keyboards are an essential ingredient of pop/rock styles. Typical pop/rock piano parts will either have very "driving" left-hand patterns with right-hand triads, or they will be based more on chordal arpeggios with syncopations. Eighth-note rhythms are the most common, although some later pop/rock styles use sixteenth notes. It's very important to "stay in the groove" (i.e., not deviate from the rhythm) in these styles!

We'll first ease into this style with a classical pop rock ballad, the song "Goodbye Yellow Brick Road" by Elton John. While the left hand plays a single-note bass line, the right hand plays the melody, filled in with lots of repeated chords. Though this is a ballad, feel free to bring out the rock style by playing strong accents as indicated on some of these powerful chords.

B♭
E♭
C7
F
Gm7
B♭
C7
F
B♭
E♭
C7
F
D♭
E♭7
A♭
D♭
B♭m
C7

F
A7
B♭
F
D7
Gm
C7
F
Dm
A
B♭
D♭
E♭
F
Am/E
Dm
Dm/C
B♭
C7
D♭
E♭
A♭
D♭
B♭m
C7
1.
F
2.
F

Next up is a classic pop/rock song from Marc Cohn, "Walking in Memphis." This piano pattern also uses arpeggios, but with a highly syncopated feel (emphasizing the "and" of 2 and the "and" of 4 in each measure). The arpeggios in measures 1–20 use only the roots and 5ths of the chords, and are spread out between both hands (note that the first 12 measures of the left-hand part are notated in treble clef). The groove becomes heavier starting in measure 20, with the right hand playing dyads and triads in the mid-range, and the left-hand roots in the lower register:

Photo courtesy of Photofest, Inc.

Marc Cohn

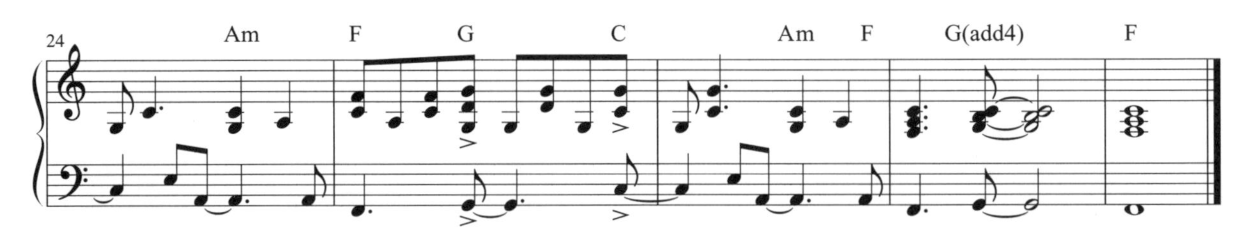

Now we'll switch gears and look at an excerpt from "A Thousand Miles" by the 21st century pop/rock artist Vanessa Carlton. This uses sixteenth-note subdivisions and syncopations, which is typical of later pop/rock styles. The instrumental sections (measures 1–4, 7–8, and 11–12) use some high arpeggios and large interval skips in the right hand, supported with syncopated single notes or octaves in the left hand. In measures 5–6 and 9–10, the right hand is playing the melody, accompanied by root–5th and root–3rd intervals in the left hand.

Photo courtesy of Photofest, Inc.

Vanessa Carlton

A Thousand Miles

Words and Music by
Vanessa Carlton

Listen to **track 63** to hear "Before I Get Old." The left-hand part is on the left channel, and the right hand part is on the right channel; to practice "hands separately," just turn down one channel or the other!

CHAPTER 21
COUNTRY

What's Ahead:

- Introduction to country styles
- "Outlaw Country" – play along with the CD!
- "Crazy" (Patsy Cline)
- "Your Cheatin' Heart" (Hank Williams)

INTRODUCTION TO COUNTRY STYLES

Country is an American music style that emerged in the 1920s, and continues to evolve up until the present day. All of the various country styles generally have lyrical themes which are "true-to-life," dealing with subjects such as home and family, relationship issues, and so on. Musically, country music traditionally features the steel guitar, mandolin, and fiddle, although the piano also plays an important role in the later country styles.

The old-time country music of the 1920s was quickly followed by the cowboy music of the 1930s and '40s, which put the "western" into country 'n' western music. Around the same time, western swing evolved, mixing country with blues and Dixieland elements. Also in the 1940s, bluegrass (with up-tempo banjo and mandolin patterns) and honky-tonk (with lyrical themes of celebration and sin) became very popular. By the late 1950s and early '60s the *Nashville* sound arrived, reaching a wide audience with a polished blend of pop and country. By the 1970s, this had been replaced by outlaw, a back-to-the-roots country sound which was a reaction to the more formula-driven Nashville era, and country-rock, a West Coast blend of country melodies and rock rhythms. From the mid-1980s up until the present day, the new country movement has successfully blended more "roots-oriented" country instrumentation with modern pop and rock production.

By the middle of the 20th century, piano players began to make a major contribution to the development of country music. Noted pianists from the Honky-Tonk period were Fred Rose (who played with Hank Williams) and Owen Bradley (who performed with Ernest Tubb). Also, the session ace Hargus "Pig" Robbins played on many records from the Honky-Tonk, Nashville, and Outlaw periods. Perhaps the most famous piano stylist in country music is Floyd Cramer, whose distinctive "slip-note" style was featured on many Nashville sessions. The more contemporary New Country period saw the rise of a new generation of session pianists, including Matt Rollins (Randy Travis and many others) and John Hobbs (Shania Twain and many others).

Our first tune gets us warmed up with a comping pattern that works on a lot of honky-tonk, Nashville, and country-pop songs. The right hand is playing triads in an "alternating eighths" style. The left hand is playing the root and 5th of the chord on beats 1 and 3, respectively. This is varied by using country "walkups" and "walkdowns" with the left hand. These are very authentic devices that you can use on your next country gig!

Listen to **track 64** (slow tempo) and **track 65** (fast tempo) to hear "Outlaw Country." You may notice that either tempo can work well for a country tune, depending on the mood. This tune is recorded with a rhythm section on the left channel, and the piano part on the right channel; so, to jam along with the band, just turn down the right channel!

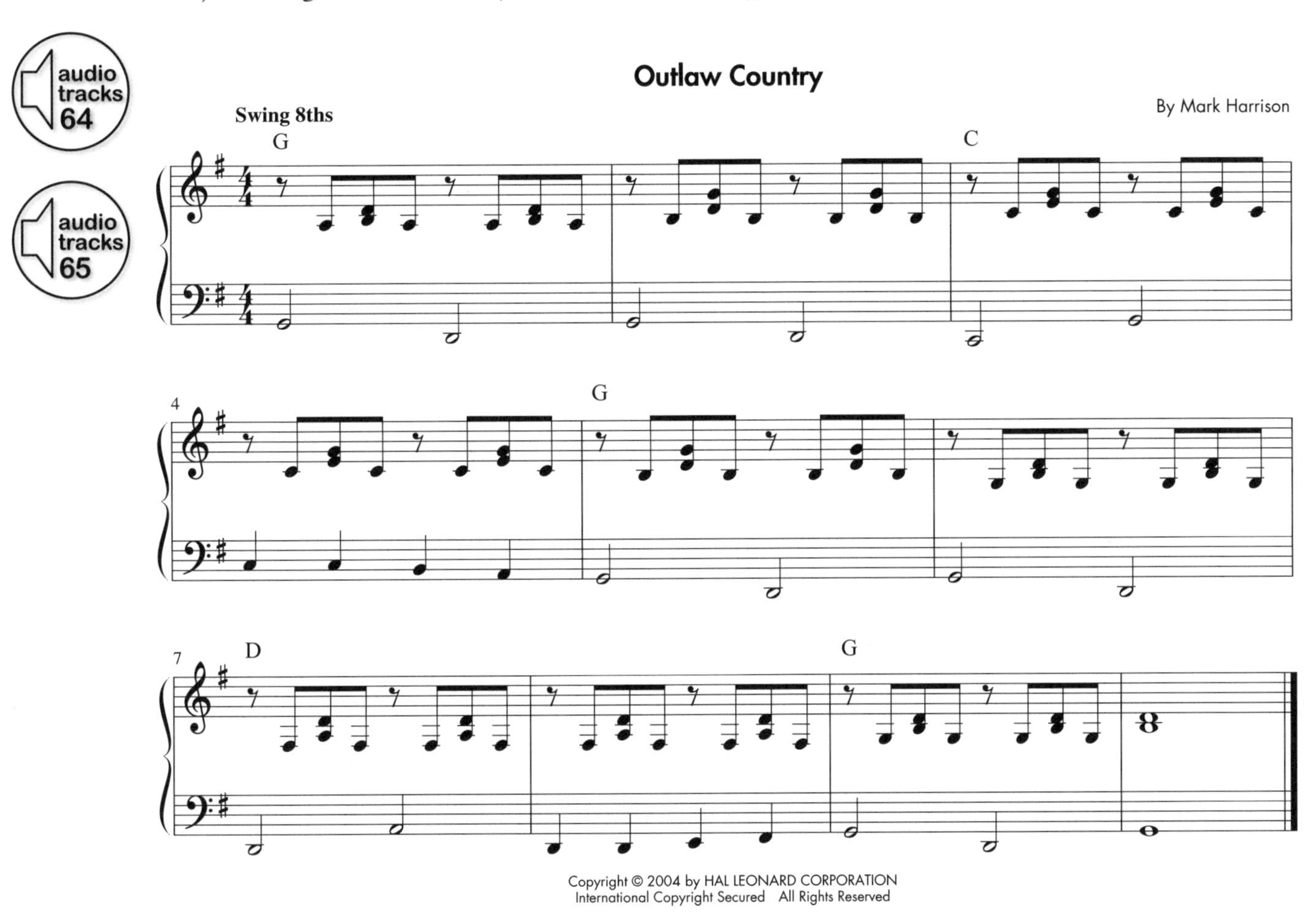

We're next going to look at the intro to the famous country song "Crazy," which was a hit for Patsy Cline, and was written by Willie Nelson (an icon of the Outlaw Country period). The song adds some blues to this Nashville country style, with the use of half-step movements and grace notes in the right hand. The left-hand part is also a little reminiscent of "stride piano," playing roots on beats 1 and 3, and mid-range chords on beats 2 and 4.

Crazy

Our last tune is a melody arrangement (the vocal melody is in the right-hand part) of "Your Cheatin' Heart," a classic country song from Hank Williams. After the 4-bar intro, the left hand plays the root of the chord on beat 1, and the 5th of the chord on beat 3, sometimes with added connecting tones and "pickups." The right hand is playing triads or four-part chords with the melody, mixed with arpeggios during the longer melody notes (for example, in measure 7). This is all very typical of mainstream country, and can serve as a model for your country melody arrangements.

Your Cheatin' Heart

5
C
C7
F
A♭7
heart will make you weep. You'll cry and
heart will pine some day and crave the
9
G7
C
G7
cry and try to sleep. But sleep won't
love you threw a - way. The time will
13
C
C7
F
A♭7
come the whole night through, your cheat - in'
come when you'll be blue, your cheat - in'
17
G7
C
C7
heart will tell on you.
heart will tell on you.
When tears come
21
F
C
D7
down like fall - in' rain, you'll toss a - round

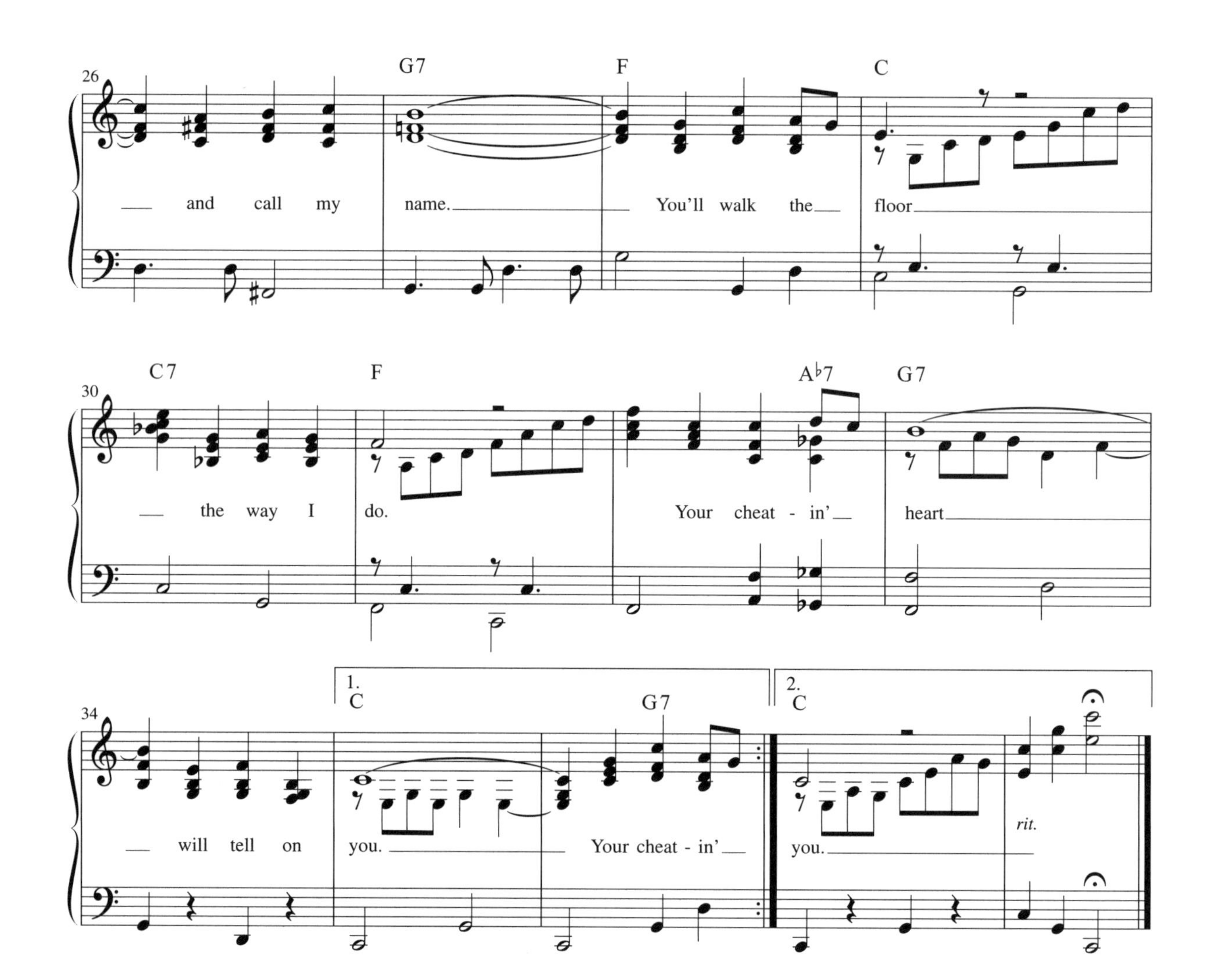
26
G7
F
C
and call my
name.
You'll walk the
floor
30
C7
F
A♭7
G7
the way I
do.
Your cheat - in'
heart
34
1.
C
G7
2.
C
will tell on
you.
Your cheat - in'
you.
rit.

CHAPTER 22
CLASSICAL

What's Ahead:

- Introduction to classical styles
- "Für Elise" (Ludwig van Beethoven)
- "Sonata in C Major" (Wolfgang Amadeus Mozart)
- "Prelude in B Minor" (Fryderyk Chopin)
- "Clair de Lune" (Claude Debussy)

INTRODUCTION TO CLASSICAL STYLES

Piano and keyboard music is probably the largest category within classical music as a whole, and many people are first introduced to classical music at the piano keyboard. Classical music (including classical piano music) can broadly be divided into different periods, as follows:

- **Baroque** period (17th century to mid-18th century): This period pre-dated the piano, and most keyboard music was played on the harpsichord. The music style was very linear and "contrapuntal" (melodies written in opposing parts). J.S. Bach emerged toward the end of this period (the piano had its early beginnings during his lifetime), and was a master of this contrapuntal style. Other noted Baroque composers included Handel and Domenico Scarlatti.
- **Classical** period (mid-18th century to early-19th century—not to be confused with "classical music" as a whole!): This period is sometimes described as "from Bach to Beethoven." The new "pianoforte" soon became the dominant keyboard instrument, and Mozart was one of the first composers to make full use of the piano's powers. This period had more emphasis on single melodies supported by accompaniments, and adhered strictly to musical forms such as sonatas and concertos. Other noted composers from the Classical period include Haydn and Schubert.
- **Romantic** period (early 19th century to early 20th century): This was the era of the pianist/composer superstars. Chopin and Liszt played their original compositions to ecstatic crowds in Paris and elsewhere. The Romantic era emphasized melody and virtuosity, extracting the full potential from the piano (which by then had evolved to a level similar to modern-day instruments). In fact, Chopin wrote almost exclusively for the piano, and became one of the instrument's greatest champions. Other prominent Romantic era pianists/composers include Rachmaninoff and Brahms.
- **Modern** period (early 20th century to the present day). This period saw a multitude of styles shooting off in many different directions. In this book, we'll cover one of them, Impressionism, which was related to the "Impressionist" movement in the visual arts, with its fuzzy colors and non-literal images. Led by the French composers Ravel and Debussy, this style produced music with shifting harmonies and rhythms, conveying somber moods while stimulating the imagination. Ravel was also influenced by the burgeoning jazz styles of the time. Other famous Impressionist composers include Satie and Faure.

We'll start out with an all-time classic from the *Classical* period, an excerpt from Beethoven's "Für Elise." The first section of this piece is very popular for early-intermediate students of the piano, as its technical demands are fairly modest. Its endearing melody, however, has made it the composer's most famous "piano miniature." There has been much debate about who "Elise" actually was—one common theory is that she was one of Beethoven's piano students. Make sure you observe the dynamic markings and slurs, and use the sustain pedal as indicated. Oh…and watch out for the clef changes in the left hand!

Listen to **track 66** to hear an excerpt from Beethoven's "Für Elise." Notice the expressive character in the playing, with gradual changes in tempo. Experiment with your own expressions to give this piece its own "life." The crescendo (<), meaning to gradually get louder, and diminuendo (>), meaning to gradully get softer, help add to the expressive quality of the music.

Next, we'll move to the "Sonata in C Major" (first movement) by Mozart, a great genius from the "classical" period. This is the most famous of all Mozart's piano sonatas, due to its relative simplicity compared to his other works. Mozart himself designated this tune "for beginners," and here we have an excerpt from the first movement of the sonata. Although the tempo is marked as "Allegro" (fast), don't forget to practice it slowly first. Oh, and it looks like we have some of those pesky clef changes again in the left hand!

W.A. Mozart

Listen to **track 67** on the CD to hear an excerpt from Mozart's "Sonata in C Major."

The left-hand pattern in "Sonata in C Major" (first 4 measures) was a very common type of accompaniment figure in the Classical period known as *Alberti bass*. The pattern consists of broken chords, usually tonic–dominant—mediant–dominant (or in inverted chords, bottom note–top note–middle note–top note, etc.) in succession. See Section 5, Song 2, "Come Sail Away," for an example of this classical figure used in popular music.

Our next piece is the "Prelude in B Minor" by Fryderyk Chopin, a towering figure in the Romantic period. This is a good example of the melody being played in the left hand, with the accompaniment being played in the right hand (for a change!). This is probably the most well-known of all Chopin's preludes. It has a very somber mood, with the left-hand melody slowly unfolding. Make sure you observe the crescendo and diminuendo markings, as well as the slurs in the left hand!

Listen to **track 68** to hear Chopin's "Prelude in B minor (Op. 28, No. 6)." Pay close attention to the left-hand part, and notice how it "sings" above the right-hand part with respect to volume.

Always know where the *melody* is in each tune you play. As we saw in "Prelude in B Minor," the melody was in the left hand. The melody must be louder than the accompaniment, so always practice bringing it out. Melodies can shift from one hand to another, and also be embedded in an inner voice, especially in classical music. It may be difficult at first, as both hands will want to play the same volume, but with careful practice, the independence needed to play one hand loudly and the other hand softly will come.

Our last piece in this chapter is Debussy's wonderful composition "Clair de Lune," one of the best-known pieces from this Impressionistic composer. The piece has subtle twists of harmony and rhythm, and evokes images of nature's beauty through its emphasis on color and texture over melody. The work is very challenging for the pianist, and the articulations and dynamics are crucial to the emotional intensity of the work. Enjoy!

Listen to **track 69**, to hear an excerpt from Debussy's "Clair de Lune." Notice how the piece seems to float without a clear pulse. This is just one interpretation to use as a guide, but you should employ a certain amount of *rubato* (freedom of rhythm and tempo) when playing it—the tempo should "expand" and "contract" as you see fit, in order to bring out the impressionistic qualities.

To emphasize the impressionistic nature of this piece, liberal use of the damper pedal is recommended. Use your ears to help judge when and where to make pedal changes. Also, the beginning is marked *con sordino* which means "with mute," indicating to employ the soft (*una corda*) pedal.

SECTION 5

Songs

"Minuet in G"

The "Minuet in G" is part of a collection of instructional pieces Bach compiled for his second wife. Long assumed to be by Bach, it was probably in fact composed by his colleague Christian Petzold. The main melody is carried by the right hand in the upper register, supported by some light harmony in the left hand.

"Come Sail Away"

"Come Sail Away" is a classic power ballad from the 1970s pop/rock band Styx, and was included on the band's 1977 triple-platinum album *The Grand Illusion*. The song also enjoyed a resurgence in the early 21st century when it was included on the soundtrack to the animated series *South Park*. Check out those left-hand arpeggios and right hand triads—all classic pop/rock piano techniques (the first three measures use the "Alberti bass" we discussed in the classical music chapter)! On the CD, you may notice a second piano part playing faintly in the background. Many groups would often add extra parts in the studio to enhance the music.

9
Am
Am/G
F
G
free,
free to face the life
that's a - head of me.
12
Am
G
Am
On board I'm the cap - tain,
so climb a - board.
We'll search for to - mor - row
15
G
C
Em/B
Am
Am/G
on ev - 'ry shore.
And I'll try,
oh Lord,
I'll try
3
18
F
G
C
Dm
Em
Dm
to car - ry on.

C
G7
C
Em/B
Am
Am/G
I look to the sea.
F
G
Re - flec-tions in the waves spark my mem - o - ry,
C
Em/B
Am
Am/G
F
some hap - py, some sad. I think of child-hood friends and the
G
Am
G
dreams we had. We lived hap-p'ly for-ev - er so the sto - ry goes.

32
Am
G
But some-how we missed out
on the pot of gold. But we'll
34
C
Em/B
Am
Am/G
F
G
try best that we can,
to car - ry
37
C
F/C
G5/C
F/C
C
F/C
on.
40
G5/C
F/C
C
F/C
G5/C
F/C
A gath-er-ing of an-gels ap-peared a-bove my head. They
ff

43
C
F/C
G5/C
F/C
sang to me this song of hope and this is what they said. They said
45
C
F/C
G5/C
F/C
come sail a - way, come sail a - way, come sail a - way with me, lads.
47
C
F/C
G5/C
F/C
Come sail a - way, come sail a - way, come sail a - way with me.
49
C
F/C
G5/C
F/C
To Coda
Come sail a - way, come sail a - way, come sail a - way with me.

C
F/C
G5/C
Come sail a - way, come sail a - way, come sail a - way with me.
C
F/C
G5/C
F/C
I
thought that they were an - gels but much to my sur - prise, we
climbed a - board their star - ship and head - ed for the skies. Sing - in'
D.S. al Coda

"Bennie and the Jets"

"Bennie and the Jets" is from Elton John's 1973 album *Goodbye Yellow Brick Road*, and was arranged around John's percussive piano downbeats that begin the tune. The percussive quality is indicated by the eighth notes with eighth rests in between, notifying the player to "hit" these rather than play them. This Top-10 hit also features honky-tonk-style playing on the verses.

G
G♯dim7
light's hit - ting some - thing that's been known to change the weath - er.
be they're blind - ed, but Ben - nie makes them age - less.
Am7
D
Em
We'll kill the fat - ted calf to - night, so stick a - round.
We shall sur - vive; let us take our - selves a - long,
You're
where we
Am
Bm
C
gon - na hear e - lec - tric mu - sic sol - id walls of sound.
fight our par - ents out in the streets to find who's right and who's wrong.
Solo ends
Say,
Gmaj7
Am
Can - dy and Ron - nie, have you seen them yet, ooh but they're so spaced out.
B - B - B - B - B

C
Gmaj7
13
Ben-nie and the Jets.
Oh but they're weird and they're won-der-ful. Oh, Ben-
Am
C
D
15
- nie, she's real-ly keen.
She's got e - lec-tric boots, a mo-hair suit; you know I
Em
Em/D
C
B♭/C
C
17
read it in a mag-a-zine,
oh.
B-B-B Ben-nie and the
To Coda
19
Gmaj7
Fmaj7
Jets.

1.
2.
D.S. al Coda
Coda
24
Gmaj7
Ben - nie,
Ben - nie,
3
26
Fmaj7
Ben-nie,
Ben - nie
and the Jets.
Repeat and fade
28
Optional Ending
Gmaj7

"Takin' Care of Business"

"Takin' Care of Business" was a Top-20 hit for Bachman-Turner Overdrive in 1974, and is still going strong into the 21st century on commercials for a well-known office supplies company. The left-hand root–5th and root–6th intervals, together with the right-hand blues phrasings, all add up to some great rock 'n' roll piano!

F7
C7
B♭7
F7
C7
gliss.
B♭7
F7
C7
B♭7
F7
C7
gliss.
B♭7
gliss.
F7
C7

38
B♭7
F7
C7
42
B♭7
F7
C7
46
B♭7
F7
C7
50
B♭7
F7
C7
54
B♭7
F7
C7
57
B♭7
F7
C7

61
B♭7
F7
C7
65
B♭7
F7
C7
68
B♭7
F7
71
C7
gliss.
B♭7
F7
75
C7
B♭7
F7
79
C7
10
10
gliss.
C7

94
B♭7
F7
C7
98
B♭7
F7
C7
102
B♭7
F7
C7
gliss.
105
B♭7
F7
108
C7
B♭7
111
F7
C7

114
B♭7
F7
C7
117
B♭7
F7
120
C7
B♭7
F7
124
C7
C
9
9
138
B♭
F
C
B♭
F
144
C
(8va)
gliss.
C7
loco
B♭7

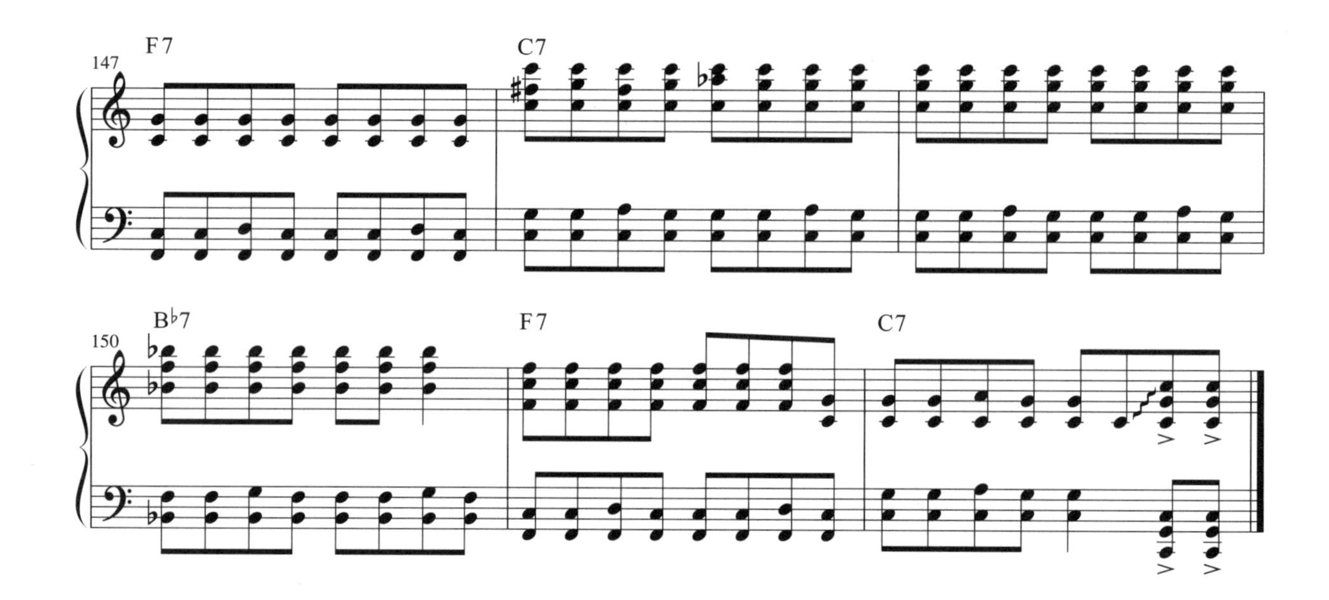

"Misty"

"Misty" is one of the best known jazz standards ever, and has been recorded by hundreds of well-known artists. This is a jazz trio version (piano, bass, and drums), with the piano comping behind the vocals.

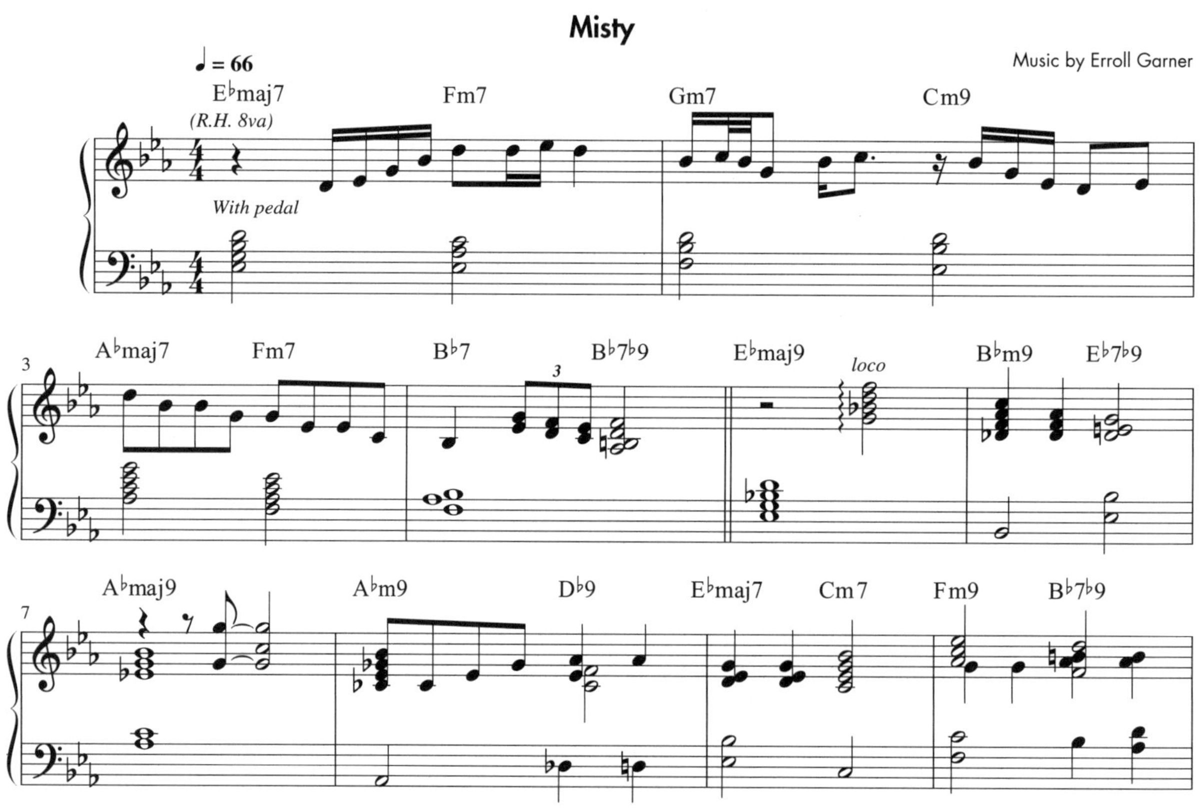

11
Gm7 C7♯9♯5 Fm7 B♭13 E♭maj9
3
3
3
14
B♭m9 E♭13♭9 A♭maj7 A♭m9 D♭9
3
17
E♭add9 Cm7 Fm7 B♭7♭9 E♭add9 D♭9
21
B♭m7 E♭13♭9 A♭maj9 E♭13 sus4 A♭maj9
25
Am7 D9 Cm9 F13♭9 Fm7 B♭9 B♭7♯9♭5
29
E♭maj9 B♭m9 E♭13♭9 A♭maj7 A♭m7 D♭9 Dmaj9

33
E♭maj9 Cm7 Fm9 B♭13♭9 E♭maj9 D♭9 E♭maj9
37
B♭m7 E♭13♭9 A♭maj7 B♭m7/A♭ A♭maj9
41
Am7 D7 Cm9 F13 Fm7 B♭13 E9♭5
45
E♭maj7 B♭m9 E♭13♭9 A♭maj9 A♭m9 D♭13
49
E♭maj7 Cm7 Fm7 B♭13♭9 Gm7 G♭13
52
Fm7 E9♯11 E♭maj9
Rubato
8va

SECTION 6

The Gig

CHAPTER 23

PREPARATION AND PERFORMANCE

What's Ahead:

- Preparing for the gig
- Interpretation and improvisation
- Showmanship and "Faking It"

PREPARING FOR THE GIG

OK, so now it's time for you to go out and do your first (or next) gig, whether it's a heavy metal bash, a cool jazz gig, or a classical piano recital. For many musicians, "playing live" is what it's all about! But what can you do to make sure your gig is a success? Well, if you follow these guidelines, you'll be well on your way!

Be prepared to play. Make sure that you've gone over your parts, not just in rehearsal time with the band, but in your own practice time. When preparing for a gig with my original jazz fusion band, I'll try to play through our whole set on the three or four consecutive days before the gig, either solo piano or with backing tracks/sequences I have prepared. As my band members are "in-demand" guys, sometimes we only get minimal rehearsal time, so everyone has to come to the gig prepared. If you're on a *chart* gig, and you have the music charts ahead of time, scan through them before the gig to make sure you know the road map and form of each song. If you're reading music at a classical recital, again make sure you've had sufficient practice time with the music, and that all of your page turns are OK. One exception to all this, of course, is if you're just showing up to a jam session (good for you!), in which case you're "winging it," using your playing skills and your ears!

Be relaxed and have a pleasant attitude. Less experienced players will sometimes suffer from "nerves" or "stage fright" when performing in public. Well, players of all levels will experience nerves from time to time, but the trick is to get that nervous energy to stimulate you into giving a great performance, instead of holding you back. Especially if you're just starting out, try to get some family or friends to come to the gig and support you, then if an anxious moment strikes, you can look around and be comforted by familiar faces who want you to do well! We're always our own worst critics when it comes to our performance, but your audience will still most likely enjoy it and have a good time (provided you keep going… see comments later in this chapter). Always be very courteous and have a pleasant attitude towards your band mates, the engineer(s), the venue staff, and any audience members you come in contact with. If you project a relaxed and sunny attitude, it will influence those around you, to everybody's benefit.

Make sure your equipment is ready. If you'll just be showing up to a jazz or classical gig playing the piano that is already there, there's just one major thing to take care of regarding equipment: try to get in some warm-up time on the instrument. All pianos are at least a little bit different from each other, and it will help in your preparation to be acquainted with the feel of the instrument.

If you have your own keyboards that you'll be transporting to the gig, there are some other things to keep in mind. Always make sure your equipment is in good working order, and that you have all of the components you need before leaving for the gig. I have a checklist that I run down for keyboards, amplifiers, speakers, pedals, cables, plug boards, extensions, and so on, before I leave for the gig. Always carry spare cables (audio, midi, a/c mains, mic cables, etc., depending on your setup). If one of your keyboards or other equipment has a technical problem, never use it on the gig in the hope that it will "behave itself." That's a disaster waiting to happen. Get it fixed, and use another piece of equipment (perhaps a rental or "loaner") in the meantime.

Be punctual. This sounds simple and obvious, but it's extremely important. If you get to the gig in plenty of time, you're likely to be more relaxed when you set up, and you'll have more time to deal with any "curve balls" with the setup, sound check, and so on (more about sound checks in a minute). Allow even more time to get to the gig if it's a venue you're playing for the first time. This will ensure that you can find the place, sort out the equipment load-in, parking, etc. When playing with my own jazz-fusion band, or with my Steely Dan tribute band in the Los Angeles area, I generally get to the gig between 2– 3 hours before show time, depending on the particular setup and logistics involved. (And I have to allow for the L.A. traffic!)

Observe sound check "etiquette." At pop, rock, and jazz gigs, a sound check is an opportunity to check the sound of each instrument and the whole band—how the band will sound "out front" through the P.A. system, and how the band will hear themselves and each other through "onstage monitoring." For example, for a 9 p.m. show, the sound check might be run from 6 p.m. until 6:30 p.m. If you're the only band on that night (typical for a jazz club), then once you've done the sound check, you can leave all your equipment in place so you're ready to go when show time rolls around. But, if you're one of several bands playing that night (typical for a rock club), then you may have to tear down all of your equipment once you've had your sound check, as the next band then needs to set up! This can get a little chaotic, and you need to keep your wits about you and focus on the task at hand. Here are some do's and don't's you should know about on the sound check:

- Normally the engineer will ask each player to play individually, in order to set levels and equalization (tone color). Next, the whole band may be asked to play sections of one or two songs to check the overall sound and monitoring. Always be available on stage during the sound check so that you're ready to play when the engineer asks. Play one or two representative parts (from each keyboard, if you have more than one) to give the engineer a good idea of what to expect.
- Always be on time for the sound check, and respond promptly to the engineer's requests so that the sound check is completed in a timely manner. This is particularly important if several bands need to sound check, one after the other. In this case, set up and then tear down your equipment as promptly as possible, as required by the club. Keep onstage chatter to a minimum—listen and concentrate.
- Even if you are not happy with your sound or monitoring at first, never be hostile or show a bad attitude toward the engineer. He or she controls how you will sound to your audience! Try to be constructive and positive in your questions and communication to the engineer, and you will get the "best out of them" to help your gig be successful.
- For rock or fusion jazz gigs: try to not have your "backline" (on-stage guitar, bass, and keyboard amps) too loud if at all possible! The louder the backline, the less the engineer can do to shape or balance the sound. Also, the onstage monitoring (necessary for vocalists and instrumentalists to hear themselves) can be ineffective and/or start to "feed back" when backline levels get too high.

Even if you don't normally wear ear protectors on stage during the gig, consider wearing them during the sound check (particularly at rock clubs!). I've played some rock gigs on Hollywood's Sunset Strip where the engineer moved the wrong fader on an "open mic" during the sound check, causing a brutal burst of feedback—not good for the ears!

INTERPRETATION AND IMPROVISATION

In my classes, I am sometimes asked whether a performing musician should play a piece exactly how it is written, and/or play it the same way at each performance. The answers to these questions depend on what style of music you are playing. For example, if you were playing at a classical recital and you started adding your own notes in the middle of Debussy's "Clair de Lune," you would probably get some strange looks from the audience! Conversely, if your jazz trio was playing for a few nights at the Blue Note in New York, and you played a "standard" exactly the same way on two consecutive nights, this might not go down well with the hard-core jazz crowd. Subject to many variations and exceptions, we can make the following broad observations about interpretation and improvisation in the different styles.

Classical: Except in certain experimental or "fringe" situations, you are expected to play the notes that are on the paper (either from memory, or by reading the music). Improvisation (adding your own notes) is not appropriate, which is perhaps ironic given that many classical composers were also noted improvisers in their day. However, classical pianists have major interpretive responsibilities in areas such as dynamics, articulation, phrasing and tempo. Through this interpretation process, the performer's musical personality will emerge. Considering this, when you play something like Debussy's "Clair de Lune," it really may not sound exactly the same each time—make it your own interpretation, while still following the composer's directions. There is a lot you can put into a performance that is not written on the page!

Jazz and Latin: The majority of jazz compositions are written just with a melody and chord symbols (see comments on lead sheets and fake books in Chapter 14). With the exception of some of the more "arranged" contemporary jazz styles, the chord voicings and melody phrasings are normally improvised by the players. Solos in particular will be improvised on the spot, and a "true jazz" performer would not play a solo the same way twice (although they might have favorite phrases or "licks" that they drop into their solos). Latin styles (such as bossa nova and samba) would also come under this general heading, as they typically use the full range of jazz melody and harmony options, and they have a similar approach in terms of improvisation.

Pop/Rock/R&B: The majority of contemporary pop, rock, and R&B songs are performed within a specific structure or *form* (intro, verse, chorus, etc.). Most bands playing these styles are performing from memory, although some may be reading from lead sheets or fake books. There is not normally very much improvisation, except for instrumental solos. Even then, the solo may be a "signature" which is played the same way each time as it is a recognizable part of the song. Some rock bands do, however, incorporate more extended improvisational "jams," notably the Grateful Dead and the Dave Matthews Band.

SHOWMANSHIP AND FAKING IT

When you're performing, (whether it's classical, pop, or jazz music, a little showmanship and "performance awareness" can go a long way. Here are some tips from the trenches:

Keep going, no matter what happens. This applies to all performance situations and musical styles! Whether you're in the middle of Beethoven's "Moonlight Sonata," Coltrane's "Giant Steps," or the Beatles' "Lady Madonna," you should never stop if you fumble in mid-performance! Instead, keep going at all costs, striving to maintain the rhythm as consistently as you can. As musicians, we always tend to be our own worst critics, but I guarantee you that the great majority of your audience will not notice those imperfections, provided that you keep going, and are "in the pocket" rhythmically speaking. I regularly play gigs attended by other musicians here in L.A., and even those guys often don't notice our little flaws (unless they're too polite to tell us!). As the old saying goes (or maybe I just made this up!?), "If you keep going, maybe 2% of your audience will know you made a mistake. If you stop, then 100% of them will notice!" If you're on a pop or jazz gig and you lose your place in the form of the song, use you ears and try to figure out where the band is (i.e., are they on the I chord, the V chord, and so on?). Worst case: if you're playing a tune with a repetitive form (like a blues, or jazz standard), try to catch up when the band returns to the top of the form again!

Make your performance visually as well as musically interesting. This is admittedly style-dependent, and is perhaps most important when playing the popular styles. Rock bands will routinely move around a lot on stage, including some keyboard players who use strap-on keyboard controllers as an alternative to (or as well as) the more conventional keyboard "rig." This kind of showmanship is much less common in the jazz world, although Chick Corea (a giant of acoustic and electric jazz) still uses his strap-on keyboard at concert performances. Otherwise, we keyboard players are stuck behind a grand piano or electronic keyboard rig! Whatever the gig, it's important to look relaxed, happy, and confident, as this will then be conveyed to your audience. As much as I recognize the profound contribution that Miles Davis made to the jazz world, I don't subscribe to his theory of "turning his back" on the crowd. If you engage your audience, they will in turn be more receptive to what you have to play, to everyone's benefit!

Talk to your audience. This again mainly applies in the pop, rock, and jazz styles. I think it's good to introduce your songs (either before or after you play them), and if they're from a CD that you have released, then you can mention that too. It's also good etiquette (particularly on jazz gigs) for the leader to introduce the band members at least once in every set, and maybe more often if some players are featured soloists on particular tunes.

CHAPTER 24
PLAYING OPPORTUNITIES

What's Ahead:

- Solo work
- Joining or forming a band
- Band work
- Studio tips

SOLO WORK

As piano players, we have an advantage over most other instrumentalists when it comes to solo work, in that we can play the melody, harmony (chords), and rhythm of a song all at once, creating an authentic "solo piano" arrangement. If you are also a vocalist, the piano is the ideal accompaniment instrument for the voice across a wide range of popular styles.

If you are new to playing solo gigs, a good place to get started would be an "open mic" session at a local club or coffee house, particularly if they have a piano already set up. The musicians at these events are mostly singer-songwriters, and you normally get to do either one, two, or three songs depending on the time available. This can be a good way to get some performance experience, before moving on to other types of work. Invite some friends along so you have some built-in support!

A lot of clubs, bars, and restaurants have solo piano players, and most (but not all) of them are also singers. The style of music will vary depending on the venue. Hiring just one piano player is more economical than hiring a full band, which is also in the solo performer's favor. Check out the venues in your area, the musical styles they feature, and the nights of the week when they have music. You can inquire directly with the management at the club, or through the agent if the club uses one. Submit a promo pack with a brief bio, photo, and music CD of your playing. You can also get to know the players currently playing, and ask if they need "subs" at any time. Of course, before doing all this, you need to be fluent in the style(s) needed, and to have sufficient "repertoire" under your fingers.

At a higher level of solo work, there is the "hotel circuit." Some of my students have played at the Beverly Hills Hotel "Polo Lounge," which is perhaps the best hotel gig in the Los Angeles area. These high-end gigs are normally found either by personal recommendation or referral, or through the hotel management or an agent. To have a shot at this type of gig, you need to be very personable and presentable, and have a good repertoire of pop and jazz standards, show tunes, and "popular" classical music.

To get the better-paying solo gigs, it is often advisable to register with an agent in your area. They will need your photo, bio, and demo CD, plus a repertoire list of tunes that you know in different styles. This can be the gateway to solo work opportunities for private parties, weddings, corporate functions, and so on. You can also advertise your own services in publications and on the internet. Networking with other musicians, and doing some of these gigs on a "sub" basis for someone else, is also a good way to get started.

Bookstores are also another venue to consider for solo (as well as band) work. Most bookstores don't pay the musicians anymore (unless there's a grand opening for a new store location), but playing there can be good publicity, and you get to sell your CDs if you have any (whether or not the store actually distributes them). Many stores don't have a lot of room for the musicians, which again favors a solo performer or duo rather than a full band.

Shopping malls and retail stores also hire piano players, normally just solo piano (without vocals). The upscale clothing store Nordstroms frequently has pianists playing background music, mostly a mixture of light classical and standards. I must admit that the pianists I have heard in Nordstroms have been rather "busy" for my taste—I keep wanting to get them a T-shirt which says "Arpeggios R Us"! (No disrespect intended if you've done a Nordstroms gig… honest!) Shopping malls also have piano players, often on a seasonal basis (i.e., playing Christmas carols during the shopping season before the holidays).

JOINING OR FORMING A BAND

Many musicians start playing in bands with friends, often at a young age. However, what happens when you want to join or form a band, and you're missing some (or all) of the band members? Well, in fact there are several options available for you to expand your "network" and meet new musician friends. Local music stores and rehearsal studios are good places to start. Sometimes they will be able to refer or recommend players, and/or they will have a bulletin board available for you to post your ads: "bass player wanted for 21st century punk band," or similar! Also, if you can find any local schools or colleges offering music ensemble classes, this can be a good way to meet and network with other musicians. (I have students who have done this as preparation for "playing out" with different bands.)

Of course, the internet offers many ways for people in all walks of life (including musicians!) to get in touch. One of the best known sites in this area is Musicians Contact Service (www.musicianscontact.com) which runs "musicians wanted" ads from all parts of the U.S., as well as some in Canada. Also here in Los Angeles, we have the *Recycler* paper, which contains free ads for virtually everything, including "musicians wanted" ads. Their website (www.recycler.com) now has listings for other major cities across the U.S. In addition, *Music Connection* (a bi-weekly West Coast music magazine) has similar ads, including "Keyboardists Wanted" and "Keyboardists Available." Check out other newspapers and magazines in your area to see if they run music-related ads.

If you're placing an ad for one or more players, be specific about what you're looking for. You should state what the music style is, and where the band is located (especially if you're on a website or in a publication serving multiple areas). For example: "Country/rock band looking for bass player. Los Angeles area. Call Dave at 999–999–9999, dave@xxxx.com." Or, if you're looking to find a band or playing situation, here's an example: "Piano player seeks working blues or R&B band. Atlanta area. Mike 999–999–9999, mike@xxxx.com." When you're receiving replies to your ad, or replying to someone else's, do your best to evaluate them over the phone (not just via email) before setting up a meeting or rehearsal. These days it is typical to exchange music examples (as MP3 files) in these situations, so be prepared to provide these should the need arise.

Whether you have a band or are looking for one, you should also think about what style or styles you want to play, and whether you're going to do cover tunes (i.e., other people's songs), your own original tunes, or some mixture of both. All the band members need to be "on the same page" regarding what songs you are playing, otherwise the situation is probably not going to work. Some bands play cover tunes by one other band only, and are known as "tribute bands." For example, here in Los Angeles, we have "Led ZepAgain" (Led Zeppelin tribute), "Cinema Show" (Genesis tribute), and so on. I play in a Steely Dan tribute band called "Doctor Wu," and we are in friendly competition with another Los Angeles-based Steely Dan tribute band called "Pretzel Logic." I enjoy playing in the Doctor Wu band, and it's a fun way to "keep my chops up"! Your band will also work better if you have broadly similar ability levels among the players. Ideally, you should strive to be with players a little better than you, so that you can improve and gain from their experience. Conversely, if you are the best musician in your band, then you may get frustrated with the other players and end up looking for a different situation. Also, you should try to make your band's rehearsal time as productive as possible (poorly organized and unproductive rehearsals are a common problem with amateur and semi-pro bands). Set a target for each rehearsal—such as learning three new songs, or going through a set list for an upcoming gig—and stick to it!

BAND WORK

So now that you have a band, where are you going to "play out?" Well, some of the same venues we mentioned earlier (for solo work) are also suitable for bands. If you play original rock, you need to hit the clubs that cater to that world (in Los Angeles, that would be the rock clubs along the Sunset Strip, such as the Whisky and the Roxy). If you play rock/pop/R&B covers, this opens up a wider range of possibilities to play at clubs, bars, and restaurants, particularly on the weekends. "Acoustic" straight-ahead jazz normally finds a home in coffee houses, bookstores, hotels, and jazz clubs/restaurants. Some jazz clubs are what I call "listening" rooms, where the crowd is there specifically to see and hear the artists, and in other jazz clubs, the musicians are there more as sophisticated "background music" for the customers in the restaurant. "Electric" (contemporary fusion) jazz is performed in the clubs specifically catering to this style, and these are normally "listening" rooms where people come and pay attention! My contemporary jazz band (Mark Harrison Quintet) plays at the Baked Potato and La Ve Lee, two of the best-known electric jazz clubs in the Los Angeles area. These venues regularly attract foreign tourists and out-of-town visitors.

Tribute bands can also find work at rock clubs, which will sometimes have a "tribute band night" (often on a weekend) featuring several bands on one bill. Outdoor events such as festivals, seasonal concerts, and arts & crafts shows are also options for cover bands, tribute bands, and jazz bands. These events are often coordinated by "city offices" or corporate sponsors. Do a Google search on "outdoor concerts" and "festivals" in your area, and see what you come up with!

If your band wants to earn some more serious cash by playing at private parties, weddings, and functions/casuals, then you need to raise the bar in terms of your repertoire, stylistic versatility, and appearance. You'll need to learn a range of pop standards from the 1950s to the present day, as well as some jazz and "classic" vocal standards. At least two (and preferably three or more) of your band members need to be singers, and if you have more than one lead singer (i.e., one male and one female), that is an advantage. You may also need to learn some songs for a particular gig, for example, the bride and groom may request you to play some specific songs for a wedding. You also need to have good "showmanship" and communication with your clients, and be dressed appropriately (normally tuxedos for the guys, and evening dress for the ladies). A lot of this higher-end work is done through agencies or referrals, although I know some musicians (including the sax player in my jazz quintet) who have set up their own agencies and websites specifically for this purpose, putting together bands as needed for their clients. If you're prepared to do all the work, and compete hard for the gigs, the rewards can be substantial!

STUDIO TIPS

There are three main stages to recording a CD: *tracking* (recording), *mixing*, and *mastering*. With today's technology, it is feasible to do all of these stages in a home studio environment. However, unless you are a solo artist working with synthesizers and "electronica," you are likely to need professional studio help during one or more of these stages. This is due to the limitations of home studios when recording acoustic instruments and full-band lineups, as well as the engineering skills needed to track, mix, and master your music to a professional standard. Although some musicians are also good engineers, in my experience this is the exception, as the skills of engineers and musicians (though related) are not the same. The following comments assume that you are making a self-produced and self-financed CD; there has been a huge growth in these "independent" recordings in the 21st century, in all musical styles. Of course, if you are lucky enough to be signed to a major label, then some of the following constraints may not apply!

Most professional-level studios charge by the hour or by the day (typically ten hours). If you're recording a band CD "from scratch," you're probably looking at a realistic maximum of four or five tunes per day when tracking, meaning at least two full days studio time for a CD of up to ten songs. Overdubs (extra parts added once the main tracks are in place) for vocals, instrumental solos, and any other parts, could also take a full day or more. These are basic minimums if you are on a budget, and, of course, your CD could take much more time depending on the nature of the project.

Before you take your band in to record, make sure you are thoroughly rehearsed, as a professional studio is a rather costly place to be wasting time! Your band should get to the studio in plenty of time to set up any equipment (especially the drummer, as the drum kit normally takes the longest to set up, mic, and sound check in the studio). All players in your band will have headphones on when "tracking." Make sure you can hear enough of yourself and everyone else in your headphones. The engineer should be able to adjust your "headphone mix" as needed.

When all the tracking is done, then it's time for mixing. This is when all of the individual tracks (piano, guitar, bass, drums, vocals, etc.) are balanced and combined into a stereo master (left and right) by the mixing engineer. For the "average" band CD (if there is such a thing!), you should allow a minimum of 2–3 hours per song for mixing. Of course, this will be more if your mixes are complex and involve a lot of layers. You don't have to do the mixing at the same studio you "tracked" at. A lot of commercial CDs are tracked and mixed at different studios.

Since the late 20th century, hard disk-based recording systems (such as ProTools) have taken over from tape-based systems in many studios. These systems provide more flexibility and editing options in all stages of the recording process. Artists can also bring tracks they have created in their home or project studios into the "main studio" to dump into ProTools as a starting point for their songs.

When all the mixing is done, it's time to "master" your record. This is the final "icing on the cake" that will make your CD sound professional and radio-ready! Some less experienced musicians make the mistake of missing out the mastering step, and just pressing CDs from the mixes. This may be OK for demos, but is not recommended for a full CD! Mastering is often done at special "mastering studios," with the room and equipment specifically set up for that purpose. Mastering involves: overall level adjustments to make the whole CD consistent (and suitable for radio broadcast), overall EQ or tone color adjustments (for example, raising the level of the highest and lowest frequencies in commercial pop styles, to make the sound "pop out" when played on different systems), "topping and tailing" (cleaning up the beginnings and endings of the tunes as needed), and track spacing (determining the time between songs on the final CD).

When you have mastered your recording, then you finally need to manufacture your CDs to sell at gigs and over the internet (as well as any other distribution channels which are available). There are many companies offering CD manufacturing services for independent musicians, and one of the best-known is DiscMakers (www.discmakers.com). DiscMakers will take your master disc, band photos, text, and any design suggestions, then design your CD artwork and cover in-house for your approval, before delivering bar-coded shrink-wrapped CDs on time and at a good price. I have used DiscMakers for two independent CDs, and would not hesitate to use them again. Another company very helpful to independent musicians is CDBaby (www.cdbaby.com). Their website is perhaps the best-known online store to buy and sell independent music on the internet. My CDs are on CDBaby, and I know a lot of other independent musicians who have CDs on there too!

SECTION 7

Instruments and Care

CHAPTER 25
DIFFERENT TYPES OF PIANOS

What's Ahead:

- Acoustic pianos
- Electric pianos and keyboards

ACOUSTIC PIANOS

Acoustic pianos are divided into two overall categories: *vertical* and *horizontal*. Vertical pianos are also sometimes referred to as "uprights," although technically an upright is just one type of vertical piano, as we'll see in a minute. Horizontal pianos are also referred to as "grand" pianos.

Spinet

Vertical pianos fall into one of the following sub-categories: spinet, console, studio, and upright. The *spinet* piano is the smallest piano made, with a height of around 3 feet. Compared to other pianos, the keys have to go through more steps before striking the string, which enables the piano to be shorter. However, there is a loss of power and balance, and as a result there are very few new spinet pianos being manufactured. The *console* piano is the next size up, with a height of around 3 feet 6 inches. Unlike the spinet, the console uses a "direct key" action, which together with the longer strings and larger soundboard, results in a better tone. The *studio* piano is the next size up, with a height of around 4 feet. This piano has very good tone quality and is often found in music schools and studios. Finally, the *upright* piano is the tallest, with a height of up to 5 feet. There are very few new upright pianos being manufactured, so if you see one, it's most likely to be old!

Console

Studio

Upright

Horizontal or "grand" pianos fall into one of the following sub-categories: petite, baby, medium, parlor (or "living room"), ballroom (or "semi-concert"), and concert. The main difference between all these types is the overall length. The *petite* is around 4 feet 8 inches, the *baby* is around 5 feet 3 inches, the *medium* is 5 feet 7 inches, the *parlor* is around 6 feet, the *ballroom* is around 7 feet, and the *concert grand* is 9 feet long. All grand pianos will have a louder and fuller tone than vertical pianos due to their longer strings and larger soundboards. The grand piano has an even louder and more resonant sound when the adjustable lid is propped open.

Baby grand piano

9' concert grand piano

Here are some famous brands of acoustic pianos that you can check out. Even though acoustic pianos have been made in pretty much the same way for a long time now, there is still a significant difference between makes and models, in terms of the overall tone color and *feel* of the instrument. If you're in the market for an acoustic piano, go for one that fits your musical needs, available space, and budget!

- **Baldwin** www.gibson.com, then click on "Pianos"
- **Bösendorfer** www.bosendorfer.com
- **Kawai** www.kawaius.com
- **Samick** www.samickmusicusa.com
- **Steinway** www.steinway.com
- **Yamaha** www.yamaha.com
- **Young Chang** www.youngchang.com

Console pianos are the most common for in the home. They are more decorative than studios, and don't take up too much space. Studio pianos are larger, and usually more "plain" looking. The various grand pianos are obviously excellent for the sound, but their size and price make them an instrument for only the truly dedicated (and wealthy!).

ELECTRIC PIANOS AND KEYBOARDS

You might remember that we conducted some basic comparisons between acoustic and electric instruments back in Chapter 1. Electric instruments fall into three broad categories: digital pianos, synthesizers and workstations, and software instruments.

Digital pianos are often the most tempting option for people who want a sound close to "the real thing," but don't want to deal with the world of computers and MIDI technology. Digital pianos have 88 weighted keys, and come with a selection of piano sounds as well as a handful of other sounds. They are designed to be used as a stand-alone instrument, either in the home or in a school classroom. As such, they normally have built-in speakers at each end, and a headphone output so you can practice without disturbing your neighbors. Roland, Yamaha, Korg, and Kurzweil all make good digital pianos. As with all keyboards, play the instrument to see if you like the sound and feel before buying. Popular models in 2006 include the Roland MP-60, Yamaha YDP223, Korg SP250, and Kurzweil RE-210.

Yamaha Digital

Synthesizers and **workstations** is a large category! Synthesizers are keyboard instruments capable of playing many different sounds, which by the late 1980s typically included "samples" (digital recordings) of real instruments, including piano. Synthesizers also allow the user to program and alter these sounds—in essence, to create your own sounds as well as use the "presets" already available on the instrument. Also in the 1980s, onboard "sequencing" (multi-channel recording) was added to these synthesizers, and "workstations" were born. Functionally, the workstations in the 2000s are similar, but with more features: memory, sounds, sound editing capabilities, and polyphony (number of "voices" sounding at once) have all increased greatly. These instruments now have a hefty selection of acoustic and electric piano sounds, hundreds or thousands of other sounds (strings, brass, organ, bass, drums, etc.), and an onboard sequencer with a large memory capacity. They normally don't have built-in speakers, so you'll need to run them through an external amplifier and speaker system (or combo amp), or listen to them on headphones. Popular models in 2006 include the Korg Triton Extreme, Yamaha Motif, and Roland Fantom.

Korg Triton Extreme

The features on today's digital pianos, synths and workstations are extensive, and you want make sure that the keyboard is what you need. Here are some areas you should consider before deciding what to buy:

- Are you going to be transporting it to gigs and/or rehearsals, or is it primarily for home use? A larger and heavier machine might be OK if you're leaving it at home, but portability is a factor if you're "playing out."
- Do you need sounds other than just piano sounds (for recording, or for live use)? If not, then a digital piano (for home use) or a "stage piano" (for live use) such as the Roland RD-700SX or the more budget-oriented M-Audio ProKeys 88 might work for you. These keyboards will all have a "weighted action," which is appropriate if you mainly need piano sounds.
- If you do need a range of other sounds as well as piano sounds: do you also need "weighted keys" (approximating the feel of an acoustic piano), or is an unweighted "synth action" OK? If you need weighted keys, then you're either looking at the 88-key versions of the workstation synths, or a weighted 88-key "controller" which sends MIDI data to another keyboard or "MIDI sound module" (or to a software instrument running on a computer...see next

section). If you don't need weighted keys, then you're probably better off going for the shorter (61- or 76-key) versions of the workstation synths.

- Do you need the onboard sequencing that the workstation synths provide? Well, maybe not if you already run a computer-based music setup. In mid 2000, Yamaha did a smart thing and brought out the S90, essentially a weighted 88-key version of their Motif workstation, but without the sequencer. The S90 has outstanding electric piano sounds, and reasonably decent acoustic piano sounds (and most of the other great sounds from the Motif). I play an S90 on gigs with my Steely Dan tribute band, and I've seen top L.A. players like David Garfield and Gregg Karukas use them as well.

With these thoughts in mind, here are some well-known manufacturers of digital pianos and synthesizers (not to mention a whole lot of other music equipment!) that you can check out.

- Korg www.korg.com
- Kurzweil www.kurzweilmusicsystems.com
- Roland www.rolandus.com
- Yamaha www.yamaha.com

Software instruments offer the greatest realism if you're looking to get as close as possible to the real sound of a piano (and who isn't?). The plug-ins discussed in the last chapter (which "plug in" to a host sequencer on your Mac or PC) are software instruments. They take advantage of the ever faster speed of today's computers (together with large hard drives and fast drive access times) to use huge sample libraries of instrument sounds, far larger than the memory available on workstation synths. For piano sounds, this not only means individual samples for each note (rather than "stretching" samples across a range of notes, as is common on workstations), but individual samples for multiple velocity (how hard and fast you hit a key) levels per note. This all adds up to the most realistic piano playing experience yet, using a computer and keyboard controller. Some software instruments will also run as "stand-alone" programs (i.e., they will run by themselves, instead of running inside a "host" application). The two main "software" pianos in 2006 are Ivory (by Synthogy) and Akoustic Piano (by Native Instruments). I've used Ivory extensively (as a plug-in inside Digital Performer on a Mac) on various projects, with excellent results. Some musicians are also using Ivory on gigs, with a keyboard controller hooked up to their laptop computer. It's a brave new world out there!

Also, some of the music instrument retailers have helpful catalogs and websites, covering all types of keyboard instruments, as well as music software. In particular, I find the Sweetwater catalog a useful guide and quick reference to what's out there and what's "hot." Check out these companies and websites for further information.

- American Music Supply www.americanmusical.com
- Musician's Friend www.musiciansfriend.com
- Sweetwater www.sweetwater.com

CHAPTER 26
CARE, MAINTENANCE, AND MOVING

What's Ahead:

- Where to put your piano
- Keeping your piano clean and healthy
- Moving your piano

WHERE TO PUT YOUR PIANO

The comments in this chapter mainly apply to acoustic pianos, as they are generally more susceptible to damage due to changes in temperature, humidity, and so on. However, there are also some care and maintenance issues to bear in mind when using electronic keyboards.

Before going to buy an acoustic piano, you should decide where you are going to put it (i.e., in which room in your house). Of course, you'll want the piano to be in a visually pleasing location, especially as it is an elegant piece of furniture. The two main places to avoid are a) near a window that gets direct sunlight, and b) near a heating or air conditioning duct, or radiator.

Sunlight is not good for acoustic pianos. The wood can become dried out or warped over time, and the ultraviolet rays can damage the finish, causing blisters or bleaching to occur. Eventually, this can also affect the keys and hammers, causing the piano to go out of tune. So although you may be tempted to place it near the window so you can be inspired by the view—don't! Electronic keyboards are somewhat "hardier," however it's still not a great idea to place them in direct sunlight.

Sudden temperature changes are also not good for your piano, and can cause the piano to go out of tune. Even worse are abrupt changes in humidity levels. These cause the wood in the piano to shrink or swell, which can result in cracking and damage to the joints. The expansion of the wood also causes the tuning pins to slip, and the piano to go out of tune. Condensation can also result from high humidity, which can then rust the metal parts. Many acoustic piano owners use a humidifier to regulate humidity levels in the room where the piano is located, and you can get these from your piano dealer, or from a department store. Good ventilation in the room also helps, as it prevents excess moisture from building up inside the piano.

You also want your piano in a place that is accessible and easy for you to play. Most people put pianos in a "main room" of the house, such as the family room or living room. This normally works, but make sure you can play the piano when you want to (i.e., if it's near the TV, you may be constrained during your family's favorite programs!). If this is a problem, consider putting the piano in a spare room (if there is enough space). If you live in an apartment, condo, or town house, you'll want to consider any potential disturbance to your neighbors. For example, you should avoid placing the piano next to a wall shared by your neighbor, or in a room above their bedroom. These factors are not a problem with electronic keyboards, which will normally have a "headphone output" for practicing, and are also more portable than their acoustic counterparts. Lighting is also an important factor to keep in mind. I've played in plenty of dimly-lit clubs over the years, but when I'm playing at home, I like plenty of light, whether or not I'm actually reading music. If the room your piano is in needs some more light, you can always set up an extra lamp near your keyboard.

KEEPING YOUR PIANO CLEAN AND HEALTHY

An important rule to remember, whether you're playing an acoustic or electronic piano: never allow yourself or anybody else to have food or drink around your keyboard. Drink spilled onto an electric keyboard is very likely to cause damage, and is also dangerous if the instrument is switched on! An acoustic piano is also very vulnerable to damage in this way, as it has many delicate moving parts and mechanisms inside. Don't even think about it!

Many acoustic piano owners use a feather duster to dust the piano keys and other parts. Periodically you'll want to get in between the keys to clean a little more thoroughly, which is ideally done with a small paintbrush (one that hasn't been used for painting!). When cleaning the wood surface, you can use a soft damp cloth, or a cleaner that is recommended by your piano dealer. In our house we use a Mirror Glaze™ finish enhancer on our Young Chang grand piano, with good results. I've always used Windex™ or a similar glass cleaner on my electronic keyboards (while they are turned off of course!) and this has worked fine.

Don't use regular furniture polish on your grand piano. This can ruin the finish!

Periodically your acoustic piano will also need to be tuned. This is done normally after the piano has been moved, and on average every 6–12 months afterwards. If your piano also doubles as a "studio" piano, you'll normally get it tuned at the beginning of each recording session.

Unless you are one of the small handful of pianists who are also expert tuners, always get a professional tuner to tune your piano, rather than tinker with it yourself. There are lots of good technical reasons for this... just take my word for it!

A piano tuning will generally last a couple of hours or so, and will cost around $70–$100 for a good technician. If you don't know any piano tuners, I suggest you get a recommendation from your teacher or local music store. Playing your piano right after it has been tuned by an expert will be a sheer delight, and well worth the cost!

If you need to get an instrument repaired (whether acoustic piano or electronic keyboard), again it's always best to use a professional technician. If you're buying a new instrument, hopefully you shouldn't have to worry about repairs for a while! If buying used, however, this situation is more likely to come up (sort of like with cars!). On acoustic pianos, you may get problems such as broken strings, broken hammers or dampers, or even a broken soundboard if the piano is not moved properly or has been exposed to humidity changes. On electronic keyboards, you may get problems such as the unit not powering on, distorted sound, no sound at all, LCD not working or showing gibberish, keys or buttons getting stuck, and so on. If you don't know a qualified technician or repair center, you can inquire at your music store or dealer, or directly with the manufacturer. Most professional-level keyboards these days are pretty sturdy, and should work hassle-free for a long time, provided they are not abused!

MOVING YOUR PIANO

I have one very important piece of advice to give you in this section:

Always use a professional, qualified piano mover when moving your piano (for example, when you're moving to another house). *Never* try to move it yourself or with a group of friends, and don't trust your regular "home movers"! Piano movers are specially trained to move these instruments, which are much more than furniture.

SECTION 8

Who's Who

Ludwig van Beethoven was one of the greatest classical composers of all time, as well as a formidable pianist. He was born in Bonn, Germany in 1770, and received his early music training from his father, who was a court musician. In the early 1790s, Beethoven moved to Vienna and studied with Haydn, before embarking on a career as a pianist and composer. In the early 1800s, he began to notice his hearing loss, but it did not prevent him from composing a series of groundbreaking works, most famously including his symphonies, string quartets, and piano sonatas. Beethoven's work was a huge influence on other 19th century symphonic composers such as Brahms and Wagner, as well as on Romantic song composers such as Schubert. Although Beethoven's music was revolutionary, it has very broad appeal due to its very human and dramatic qualities.

Recommended listening:

- Piano Sonata No. 14 ("Moonlight") in C sharp minor, Opus 27/2.
- Piano Sonata No. 23 ("Appassionata") in F minor, Opus 57.
- Piano Concerto No. 5 ("Emperor") in E flat major, Opus 73.

Franz Liszt has been called the greatest virtuoso pianist of all time, and a visionary composer. An icon of the Romantic period, he had a tremendous instinct for showmanship, and was definitely a "rock star" in his time. In his youth, he was already a prodigious improviser, but it was not until he was an adult that his compositional brilliance began to emerge. Liszt studied with Czerny in Vienna, and then tried but failed to get into the Paris Conservatory. Nonetheless, he became a well-known society figure in Paris, where both his romantic life and his piano wizardry caused much sensation. Inspired by the phenomenal technique and stage presence of the violinist Nicolò Paganini, he wrote progressively more challenging works for the piano, mostly for his own use. In his later years, Liszt mellowed somewhat, writing sacred works and more introspective compositions.

Recommended listening:

- Piano Concerto No. 1 in E flat major, S. 124.
- Hungarian Rhapsody for Piano No. 2 in C sharp minor, S. 244/2.
- Transcendental Etude for Piano No. 11, S. 139/11.

Art Tatum was one of the most phenomenally gifted jazz pianists of the 20th century. The sophistication and complexity of his boogie-woogie, stride, and swing playing left his competitors in the dust. Apart from some early training at the Toledo School of Music, he was largely self-taught. By the early 1930s, Tatum was stunning audiences with solo piano tunes like "Tiger Rag" which sounded like multiple pianists playing together. Although he worked in various trio and other lineups in the 1940s and '50s, the bulk of his work was done on solo piano. He was not a composer, but his highly inventive re-workings of standard tunes were in a class by themselves. Tatum's harmonic concepts were easily a generation ahead of their time, and his recordings still inspire (and intimidate!) modern-day pianists.

Photo by William Gottleib/Redferns Music Picture Library

Recommended listening:

- *Art Tatum Live, Volume 3*, 1945-49 (Storyville)
- *Art Tatum Solo Masterpieces, Volume 1*, 1953 (Pablo)
- *The Best of the Pablo Group Masterpieces*, 1975 (recorded 1954-56) (Pablo)

Photo by David Redferns/Redferns Music Picture Library

Bill Evans remains a huge influence on modern-day jazz pianists. He came to the fore in the late 1950s with the Miles Davis Sextet, and co-wrote and played on their 1959 album *Kind of Blue*, perhaps the most famous acoustic jazz record of all time. Evans used the impressionist influences of Debussy and Ravel to craft a new, more "open" chord voicing method, which together with his relaxed sensibility was well suited to the "cool jazz" pioneered by Davis at the time. He also went on to record as a leader in various lineups, most famously in trios with bassists including Scott LaFaro, Gary Peacock, and Marc Johnson, and drummers including Paul Motian, Jack DeJohnette, and Joe La Barbera. Evans also unselfishly shared the spotlight with the other members of his trios, another way he influenced the many pianists who followed in his footsteps.

Recommended listening:

- *Kind of Blue* by Miles Davis, 1959 (Columbia/Legacy)
- *Sunday at the Village Vanguard*, 1961 (Riverside/OJC)
- *Conversations With Myself*, 1963 (Verve)

Keith Jarrett is one of the most significant pianists to emerge in the last fifty years. He is perhaps most renowned for his solo performances and recordings, many of which are spontaneously improvised. He collaborated with Miles Davis in the early days of jazz-fusion, which was the only time he has used electronic keyboards in his career. By the 1970s, he was leading various jazz trios and quartets, and in the 1980s he began performing a lot of classical music as well as jazz. By the 1990s, he was also interpreting standards in a jazz trio with Gary Peacock and Jack DeJohnette,

Photo courtesy of Photofest, Inc.

and this group is documented extensively on recordings. Anyone familiar with Jarrett's work knows that he sometimes "sings along" when playing the piano, which can be distracting. However, he remains a formidable force in jazz and improvised music.

Recommended listening:

- *The Köln Concert*, 1975 (ECM)
- *The Survivor's Suite*, 1976 (ECM)
- *Tokyo 96*, 1998 (recorded 1996) (ECM)

Chick Corea has continually re-invented himself since emerging on to the scene in the 1960s. He came to the fore around the same time as Keith Jarrett and Herbie Hancock, and these three pianists are considered the main successors to mid-20th century jazz icons Bill Evans and McCoy Tyner. Corea started recording albums as a leader in the 1960s, before collaborating with Miles Davis on his classic album *Bitches Brew* (which is credited with launching the jazz-rock era). By the 1970s, he was playing high-octane fusion with his band Return to Forever. After this band broke up, he played acoustic piano in a variety of all-star lineups, before forming his Elektric band in the mid-1980s, adding a heavy dose of funk to his inventive jazz stylings. In the 21st century, he continues to juggle straight-ahead acoustic jazz with cutting-edge fusion, and remains a potent force in the jazz world.

Photo courtesy of Photofest, Inc.

Recommended listening:

- *Return to Forever*, 1972 (ECM)
- *Three Quartets*, 1981 (Warner Bros)
- *Eye of the Beholder*, 1988 (GRP)

Photo courtesy of Photofest, Inc.

Elton John is one of the biggest pop superstars of the late 20th century, and is also an innovative and influential piano stylist. Elton met his long-time lyricist collaborator Bernie Taupin in the late 1960s, and they started off writing songs for other artists. By the early 1970s, Elton's solo albums were charting in Britain and America, and he hit the peak of his commercial success between 1972 and 1976, with seven consecutive Number One albums and sixteen consecutive Top 20 hit singles. He effortlessly blended pop, rock, and soul styles, and brought a unique melodic sensibility to his song craft. In the late 1970s and early '80s, his sales slumped somewhat, but he bounced back strongly with 1983's *Too Low for Zero* album, which generated another string of hit singles. In the '90s, he began writing songs for Disney productions (*The Lion King* and *Aida*) and in 1997 he recorded a new version of his song "Candle in the Wind" as a tribute to Princess Diana, which became his biggest-ever hit.

Recommended listening:

- *Tumblewood Connection*, 1971 (UNI)
- *Goodbye Yellow Brick Road*, 1973 (Rocket/Island)
- *Two Low for Zero*, 1983 (MCA)

Keith Emerson has been an idol of many piano and keyboard players since his days with the progressive rock band The Nice in the 1960s. He is an acknowledged master of classically-influenced rock, and is known for both his showmanship and his technical accomplishments. He formed ELP (Emerson, Lake and Palmer) in 1970, and they became the first supergroup of the progressive rock era. ELP significantly increased the audience for this type of music (due in part to the heavy radio airplay they received), and they paved the way for successor "prog" bands such as Yes and Genesis. These bands collectively produced some of the most creative and interesting rock music of the 1970s. After ELP broke up in 1980, Emerson began scoring movies (including *The Inferno* and *Nighthawks*), and the band re-united in the early 1990s for a successful tour and album.

Photo by David Warner/Redferns Music Picture Library

Recommended listening:

- *Emerson, Lake and Palmer*, 1970 (Rhino)
- *Brain Salad Surgery*, by ELP, 1973 (Manticore)
- *Emerson Plays Emerson*, 2002 (EMI)

APPENDIX

REFERENCE SHEET

Know your keys!

This handy little chart will help you learn the names of the white and black keys on your piano…

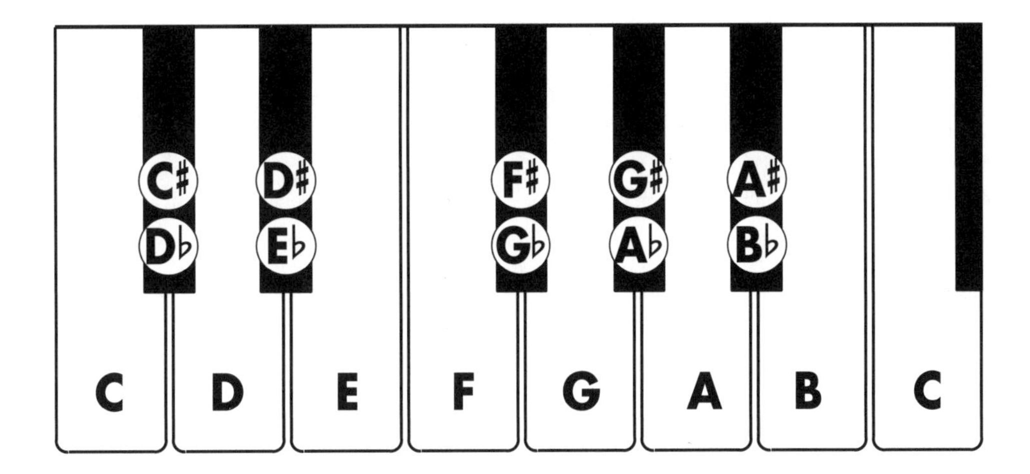

… and here are the corresponding notes shown in the treble and bass clefs:

Musical terms and symbols

These terms and symbols will come in handy when you're practicing the piano!

CLEFS

FREQUENTLY USED TIME SIGNATURES

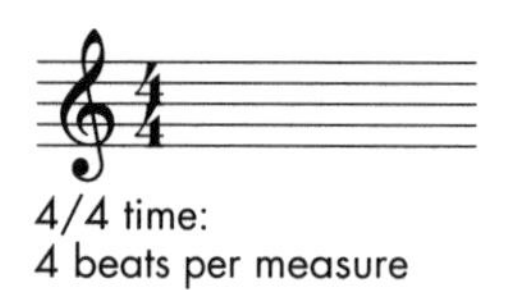

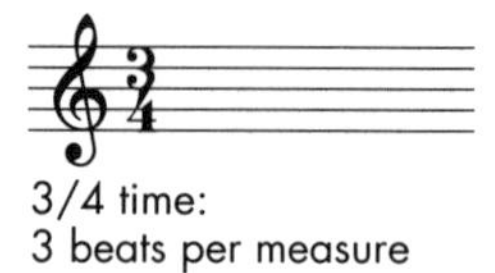

RHYTHMIC VALUES: NOTES

RHYTHMIC VALUES: RESTS

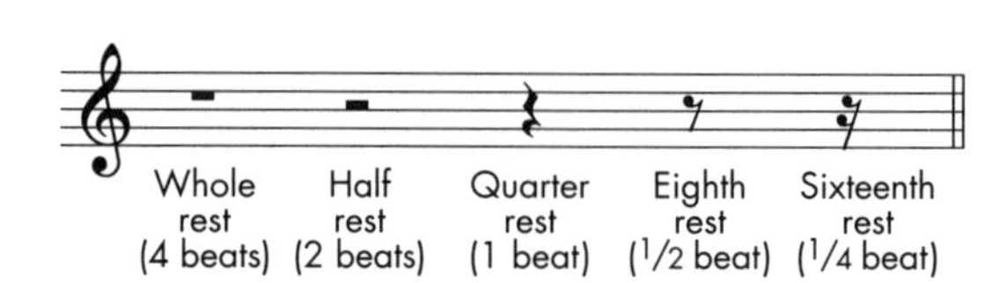

DOTTED NOTES

TIED NOTES

COMMON MAJOR SCALES AND CHORDS

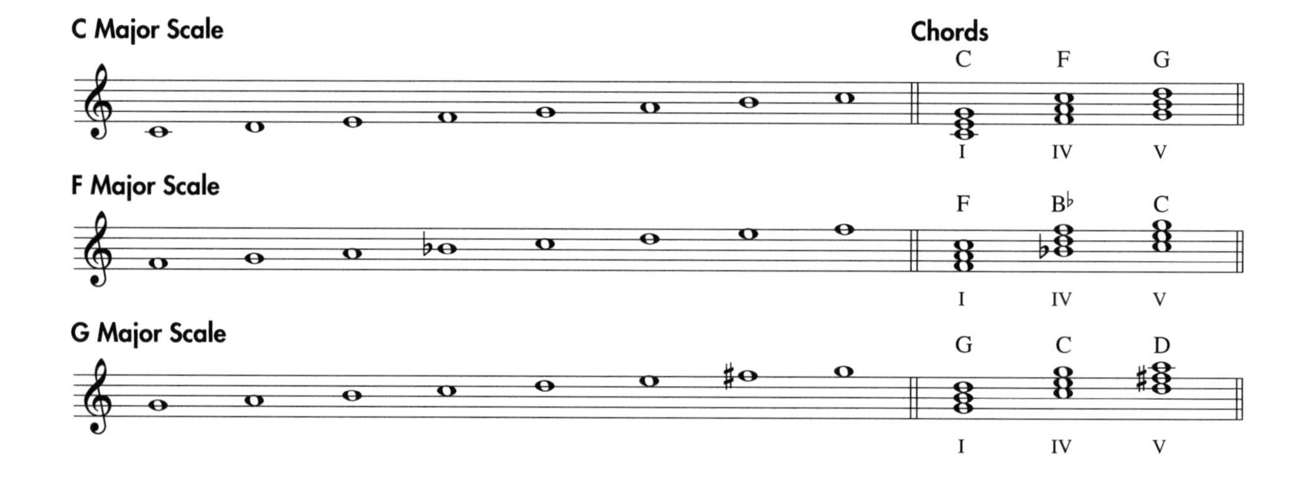

WHO'S WHO BIG LIST – 100 PIANO PLAYERS

For artists primarily associated with one band or group, that group is also shown.

Mose Allison (soul jazz)
Albert Ammons (boogie-woogie)
Tori Amos (pop/rock)
Martha Argerich (classical)
Johann Sebastian Bach (classical, composer)
Tony Banks (progressive rock): Genesis
Count Basie (jazz)
Ludwig van Beethoven (classical, composer)
David Benoit (jazz)
Roy Bittan (rock): The E Street Band
Alfred Brendel (classical)
Dave Brubeck (jazz)
Robbie Buchanan (pop/R&B)
Kate Bush (pop/rock)
Michel Camilo (Latin jazz)
Ray Charles (R&B)
Fryderyk Chopin (classical, composer)
Van Cliburn (classical)
Chick Corea (jazz)
Floyd Cramer (country)
George Duke (jazz/R&B)
Duke Ellington (jazz, composer)
Keith Emerson (progressive rock)
Bill Evans (jazz)
Donald Fagen (jazz/rock): Steely Dan
Russell Ferrante (jazz): Yellowjackets
Ben Folds (pop/rock)
Erroll Garner (jazz)
George Gershwin (jazz, composer)
Glenn Gould (classical)
Don Grolnick (jazz)
Dave Grusin (jazz)
Don Grusin (jazz)
Herbie Hancock (jazz)
Gene Harris (soul jazz)
Earl Hines (jazz)
Jools Holland (rock): Squeeze
Nicky Hopkins (rock): The Who
Bruce Hornsby (pop/jazz/R&B)
Vladimir Horowitz (classical)
Keith Jarrett (jazz)
Billy Joel (pop/rock)
Dr. John (New Orleans blues/R&B)
Elton John (pop/rock)
James P. Johnson (jazz)
Pete Johnson (boogie-woogie)
Scott Joplin (ragtime)
Tony Kaye (progressive rock): Yes
Wynton Kelly (jazz)
Kenny Kirkland (jazz)
Evgeny Kissin (classical)
Diana Krall (jazz)
Wanda Landowska (classical)
David Lanz (new age)
Liberace (various)
Chuck Leavell (rock/R&B): The Rolling Stones
John Legend (pop/gospel/R&B)
Professor Longhair (New Orleans blues)
Little Richard (rock)
Jerry Lee Lewis (rock)
Franz Liszt (classical, composer)
Jon Lord (rock): Deep Purple
Lyle Mays (jazz): The Pat Metheny Group
Brad Mehldau (jazz)
Max Middleton (jazz/funk)
Thelonious Monk (jazz)
Jelly Roll Morton (jazz)
Wolfgang Amadeus Mozart (classical, composer)
Ignacy Jan Paderewski (classical)
David Paich (pop/rock): Toto
Oscar Peterson (jazz)
Greg Philinganes (pop/rock/R&B)
Bud Powell (jazz)
Sergei Rachmaninoff (classical, composer)
Hargus Robbins (country)
Matt Rollins (country/rock)
Arthur Rubinstein (classical)
Jordan Rudess (progressive rock): Dream Theater
Gonzalo Rubalcaba (Latin jazz)
Michael Ruff (pop/rock/R&B)
Joe Sample (jazz/R&B)
Tom Schuman (Latin jazz): Spyro Gyra
Horace Silver (jazz)
Memphis Slim (blues)
Otis Spann (blues)
Liz Story (new age)
Roosevelt Sykes (blues)
Art Tatum (jazz)
Cecil Taylor (avant-garde jazz)
Richard Tee (gospel)
Lennie Tristano (jazz)
Big Joe Turner (blues)
McCoy Tyner (jazz)
Rick Wakeman (progressive rock): Yes
Fats Waller (jazz, composer)
Teddy Wilson (jazz)
George Winston (new age)
Steve Winwood (pop/R&B)
Stevie Wonder (pop/R&B)
Yanni (new age)
Joe Zawinul (jazz)

STAFF PAPER

After you've made it through this book, you'll be equipped with the tools to start creating your own piano lines. Therefore, we've included some pages here with which you can start working right away. Remember to only make copies of these pages, though; that way, you'll never run out.

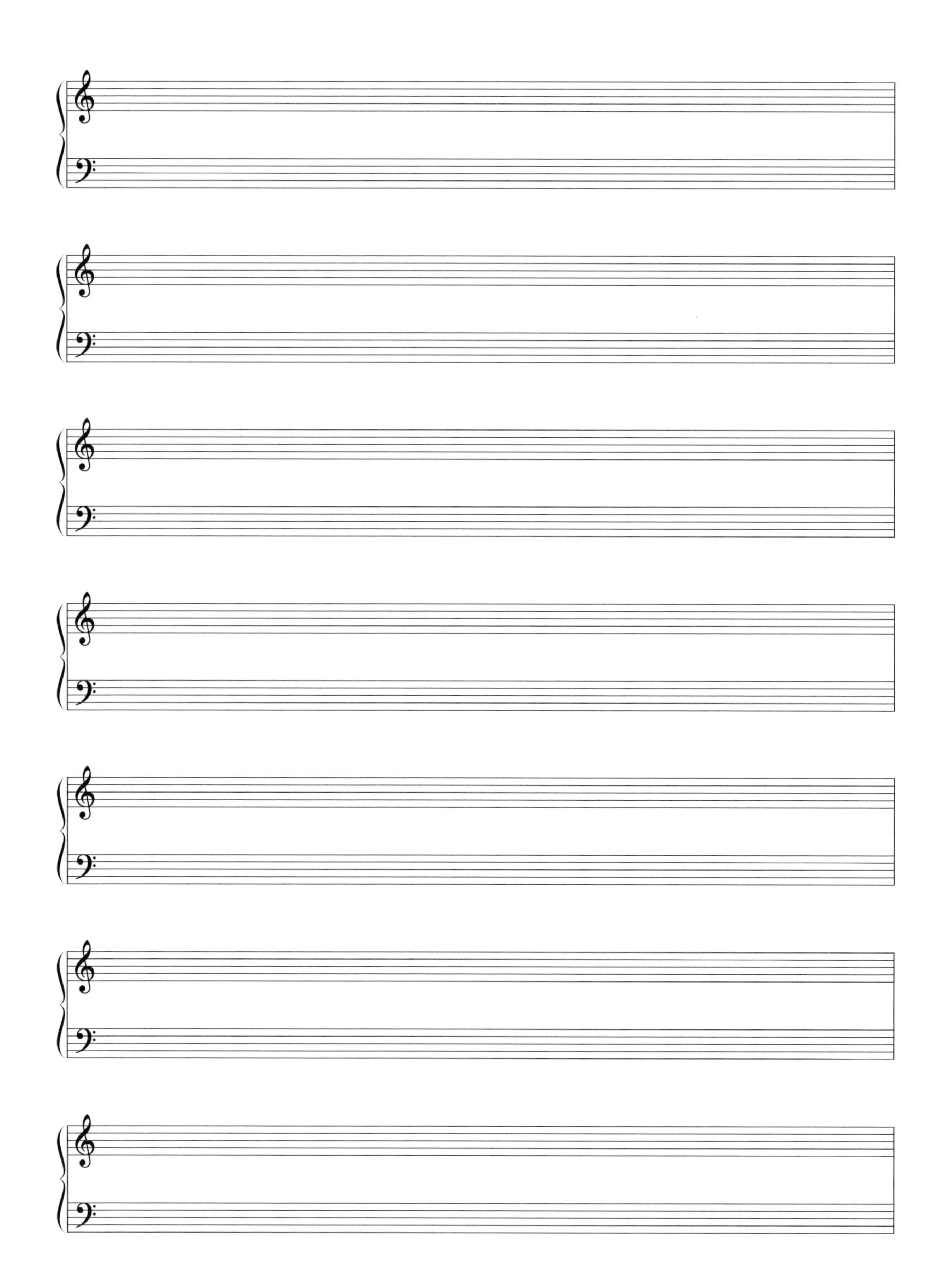

GLOSSARY

Accidental: A sign to the left of a note: either a natural, sharp, or flat. See individual glossary entries.

Add9 chord: Chord created by adding a ninth (9th) to a major or minor triad.

Alternating eighth notes: Right-hand comping pattern used in pop and country styles.

Anticipation: See *syncopation*.

Arpeggio: Playing the notes of a chord one at a time, or "broken chord" style.

Articulation: How the note is played, i.e., *staccato* (short) or *legato* (smooth and connected), etc.

Augmented triad: A triad created by raising the 5th of a major triad by one half step.

Ballad: A song performed at a slow tempo.

Bar: See *measure*.

Barline: Vertical line on the staff which divides the music into measures.

Bass clef: Sign at the beginning of piano music indicating notes to be played on the lower portion of the keyboard, usually with the left hand.

Beam: Horizontal line that connects the stems of adjacent eighth or sixteenth notes.

Beats: A basic unit of musical time. Different rhythmic lengths (of notes and rests) are expressed in *numbers of beats*.

Blues: An indigenous American music that first emerged in the late 19th century as an African-American vocal style.

Blues form: A twelve-bar form or sequence which is used for the majority of blues songs.

Blues scale: A six-note scale with the following internal intervals: minor 3rd, whole step, half step, half step, minor 3rd, and whole step.

Boogie-Woogie: An early 20th century blues style using driving left-hand patterns and fast tempos.

Chart: Notated version of a song, showing the melody and chord symbols, or just the chord symbols (without the melody). Also see *lead sheet*.

Chord: Three or more different notes played at the same time. Chords are usually (but not always) built in stacks of thirds.

Chord chart: Version of a chart (see above) only containing chord symbols.

Chord function: Where the chord occurs within a key and the resolution tendancies of that chord. For example, G major is a *V* chord in the key of C, and its function is to resolve to the *I* chord.

Chord inversion: A chord re-arranged so that the root is no longer on the bottom.

Chord progression: A sequence of chords used in a song.

Chord root: The first note or *foundation pitch* of a chord, for example, the root of a C major triad is the note C.

Chord symbol: Symbol placed above the staff, telling you which chord is being used at that point in the music.

Chord "upgrading": Adding notes to the chord beyond the chord symbol, for example, using "upper structure" voicings (adding 9ths, 11ths, and 13ths).

Chord voicing: An interpretation of a chord symbol by the pianist, i.e., which notes to play in each hand, whether to add or subtract any notes depending on the style, and so on.

Cluster: A type of chord containing one or more seconds, producing a dissonant sound.

Common time: Another name for a 4/4 time signature.

Comping: Musical slang for *accompaniment*.

Country: An American music style which emerged in the 1920s, with storytelling lyrics, and mostly straightforward/simple harmonies.

Crescendo: A dynamic marking instructing to play louder.

"Crossover" lick: A descending right-hand piano embellishment typical in blues styles.

Cut time: Same as a 2/2 time signature (two half-note beats in each measure).

Decrescendo: A dynamic marking instructing to play softer.

Diatonic four-part chords: Four-part chords which belong to (i.e., are contained within) the major key or scale.

Diatonic triads: Triads which belong to (i.e., are contained within) the major key or scale.

Digital piano: An electric piano which plays "digital" recordings (or "samples") of a real piano when the keys are played. A more portable and lower-cost alternative to a real piano.

Diminished triad: A triad created by lowering the 3rd and 5th of a major triad by one half step.

Dominant seventh chord: A four-part chord created by building major 3rd, perfect 5th, and minor 7th intervals up from the root.

Dotted notes: A dot placed after a note adds half as much again to the duration, i.e., a dotted quarter note lasts for one and a half beats.

Double flat: A symbol indicating to lower the given pitch by two half steps, i.e., the note "E double flat" is equivalent to the note D.

Double sharp: A symbol indicating to raise the given pitch by two half steps, i.e., the note "D double sharp" is equivalent to the note E.

Downbeat: The first beat of a measure, or, a note falling "on the beat" of a measure as opposed to "between the beats."

Dynamic marking: A marking in the music signifying how soft or loud to play.

Eighth note: A note which lasts for a half of a beat (in time signatures with a "4" on the bottom).

Eighth rest: A rest which lasts for a half of a beat (in time signatures with a "4" on the bottom).

Electric piano/keyboard: A general term applied to a keyboard instrument which makes its sound "electronically" instead of "acoustically."

Enharmonics: Alternative names for the same note. For example, the note "C sharp" is enharmonic to the note "D flat."

Fake book: A book containing lead sheets of songs (see "lead sheet"). Musicians will improvise their arrangement of the songs, working from the fake book.

Faking it: The art of improvising the piano arrangement from a lead sheet or fake book, as above.

Fallboard: The long piece of wood that is hinged to the piano at the top of the keys.

Fermata sign: A sign over the music indicating a held note/chord or pause. Sometimes used at the end of a chart, on the last note/chord.

Fingering: Assigning different fingers to the notes in the music in order to play them. Also see "hand position."

Fingering groups: A way of splitting up or grouping the notes in a scale to see the fingering more easily.

Finger numbers: The numbers 1–5 to indicate which fingers are to play which notes:

1 = Thumb
2 = Index finger
3 = Middle finger
4 = "Ring" finger
5 = Pinkie or little finger

Flags: The "tail" added to the end of the stem, for individual (not beamed) eighth or sixteenth notes.

Flat: A sign to the left of a note which lowers it by one half step.

Forte (loud): A dynamic marking (signaled by the letter "*f*") instructing the pianist to play loudly.

Fortissimo (very loud): A dynamic marking (signaled by the letters "*ff*") instructing the pianist to play very loudly.

Four-part chords: Chords consisting of four notes: typically the root, 3rd, 5th, and 7th.

Funk: A sub style of R&B which emphasizes groove and syncopation.

Fusion: A term used to describe the blending of jazz with rock and/or funk styles.

Gig: Live performance (paid or not!).

Grace note: A note of very short duration which is "squeezed in" before another note.

Grand piano: See *horizontal piano*.

Grand staff: A combination of treble and bass staves which is used to notate piano music (one staff for each hand).

Half note: A note which lasts for two beats (in time signatures with a "4" on the bottom).

Half rest: A rest which lasts for two beats (in time signatures with a "4" on the bottom).

Half step: The distance between any note on the keyboard, and the very next note (either higher or lower). The half step is the smallest interval measurement in conventional Western music.

Hand position: Placement of the hand which enables you to reach the notes in the music. Except in the simplest tunes, hand positions are likely to change while playing the piece.

Hanon exercises: A set of exercises written by C.L. Hanon which emphasize finger independence and are used for developing technique.

Harpsichord: An early forerunner of the piano. Strings are plucked as opposed to struck.

Horizontal piano: Also known as a *grand* piano. The strings and soundboard are horizontal (as opposed to a *vertical* piano).

Improvised solo: A spontaneous sequence of notes, normally played "over" the chord progression of a song (or section).

Interval: The distance between two notes.

Inversion: See *chord inversion*.

Jazz: An American music style emphasizing improvisation and sophisticated harmony.

Jazz-blues: Music which combines jazz and blues elements. One method is by applying more sophisticated harmony and improvisation to tunes which have a blues form.

Jazz standard: A well-established tune in the jazz repertoire, commonly played by successive generations of players.

Key: The key indicates the principal note or *tonic* of the piece, and which scale the piece is based on (subject to any *accidentals* in the music).

Keyboard: The arrangement of black and white keys on the piano, or a general term used to describe an electronic keyboard instrument.

Key signature: A series of sharps or flats at the beginning of the music indicating which key you are in via which notes are to be played flat or sharp.

Lead sheet: Notated version of a song, showing the melody and chord symbols.

Ledger lines: Small staff lines placed above or below the staff in order to write notes which are too high or too low to be placed on the staff.

Legato: Play in a smooth and connected style.

Line note: Note which is written on a line (rather than in a space) on the staff.

Major intervals: Intervals contained within the major scale, from the tonic to other scale degrees (apart from 4ths, 5ths and octaves). Also see *perfect intervals*.

Major scale: A seven-note scale made up of the following internal intervals: whole step, whole step, half step, whole step, whole step, whole step, and half step.

Major seventh chord: A four-part chord created by building major 3rd, perfect 5th, and major 7th intervals up from the root.

Major triad: A three-part chord created by building major 3rd and perfect 5th intervals up from the root.

Measure: A section of music between two consecutive barlines, containing a specific number of beats.

Metronome: A mechanical or electronic device which "clicks" on each beat. An essential practice aid.

MIDI: Stands for "Musical Instrument Digital Interface." The protocol via which keyboards, computers, and other musical equipment communicate with one another.

Middle C: The note C in the middle of the piano keyboard.

Minor seventh chord: A four-part chord created by building minor 3rd, perfect 5th, and minor 7th intervals up from the root.

Minor seventh (flat 5) chord: A four-part chord created by building minor 3rd, diminished 5th, and minor 7th intervals up from the root.

Minor sixth chord: A four-part chord created by building minor 3rd, perfect 5th, and major 6th intervals up from the root.

Minor triad: A three-part chord created by building minor 3rd and perfect 5th intervals up from the root.

Music alphabet: The letters which are used for note names: A, B, C, D, E, F, and G.

Natural: A sign placed before a note to cancel a flat or sharp, either that from within the same measure, or from the key signature.

New Age: A late 20th century style of music with an emphasis on calming sounds and avoidance of harsh textures.

Octave: The interval distance between any note to the next-occurring note of the same name, either higher or lower on the keyboard.

Open triad: A triad (either in root position or inverted) in which two or more of the notes span more than one octave. Used for left-hand arpeggio patterns in ballad styles.

Pentatonic scale (major): A five-note scale with the following internal intervals: whole step, whole step, minor 3rd, whole step, and minor 3rd.

Pentatonic scale (minor): A five-note scale with the following internal intervals: minor 3rd, whole step, whole step, minor 3rd, and whole step.

Perfect intervals: Unison, 4th, 5th, and octave intervals which are contained within the major scale. Also see *major intervals*.

Piano (soft): A dynamic marking (signaled by the letter "*p*") instructing to play softly.

Pianissimo (very soft): A dynamic marking (signaled by the letters "*pp*") instructing to play very softly.

Pickup measure: An incomplete measure at the beginning of a song. Used if the melody does not begin on beat 1.

Plug-in software: Software instruments or effects which "plug into" a host, such as a sequencer program.

Polyphony: The number of notes an electronic keyboard or synthesizer can "sound" at once.

Pop ballad: A contemporary music style using slow-to-medium tempos, and eighth or sixteenth-note subdivisions.

Pop/Rock: A contemporary music style using medium-to-fast tempos, combining the melodic hooks of pop music with the driving energy of rock music.

Progression: See *chord progression*.

Quarter note: A note which lasts for one beat (in time signatures with a "4" on the bottom).

Quarter rest: A rest which lasts for one beat (in time signatures with a "4" on the bottom).

R&B (rhythm and blues): An American music style which emerged in the 1950s. Nowadays, the term encompasses all "black popular music," such as soul, funk, dance-pop, hip-hop, neo-soul, etc.

Rest: A rest indicates silence—that you don't play for the specified number of beats (depending upon the length of the rest).

Rock 'n' roll: A highly rhythmic blend of pop, blues, country, and gospel which emerged in the 1950s, and influenced all subsequent popular music styles.

Root: The fundamental note of a chord. For example, the root of a C major triad is the note C.

Root position: A chord which has not been inverted, i.e., the root is still the bottom note.

Scale: A sequence of notes built using a specific set of intervals.

Sequencer: Software program which allows you to multitrack record (and more!) on your computer. Can also refer to the recording component of a workstation keyboard/synthesizer.

Seventh chords: Alternate name for four-part chords.

"Seven-three" (7–3) voicings: Voicing technique using the seventh and third of the chords in a song. Commonly used in jazz styles.

Sharp: A sign to the left of a note which raises it by one half step.

Shuffle: An alternate term for a *swing eighths* feel.

Sixteenth note: A note which lasts for a quarter of a beat (in time signatures with a "4" on the bottom).

Sixteenth rest: A rest which lasts for a quarter of a beat (in time signatures with a "4" on the bottom).

Slash chart: See *chord chart*.

Slash chord: Chord symbol which places a chord over a bass note (other than its root), i.e., C/E. This is often done to place the chord over its 3rd or 5th in the bass.

Slur: A curved line in the music which groups certain notes together, indicating that they are to be played legato (smooth and connected).

Soft pedal (una corda): The leftmost pedal, which moves all the keys to the left, resulting in a softer sound.

Software piano: A computer program which accesses a large library of recorded piano sounds, and, therefore, gives a very realistic piano emulation when playing a MIDI keyboard hooked up to the computer. Can also be a "plug-in."

Sostenuto pedal: The middle pedal, which sustains the notes currently being held down on the keyboard, without sustaining notes played afterwards.

Space note: Note which is written in a space (rather than on a line) on the staff.

Sound check: A procedure before an "amplified" gig where the sound engineer checks the individual sounds of each instrument, as well as the whole band playing together.

Staccato: A kind of short and bouncy style, with considerable separation between notes.

Staff: The system of five parallel lines on which music is written.

Standard songs: Well-known songs in a particular genre.

"Straight eighths" feel: A rhythmic style in which each eighth note gets exactly one half of the beat.

Suspended triad: A triad in which the 3rd has been replaced by another note, normally either the second or fourth, i.e., in a C major chord, the E would be replaced by a D or F to make it a Csus chord.

Sustain (or damper) pedal: The rightmost pedal, which lifts all of the dampers off the strings, enabling them to vibrate after the notes are released from the keyboard.

"Swing eighths" feel: A rhythmic style in which the first eighth note in each "pair" gets two-thirds of the beat, and the last eighth note gets one-third of the beat.

Syncopation: Rhythmic emphasis on upbeats (i.e., on notes not falling on the beat).

Synthesizer: An electronic keyboard or module capable of producing many different instrument and synthetic sounds.

Tempo: Speed of the song, normally expressed in "beats per minute."

Thumb turn: Passing the thumb underneath the other fingers when playing a scale, or playing blues "crossover" phrases.

Tie: A curved line in the music connecting two notes of the same pitch, indicating that only the first note is to be played, and then held for the combined duration of both tied notes.

Time signature: A numeric symbol at the beginning of the music telling you how many beats there are in each measure, and what rhythmic value is assigned to the beat.

Treble clef: Sign at the beginning of piano music, indicating to play notes on the upper portion of the keyboard, usually with the right hand.

Triads: Three-note chords, built in thirds.

Tribute bands: Bands performing cover tunes by one well-known band or artist only, i.e., they are a "tribute" to that band or artist.

Triplets: Three notes fitting into the space normally occupied by two, for example, an eighth-note triplet divides the quarter note into three equal parts.

Upbeats: A note falling "between the beats" (i.e., on the "and" of 1, or halfway through beat 1, as opposed to "on the beat").

"Upper structure" voicing: The upper tones of a chord (for example, the 3rd, 5th, and 7th) played in the right hand, over the bass note played in the left hand.

Vertical piano: Also known as an "upright" piano (although "upright" is in fact just one type of vertical piano). The strings and soundboard are vertical (as opposed to a "horizontal" or grand piano).

Voice leading: Using inversions for smooth movement between chords (i.e., without large interval skips).

Voicing: See *chord voicing*.

Waltz: A piece of music which is in 3/4 time, usually used for dancing.

Weighted keyboard: A feature of some electronic keyboards, which attempts to duplicate the weight and feel of an acoustic piano keyboard.

Whole note: A note which lasts for four beats (in time signatures with a "4" on the bottom).

Whole rest: A rest which lasts for four beats (in time signatures with a "4" on the bottom).

Whole step: An interval twice the size of a half step. Also equivalent to a major second (2nd) interval.

Workstation keyboard: An electronic keyboard or synthesizer with a built-in sequencer, allowing for multitrack recording capability.

CD TRACK LISTING

Track	Track Title	Chapter
1	Rhythm example #1	3
2	Rhythm example #2	3
3	"Go Tell Aunt Rhody"	4
4	"When the Saints Go Marching In"	4
5	"Dry Bones"	5
6	"Home Sweet Home"	5
7	Eighth-note rhythm example	6
8	Dotted notes example	6
9	Tied note example 1	6
10	Tied note example 2	6
11	Mixed notes and rests example	6
12	Eighth-note triplet example 1	6
13	Eighth-note triplet example 2	6
14	Straight and swing eighth note examples (parts 1–2)	6
15	Sixteenth-note rhythm example	6
16	Melody example with sixteenth notes	6
17	Melody example with sixteenth notes and rests	6
18	"Marianne"	8
19	"Michael Row the Boat Ashore"	8
20	"Shenandoah"	8
21	"For He's a Jolly Good Fellow"	9
22	"Lavender's Blue"	9
23	"Hail, Hail, the Gang's All Here"	9
24	"Jingle Bells"	11
25	"Ode to Joy"	11
26	"Auld Lang Syne"	11
27	"Buffalo Gals"	11
28	Left-hand triad progression	12
29	Left-hand triad progression w/ inversions	12
30	Left hand 4-part chord progression	12
31	Left hand 4-part chord progression w/ inversions	12
32	"Sonatina in C Major"	13
33	"Gymnopédie No. 1"	13
34	Pop ballad & rock comping example, Stage 1	14
35	Pop ballad & rock comping example, Stage 2	14
36	Pop ballad & rock comping example, Stage 2	14
37	R&B ballad & funk comping example, Stage 1	14

Track	Track Title	Chapter
38	R&B ballad & funk comping example, voice led	14
39	R&B ballad & funk comping example, Stage 2	14
40	R&B ballad & funk comping example, Stage 2	14
41	"Let Somebody Love You" piano only	14
42	"Let Somebody Love You" full band	14
43	"You Can't Hide" piano only	14
44	"You Can't Hide" full band	14
45	Left hand open triad arpeggios example 1	15
46	Left hand open triad arpeggios example 2	15
47	Left hand open triad arpeggios example 3	15
48	Left hand open triad arpeggios example 4	15
49	"Easy Going" (version 1)	15
50	"Easy Going" (version 2)	15
51	"Easy Going" (version 3)	15
52	"Chicago Breakup" (slow)	16
53	"Chicago Breakup" (full speed)	16
54	"Rock My Soul"	17
55	Blues crossover licks (parts 1–7)	18
56	"Every Night I Have the Blues" (slow)	18
57	"Every Night I Have the Blues" (full speed)	18
58	"Blue Bop" (slow)	18
59	"Blue Bop" (full speed)	18
60	"Bird of Prey"	19
61	"Hand Prints" (slow)	19
62	"Hand Prints" (full speed)	19
63	"Before I Get Old"	20
64	"Outlaw Country" (slow)	21
65	"Outlaw Country" (full speed)	21
66	"Für Elise"	22
67	"Sonata in C Major"	22
68	"Prelude in B Minor"	22
69	"Clair de Lune"	22
70	"Minuet in G"	
71	"Come Sail Away"	
72	"Bennie and the Jets"	
73	"Takin' Care of Business"	
74	"Misty"	

ABOUT THE AUTHOR

Mark Harrison studied classical piano as a child, and by his teenage years was playing in various rock bands in his native Southern England. In the 1980s, he began writing music for TV and commercials, including a piece that was used for the *British Labor Party* ads in a national election. He also appeared on British television (BBC), and became a fixture on London's pub-rock circuit.

In 1987, he relocated to Los Angeles to experience the music business in the U.S.A. He soon began performing with top musicians such as John Molo (Bruce Hornsby band), Jay Graydon (Steely Dan), Jimmy Haslip (Yellowjackets), and numerous others. Mark currently performs with his own contemporary jazz band (Mark Harrison Quintet), as well as with the popular Steely Dan tribute band Doctor Wu.

Mark continues to write music for television, and his recent credits include *Saturday Night Live*, *The Montel Williams Show*, *American Justice*, *Celebrity Profiles*, *America's Most Wanted*, *True Hollywood Stories*, the British documentary program *Panorama*, and many others.

Mark has also become one of the top contemporary music educators in Los Angeles. He taught at the renowned Grove School of Music for six years, instructing hundreds of musicians from around the world. Mark currently runs a busy private teaching studio, catering to the needs of professional and aspiring musicians alike. His students include Grammy-winners, hit songwriters, members of the Boston Pops and L.A. Philharmonic orchestras, and first-call touring musicians with major acts.

Mark's music instruction books are used by thousands of musicians in over twenty countries, and are recommended by the Berklee College of Music for all their new students. He also writes *Master Class* articles for *Keyboard* and *How To Jam* magazines, covering a variety of different keyboard styles and topics.

You're welcome to visit Mark at **www.harrisonmusic.com**, where you'll find information about his educational products and services, as well as his live performance activities and schedule.